Greenwich Council
Library & Infor~~mation Service~~

Please return by the last date shown

8/09.

BEACHAM CLOSE
-- DEC 2018

-- AUG 2014

Thrasher
APR 2015

Rose Ct
-- MAR 2019

- 6 JUN 2011

-- FEB 2016

-- JUL 2011
-- DEC 2011
-- MAR 2012

- 1 AUG 2016

-- JUL 2012

Wicker
Ramsay
-- JAN 2017

-- JAN 2013

Hider
-- OCT 2017

-- JUN 2013

-- DEC 2017

-- AUG 2013

BISHOPS CLOSE
MAR 2018

-- NOV 2013

PENNYFIELDS 2018
BILL WALDEN
-- OCT 2018

Jerry Lewis and Dean Martin made sixteen films during their ten-year partnership. Lewis was the creator and star of a series of successful movie comedies, including *The Nutty Professor* (1963). He has received numerous honours, including appointment to the Légion d'honneur. In 1982, he was declared clinically dead after a heart attack, but came back the following year with an acclaimed portrayal of a kidnapped quiz show host in Martin Scorsese's *King of Comedy*. In 2000, at the age of seventy-four, he returned to performing in Las Vegas.

DEAN & ME

Before the Rat Pack, the hit songs and the stellar movie career, Dean Martin spent ten years partnering Jerry Lewis in a successful double act. In this candid memoir, Lewis remembers his relationship with Dean: from their early performances in Mob-owned nightclubs to the giddy days of Hollywood super-stardom. But their high-rolling lifestyle came to an end. On July 24 1956, Dean and Jerry split and the two men didn't speak to one another for twenty years. Jerry Lewis reveals much about Dean Martin's crafts-manship and enigmatic charm. He evokes the glamour of the era — the casinos, the cocktails, the mobsters, and the women. He recalls the thrill of the youthful duo's sudden, startling success, and the slow sad erosion of the fun that followed.

JERRY LEWIS
& JAMES KAPLAN

DEAN & ME

Complete and Unabridged

CHARNWOOD
Leicester

First published in Great Britain in 2006 by
Pan Macmillan Limited
London

First Charnwood Edition
published 2009
by arrangement with
Pan Macmillan Limited
London

British Library CIP Data

Lewis, Jerry, *1926 –*
    Dean & me.—Large print ed.—
    Charnwood library series
    1. Lewis, Jerry, *1926 –* —Friends and associates
    2. Martin, Dean, *1917 – 1995* 3. Entertainers—
    United States—Biography 4. Large type books
    I. Title II. Kaplan, James, *1951 –*
    791′.0922

    ISBN 978–1–84782–502–5

Published by
F. A. Thorpe (Publishing)
Anstey, Leicestershire

Set by Words & Graphics Ltd.
Anstey, Leicestershire
Printed and bound in Great Britain by
T. J. International Ltd., Padstow, Cornwall

This book is printed on acid-free paper

For Dani, the young lady who is the air in my lungs, and her young mother, who is the beat in my heart, thank you both for getting me to here.

Philippe Halsman, *Life*, 1951

PROLOGUE: BREAKING UP

Most of the outside world wasn't aware of the gulf that had grown between us, and we were still making money like the U.S. Mint. But there was no getting around it: The time had come to call it a day. In the coolest, most practical way, Dean and I decided to go out on top.

On Tuesday night, July 24, 1956 — ten years to the day after our first appearance together at Skinny D'Amato's 500 Club in Atlantic City — we played our last three shows, ever, at the Copacabana, on East Sixtieth Street in Manhattan.

The evening quickly took on the magnitude of a great event. After all, for the past decade, Martin and Lewis had delighted America and the world. We'd been loved, idolized, sought after. And now we were shutting the party down.

The celebrity guest list for this night of nights grew and grew. With about a half hour before our first show, Dean and I had very little to say to each other. It was going to be a rough night, but wc both knew we couldn't allow ourselves to be sloppy or unprofessional. So our plan was to have fun, if possible, and to do the best show we knew how to do.

I walked across the hall to my partner's suite at about 7:35 for absolutely no reason other than to announce that I needed ice. Dean always had

1

ice. I walked over to the bar and put some in my glass. He gave me a knowing glance — he felt what I felt and we didn't have to expound on it. I managed to get myself to the door and croaked out, 'Have a good show, Paul.' (That was his middle name, what I always called him.) He said, 'You too, kid.'

I walked out into the hallway and thought my heart would break. I was losing my best friend and I didn't know why. And if I had known why, would that have made a difference? I now think that since it had to happen, at least it happened quickly. When husbands and wives break up, it can take years, or they stay together for all the wrong reasons.

Dean and I knew we had to get on with our lives, and being a team no longer worked. As sentimental as it sounds, we both had the hand of God on us until even He said, 'Enough!'

I think for the most part we understood what was happening. We were just scared, and didn't want anyone to know. Scared about where we were going and what we would be doing. We had become accustomed to our fabulous lifestyle. Would the autograph-seekers still seek? Could we do *anything* without each other? Would we be accepted as anything other than what we had been?

Dean had this uncanny way of making everything bad look like it wasn't all *that* bad. It wasn't denial, it was that he never had sweaty palms. No matter how things turned out, Dean could make it seem as if that was the way he'd planned it.

One look at my face and you knew despair . . . joy . . . happiness . . . sorrow. My dad called me 'Mr. Neon' — and he was right. I always had to let everyone know what I was feeling. Anything else and I felt like a liar. Truth was my greatest ally. Painful, yes, but I found it was the only way for me. Dean could lie if it would spare someone's feelings. I had difficulty with that.

Well, however we felt, my partner and I still had three final shows to do at the Copa, and it was getting to be that time.

I always went on before Dean, did my shtick and introduced him. He would hang back on the top level of the Copa, greeting people and making nice while I was out there, setting them up for his entrance. But this night, when it came time for me to say, 'And here's my partner, Dean Martin,' the words stuck in my throat. The audience knew it was the last night I would ever say those words, and the air was filled with a kind of exquisite trauma, the star-studded crowd hoping — perhaps — for a last-minute reprieve.

It was an eerie and uncertain feeling out there. I wasn't sure myself if the powerful vibrations in the Copa were good or bad. We had to do that first show to find out a lot of things.

So Dean strolled out, as he always did . . . cool, relaxed-looking — but I knew my partner. His eyes told me he was feeling the same pain and uncertainty that I was.

We shook hands, as we always did, but this time a murmur swept through the audience. 'Maybe there *is* a chance?'

It vibrated through the entire building.

3

Dean did his three songs, uneventfully, pretty much the way he'd always done them, and out I came to go into our routine. 'It's nice that you cut down your songs to only eleven numbers. I thought I'd have to shower again! It don't say outside, 'Dean Martin,' period . . . it says 'Dean Martin and Jerry Lewis'! Did you forget, or are you anxious to be out of work?'

All of that was what we always did, only on this night every joke had too much significance. We forged ahead, knowing that soon we would be finished: Only two more shows to go, and it would be over.

We barreled through what we had to do and came to the last song in the act, 'Pardners.'

You and me, we'll always be pardners,
You and me, we'll always be friends.

Now, singing that number could have been a mistake, because once we got into it, that audience changed from uncertain to sure; it was over, and they were watching everything but the burial. We finished the song, and the applause was deafening.

We finished the second show, and the third went on at 2:30 a.m. sharp. This time Dean and I both knew: *This is it! The last time . . . never again . . . all over . . .*

It felt like being choked without hands on your throat. But here it is. It's 2:25, and Dean is standing at his place at the foot of the stairs, stage right . . . and I'm standing at the foot of the stairs, stage left. The Copa Girls go by us as

4

they finish the opening production number, and as they pass, they too are teary-eyed. Rather than rush to their dressing rooms, they stand along the staircases on both sides of the stage to watch. They all felt the death knell, and they wanted to be a part of it.

So we went on and killed them, and killed ourselves as well. We were both shattered by the time we got to 'Pardners,' and we didn't even do it too terribly well, but we got through it, and as that audience rose to celebrate all we had ever done, they knew it was over. There were shouts, tears, applause. It was midnight on New Year's Eve all over again — and in July, yet.

Dean and I both headed for the elevator, waving off all comers. When the door closed, we put our arms around each other, just letting go the floodgates. We arrived at our floor and got out, and thank God, no one was around. We went to our suites and closed the doors. I grabbed the phone and dialed Dean.

'Hey, pally,' he said. 'How're you holdin' up?'

'I don't know yet. I just want to say — we had some good times, didn't we, Paul?'

'There'll be more.'

'Yeah, well, take care of yourself.'

'You too, pardner.'

We hung up and closed the book on ten great years — with the exception of the last ten months. They were horrific. Ten months of pain and anger and uncertainty and sorrow.

Now it was time to pick up the pieces. Not so easy . . .

1

In the age of Truman, Eisenhower, and Joe McCarthy, we freed America. For ten years after World War II, Dean and I were not only the most successful show-business act in history — we were history.

You have to remember: Postwar America was a very buttoned-up nation. Radio shows were run by censors, Presidents wore hats, ladies wore girdles. We came straight out of the blue — nobody was expecting anything like Martin and Lewis. A sexy guy and a monkey is how some people saw us, but what we really were, in an age of Freudian self-realization, was the explosion of the show-business id.

Like Burns and Allen, Abbott and Costello, and Hope and Crosby, we were vaudevillians, stage performers who worked with an audience. But the difference between us and all the others is significant. They worked with a script. We exploded without one, the same way wiseguy kids do on a playground, or jazz musicians do when they're let loose. And the minute we started out in nightclubs, audiences went nuts for us. As Alan King told an interviewer a few years ago: 'I have been in the business for fifty-five years, and I have never to this day seen an act get more laughs than Martin and Lewis. They didn't get laughs — it was pandemonium. People knocked over tables.'

7

Like so many entertainment explosions, we happened almost by accident.

★ ★ ★

It was a crisp March day in midtown Manhattan, March of 1945. I had just turned nineteen, and I was going to live forever. I could feel the bounce in my legs, the air in my lungs. World War II was rapidly drawing to a close, and New York was alive with excitement. Broadway was full of city smells — bus and taxi exhaust; roast peanuts and dirty-water hot dogs; and, most thrilling of all, the perfumes of beautiful women. Midtown was swarming with gorgeous gals! Secretaries, career girls, society broads with little pooches — they all paraded past, tick-tock, tick-tock, setting my heart racing every ten paces. I was a very young newlywed, with a very pregnant wife back in Newark, but I had eyes, and I looked. And looked. And looked.

I was strolling south with my pal Sonny King, heading toward an appointment with an agent in Times Square. Sonny was an ex-prizefighter from Brooklyn trying to make it as a singer, a knock-around guy, street-smart and quick with a joke — kind of like an early Tony Danza. He prided himself on his nice tenor voice and on knowing everybody who was anybody in show business. Not that his pride always matched up with reality. But that was Sonny, a bit of an operator. And me? I was a Jersey kid trying to make it as a comic. My act — are you ready for this? — was as follows: I would get up on stage and make funny faces while I lip-synched along to phonograph records. The professional term for what I did was *dumb act*, a phrase I didn't want to think about too much. In those days, it felt a little too much like a bad review.

You know good-bad? Good was that I was young and full of beans and ready to take on the world. Bad was that I had no idea on earth how I was going to accomplish this feat. And bad was also that I was just eking out a living, pulling down $110 a week in a good week, and there weren't that many good weeks. On this princely sum I had to pay my manager, Abner J. Greshler, plus the rent on the Newark apartment, plus feed two, about to be three. Plus wardrobe, candy bars, milk shakes, and phonograph records for the act. Plus my hotel bill. While I was working in New York, I stayed in the city, to be close to my jobs — when I had them — and to stick to where the action was. I'd been rooming at the Belmont Plaza, on Lexington and Forty-ninth, where I'd also been performing in the Glass Hat, a nightclub in the hotel. I got $135 a week and a room.

Suddenly, at Broadway and Fifty-fourth, Sonny spotted someone across the street: a tall, dark, and incredibly handsome man in a camel's-hair coat. His name, Sonny said, was Dean Martin. Just looking at him intimidated me: *How does anybody get that handsome?*

I smiled at the sight of him in that camel's-hair coat. *Harry Horseshit*, I thought. That was what we used to call a guy who thought he was smooth with the ladies. Anybody who wore a camel's-hair overcoat, with a camel's-hair belt and fake diamond cuff links, was automatically Harry Horseshit.

But this guy, I knew, was the real deal. He was standing with a shorter, older fellow, and when he saw Sonny, he waved us over. We crossed the street. I was amazed all over again when I saw how good-looking he was — long, rugged face; great profile; thick, dark brows and eyelashes. And a suntan in March! How'd he manage that? I could see he had kind of a twinkle as he talked to the older guy. *Charisma* is a word I would learn later. All I knew then was that I couldn't take my eyes off Sonny's pal.

'Hey, Dino!' Sonny said as we came up to them. 'How ya doin', Lou?' he said to the older man.

Lou, it turned out, was Lou Perry, Dean's manager. He looked like a manager: short, thin-lipped, cool-eyed. Sonny introduced me, and Perry glanced at me without much interest. But Sonny looked excited. He turned to his camel-coated friend. 'Dino,' Sonny said, 'I want you to meet a very funny kid, Jerry Lewis.'

Camel-Coat smiled warmly and put out his hand. I took it. It was a big hand, strong, but he didn't go overboard with the grip. I liked that. I liked *him*, instantly. And he looked genuinely glad to meet me.

'Kid,' Sonny said — Sonny called me Kid the first time he ever met me, and he would still call me Kid in Vegas fifty years later — 'this is Dean Martin. Sings even better than me.'

That was Sonny, fun and games. Of course, he

had zero idea that he was introducing me to one of the great comic talents of our time. I certainly had no idea of that, either — nor, for that matter, did Dean. At that moment, at the end of World War II, we were just two guys struggling to make it in show business, shaking hands on a busy Broadway street corner.

We made a little chitchat. 'You workin'?' I asked.

He smiled that million-dollar smile. Now that I looked at him close up, I could see the faint outline of a healing surgical cut on the bridge of his nose. Some plastic surgeon had done great work. 'Oh, this 'n' that, you know,' Dean said. 'I'm on WMCA radio, sustaining. No bucks, just room.' He had a mellow, lazy voice, with a slightly Southern lilt to it. He sounded like he didn't have a care in the world, like he was knockin' 'em dead wherever he went. I believed it. Little did I know that he was hip-deep in debt to Perry and several other managers besides.

'How 'bout you?' Dean asked me.

I nodded, quickly. I suddenly wanted, very badly, to impress this man. 'I'm just now finishing my eighth week at the Glass Hat,' I said. 'In the Belmont Plaza.'

'Really? I live there,' Dean said.

'At the Glass Hat?'

'No, at the Belmont. It's part of my radio deal.'

Just at that moment, a beautiful brunette walked by, in a coat with a fur-trimmed collar. Dean lowered his eyelids slightly and flashed her that grin — and damned if she didn't smile right back! How come I never got that reaction? She gave him a lingering gaze over her shoulder as she passed, a clear invitation, and Dean shook his head, smiling his regrets.

'Look at this guy,' Sonny said in his hoarse Brooklyn accent. 'He's got pussy radar!'

One look at Sonny's eyes was enough to tell me that he idolized Dean — whose attention, all at once, I felt anxious to get back. 'You ever go to Leon and Eddie's?' I asked, my voice sounding even higher and squeakier than its usual high and squeaky. Leon and Eddie's was a restaurant and nightclub a couple of blocks away, on fabulous Fifty-second Street — which, in those days, was lined with restaurants and former speakeasies, like '21,' and music clubs like the Five Spot and Birdland. Live entertainment still ruled America in those pre-television days, Manhattan was the world capital of nightclubs, and Leon and Eddie's was a mecca for nightclub comics. Sunday night was Celebrity Night: The fun would start after hours, when anybody in the business might show up and get on to do a piece of their act. You'd see the likes of Milton Berle, Henny Youngman, Danny Kaye. It was magical. I used to go and gawk, like a kid in a candy store. *Someday*, I thought . . . But for now, no chance. They'd never use a dumb act — one needing props, yet.

'Yeah, sometimes I stop by Sunday nights,' Dean said.

'Me too!' I cried.

He gave me that smile again — warm but ever so slightly cool around the edges. It bathed you in its glow, yet didn't let you in. Men don't like to admit it, but there's something about a truly handsome guy who also happens to be truly masculine — what they call a *man's man* — that's as magnetic to us as it is to women. *That's what I want to be like*, you think. *Maybe if I hang around with him, some of that'll rub off on me.*

'So — maybe I'll see you there sometime,' Dean told me.

'Yeah, sure,' I said.

'Go get your tux out of hock,' he said.

I laughed. He was funny.

★ ★ ★

Sonny King was a pal, but not a friend. I badly needed a friend. I was a lonely kid, the only child of two vaudevillians who were rarely around. My dad, Danny, was a singer and all-around entertainer: He did it all — patter, impressions, stand-up comedy. My mom, Rachel (Rae), was Danny's pianist and conductor. So I grew up shuttled from household to household, relative to relative. I cherished the precious times Mom and Dad would take me on the road with them. And for them, the highest form of togetherness was to put me right in the act: My first onstage appearance was at age five, in 1931, at the President Hotel, a summer resort in Swan Lake, New York. I wore a tux (naturally) and sang that Depression classic 'Brother, Can You Spare a Dime?' From that moment on, showbiz was in my blood. So was loneliness.

By the time I was sixteen, I was a high-school dropout and a show-business wannabe. *A desperately*-wanting-to-be wannabe. I worked the Catskill resorts as a busboy (for pay) and (for free) a tummler — the guy who cuts up, makes faces, gets the guests in a good mood for the real entertainment. That's what I wanted to be, the real entertainment. But what was I going to do? I was tall, skinny, gawky; cute but funny-looking. With the voice God had given me, I certainly wasn't going to be a singer like my dad, with his Al Jolson baritone. I always saw the humor in things, the joke possibilities. At the same time, I didn't have the confidence to stand on a stage and talk.

Then I hit on a genius solution — or what seemed at the time like a genius solution. One night, at a New Jersey resort where my parents were doing their act, a friend of mine, an aspiring performer, Lonnie Brown — the daughter of Charlie and Lillian Brown, resort hotelkeepers who were destined to become very important in my life — was listening to a record by an English singer named Cyril Smith, trying to learn those classy English intonations. I had a little crush on Lonnie, and, attempting to impress her, I started to clown around, mouthing along to the music, rolling my eyes and playing the diva. Well, Lonnie broke up, and *that* was music to my ears. An act was born.

After a couple of hard years on the road, playing burlesque houses where the guys with newspapers on their laps would boo me off the stage so they could see the strippers, I became a showbiz veteran (still in my teens) with an act called 'Jerry Lewis — Satirical Impressions in Pantomimicry.'

I had perfected the act, and to tell the absolute truth, it was pretty goddamn funny. I would put on a fright wig and a frock coat and lipsynch to the great baritone Igor Gorin's 'Largo Al Factotum' from *The Barber of Seville*. I'd come out in a Carmen Miranda dress, with fruit on my hat, and do Miranda. Then into a pin-striped jacket, suck in my cheeks, and I'd do Sinatra singing 'All or Nothing at All.' I knew where every scratch and skip was on every record, and when they came up, I'd do shtick to them. I had gotten better and better at contorting my long, skinny body in ways that I knew worked comedically. I practiced making faces in front of a mirror till I cracked myself up. God hadn't made me handsome, but he'd given me *something*, I always felt: funny bones.

And I never said a word on stage.

The dumb act was a rapidly fading subspecialty in those rapidly fading days of baggy-pants comedy, and my own days doing it were numbered. There were a few of us lip-synchers out there, working the circuit, and while I liked (and still like) to think that I was the best of the bunch — nobody could move or pratfall or make faces like Jerry Lewis — I only had around three to eleven audience members per show who agreed with me. Those three or four or nine people would be wetting themselves while I performed, as the rest of the house (if anyone else was there) clapped slowly, or booed . . .

15

Bring on the strippers!

And I never said a word.

The truth is, funny sentences were always running through my brain: I *thought* funny. But I was ashamed of what would come out if I spoke — that nasal kid's voice. So I was funny on stage, but I was only part funny: I was still looking for the missing piece.

★　★　★

Room 1412 at the Belmont Plaza Hotel was more like a cubicle than a room — there was a bed, a couch, a chest of drawers, and . . . that was it. You couldn't go to the john without bruising your shin. Sonny and I were visiting with Dean, who was fresh from a not-so-hot date.

'She had a roommate,' he said, rolling his eyes. 'Where the hell can a fella get laid in peace and quiet in this damn town?'

He poured himself a Scotch to calm down, then gave us a look. 'You're not gonna let me drink this all by myself, are you?'

Hot cocoa was about the strongest thing I'd had at that point in my life, but I gamely accepted a bathroom tumbler half-filled with what smelled like cleaning fluid. I even pretended to take a sip or two as Dean put some 78s on his record player and the three of us proceeded to get into an all-night bull session. To the sounds of Billie Holiday, Tommy Dorsey, Benny Goodman, and Louis Armstrong, we sat and shot the breeze till all hours — or, I should

16

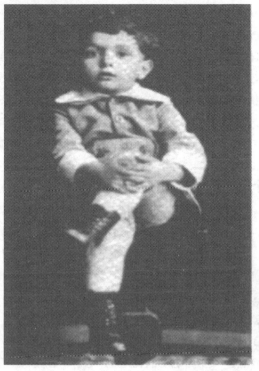

He'd already drunk a fifth.

say, one of us did. After Sonny nodded off, I just sat in awe as Dean held forth.

The time of night and a glass or two of Scotch had put him in a philosophical mood, and he proceeded to tell me the story of how Dino Crocetti had emerged from Steubenville, Ohio, and become Dean Martin. It all sounded like a fairy tale to me: the rough-and-tumble Ohio River town full of steel mills, speakeasies, and whorehouses. The close-knit Italian family, his father the barber giving shaves and haircuts all day at a quarter apiece while his mother made pots of spaghetti and meatballs for all the relatives. Dino dropping out of school ('That wasn't for me,' he said) and going to work in a foundry, then quickly realizing he wasn't cut out for factory work. He ran liquor for a bootlegger; he fought as a professional boxer called Kid Crochet. He dealt black-jack and poker in the biggest of Steubenville's many illegal casinos, the back of the Rex Cigar store. He quit boxing before that face got ruined. And he sang.

'I just had it in me,' Dean said simply. Wherever there was a chance to use his pipes — at a bar, a party, or just cruising down the street with his gang — he didn't have to be persuaded. Before long, his reputation got around and a bandleader from Cleveland, named Sammy Watkins, hired him. And then an amazing thing happened: Frank Sinatra canceled a gig at the Riobamba nightclub in New York, and the Music Corporation of America, MCA, whose man in Cleveland liked Dean's act, hired him to come east and fill in. He'd been Manhattan-based ever since.

It sounded like a fairy tale, but then I wondered: What was he doing in this shoe box of a hotel room? Like me, Dean had made it to the big town but not the big time. From traveling the circuit, I was all too aware of how long the odds were against really making it. You had to really want it, for one thing. I wanted it so badly it affected my breathing. But I wasn't so sure about this guy.

And as dazzled as I was by him, I could see there was still a lot of Steubenville in Dean. Those red-and-white patent leather shoes he was wearing, for example — pimp shoes! And from time to time, I noticed, his speech lapsed into

18

deze-dem-and-dose accents — partly his Italian-immigrant heritage (he spoke no English till age five, he told me), with a touch of Southern from West Virginia, right across the river from Steubenville. I noticed those big hands of his again, hands that had carried steel, fought in a ring, dealt cards. Life was tough, and this guy, great-looking as he was, knew it.

'They call me the Boy with the Tall, Dark, and Handsome Voice,' he said with a smile that was half proud, half self-mocking.

I just stared at him. The name certainly fit.

'And look at me, a family man, too,' he said, pulling out a couple of snapshots. His wife, Betty, was pretty — she looked like the girl next door in an MGM movie. And there were three little kids: a boy, Craig, and two girls, Claudia and Gail. Quick work for a young guy! The fact that he'd been out looking for quiff earlier that evening didn't faze me: This was showbiz.

'I've got a kid on the way, too,' I told Dean.

He snapped out of his reverie. 'You're kiddin' me,' he said. 'How old are you, pally?'

Suddenly, I felt as shy as a girl. 'I just turned nineteen,' I said. 'But I've been married to Patti since October, and we have a baby due in July.' I couldn't help smiling proudly. 'How old are you?' I asked, like a kid at grade school.

'Gettin' up there,' Dean said. 'About to turn twenty-eight.'

Nine years' difference, I thought. *He could be my big brother.* I smiled at the idea.

★ ★ ★

While Patti got more and more pregnant, I ran up and down the Eastern Seaboard, doing my act in little clubs and old theaters in Baltimore and D.C. and Philadelphia, always for the same princely salary: a hundred twenty-five a week. The big money came from the Big Apple, where my periodic gigs at the Glass Hat landed me an extra ten bucks per. And I was happy for that sawbuck, believe me: It bought Patti a maternity dress, which she wore until the eleventh month. The baby came, but a dress is a dress when you take it in.

It was funny — wherever I happened to land a job that spring and summer of 1945, Dean always seemed to be there, too, usually a week or two ahead of me or behind; it was like the two of us had a mini-circuit within the circuit. Sometimes, if I saw he was booked after me, I'd leave a note for him in the dressing room (which was a nail on the wall), something about the classy surroundings we were privileged to work in. I never got a note back. He didn't seem like much of a one for writing.

Then I returned to New York, this time to a nightclub on Broadway between Fiftieth and Fifty-first called the Havana-Madrid — to find that, miracle of miracles, Dean and I were both booked there at the same time, March of 1946.

The Havana-Madrid was one of a number of Latin-themed clubs that had sprung up in Manhattan with the rise of the rumba craze in the late thirties. The owner was a guy named Angel Lopez, and he liked to alternate Anglo and Hispanic acts. Dean was the singer; I was there

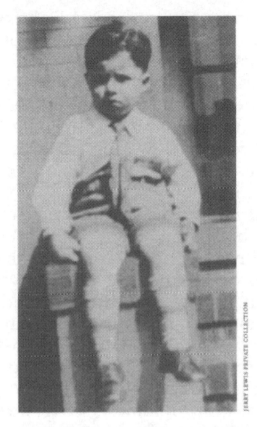

My impression of Dom DeLuise.

with my fright wig and records. On the bill with us were a dance team called the Barrancos, Pupi Campo and his orchestra, and the headliner, the great Cuban singer Diosa Costello.

I was thrilled to be on the same show, at last, with my fantasy big brother. But it wasn't enough for me to just be in the same place with him at the same time. Like all little brothers, I craved attention. And one night during the third show, as Dean stood on the Havana-Madrid stage entrancing the audience (but especially the ladies) with his honeyed version of 'Where or When,' I figured out how to get it.

The Barrancos had preceded Dean on the bill, finishing up with a hand-clapping, foot-stamping number that climaxed with Mr. Barranco bending Mrs. Barranco over a pot of fire. Very dramatic. They left the stage to big applause, and they also left their fire pot burning. With the houselights down low for Dean's romantic number, the flickering flame in the pot behind him cast a cozy glow.

The third show was in the wee hours of the morning, when there were only around eight people in the audience. In fact, at that time of night, there were more waiters in the house than customers — the waiters and captains were standing around with their napkins over their arms. It was a good time to go for broke, and that was exactly what I decided to do.

The spotlight was on Dean and the rest of the stage was in shadows, so it was easy for me to sneak out from the wings in my borrowed waiter's suit. I'd prepped the man on the lighting board. As Dean began to sing, I suddenly went into a tremendous coughing fit, and a second spotlight shone on me. I was standing there with a three-pound hunk of raw meat stuck on a fork.

'Who ordered steak?' I yelled at the top of my lungs.

Needless to say, Dean was compelled to interrupt his number.

I have to admit, there was a heart-stopping instant when I wasn't sure how he would react. Most any serious performer would be furious at being upstaged by such an asinine prank. But I had made a calculation about Dean: Remembering the incredulous smile on his face as he told me his life story, I figured him for a guy who didn't take himself too seriously, who saw all of life as one big crazy joke.

And in the next instant, my calculation proved correct. Dean did a long, slow take for the audience, looked to the side of the stage where I wasn't, and then — slowly, milking it for all it was worth — turned to face the monkey who had ruined his song. Our eyes met, and in that precious second, I saw the indulgent smile of the older brother I had always longed for. Dean was shaking his head at me, but he was grinning ear to ear.

★   ★   ★

Now and then, over the following weeks at the Havana-Madrid, Dean and I would get up together at two or three in the morning and ad-lib some comedy for the late-night audience. After my initial foray, he had taken to retaliation, banging my record player while I was in the middle of my act, making it jump at unexpected moments. Of course, I had to retaliate back. And escalate.

I'd put on a busboy's jacket and run around the place at top speed, chasing the cigarette girl and dropping plates. I'd borrow a maître d's jacket and seat people at the wrong tables. I'd take a trumpet or drumsticks from one of the guys in the band and blow that horn or bang those drums as loudly as I possibly could. I'd come out with a mop and bucket and swab the floor, very messily, as Dean sang. And while I went nuts, Dean, with the brilliant comic instincts that nobody but me had suspected him of, flawlessly played it straight. He kept right on singing, giving me that far-off stare of his (with an indulgent smile always playing around the edges), which gave the audience the space to work itself into a frenzy. Then, when I did my act, he'd heckle me right back. The people, instantly sensing how totally we clicked, ate it all up.

We were just screwing around, really, but an eerily farsighted journalist named Bill Smith sensed that something was cooking. 'Martin and Lewis do an after-piece that has all the makings of a sock act,' he wrote in *Billboard*. 'Boys play straight for each other, deliberately step on each other's lines, mug and raise general bedlam. It's a toss-up who walks off with the biggest mitt. Lewis's double-takes, throw-aways, mugging and deliberate over-acting are sensational. Martin's slow takes, ad libs and under-acting make him an ideal fall guy. Both got stand-out results from a mob that took dynamite to wake up.'

Martin and Lewis, the man wrote. Those two names, together in that odd, unalphabetical order, had never appeared in print before. The phrase had a nice sound to it, but at that point, in early 1946, it was meaningless. We weren't an act; we were just two young guys battling the show-business odds. If we'd never met that day on Broadway and Fifty-fourth, if we'd never both happened to play the Havana-Madrid, we

24

would have gone our own middling ways through the entertainment industry. Together, we ignited, and made America scream. Why? You tell me. Chemistry is chemistry. But I have a few pretty good ideas.

2

Atlantic City in the summer of 1946 was a very different place than it is today. Before the Bally and the Trump Taj Mahal and the rest of the megacasinos, long before gambling got legalized and the street life went indoors, there was a lively, milling, seaside-carnival feeling about the Boardwalk: You heard the sounds of hurdy-gurdies and happily screaming kids, you smelled the salt air and hot buttered corn on the cob and sarsaparilla. Of course, there were more grown-up amusements, too ... And, just as Vegas used to be, AC was very much in the pocket of organized crime. Philadelphia, the closest big city, was the guiding influence.

Paul D'Amato (everyone called him Skinny; he'd picked up the nickname in his teenage years and held on to it even after he filled out a bit) was a rough-and-tumble character with a good heart, a guy who stayed on the right side of some very influential people by minding his business. He was always suspected of being — as they say — a friend of the friends, but no one ever knew for sure. That was a big part of Skinny's mystique: He kept you guessing. Still, his hand-tailored suits, Parisian silk ties, and custom-made shoes seemed like a big clue. With a little help from his Philadelphia pals, and along with a partner, Irvin 'Wolfie' Wolf, Skinny ran the biggest nightclub in Atlantic City, in a yellow-brick-fronted building with a theater-style marquee on South Missouri Avenue, just a couple of blocks up from the Boardwalk. The marquee read '500 Café,' but most everyone knew it as the 500 Club, or the Fives, for short.

Inside were sixty tables, zebra-skin bar stools, an ever-present blue cloud of cigarette smoke, and an off-the-books gambling casino in the back room. Nightclub paradise. The Fives was where Abner Greshler had booked me that July, for the princely sum of a hundred fifty bucks a week, on a bill with the headliner, Jayne Manners, a busty blonde who told a few jokes and sang a few songs and wound up in the papers a lot, and a long-lashed tenor named Jack Randall.

A hundred fifty a week! It may not sound like much, but it was a 50 percent raise over what I'd been earning. And when you consider that a dollar in 1946 was worth about ten today, 150 per meant I could bring my bride and my almost-one-year-old Gary down for a real beach vacation, complete with a twelve-dollar-a-night room at the Princess Hotel, one block off the Boardwalk. And this, my friends, was paradise.

Except that there was trouble in paradise. Skinny, who micromanaged every detail of what went on in his club, from the precise proportion of water in his watered-down Scotch to the exact depth of the décolletage on Jayne Manners's gown, hated Jack Randall with a passion. 'Christ, what was I thinking when I booked this *finocchio?*' Skinny said. 'He sings like his nuts are caught in his zipper.'

The child no one would own.

Nor did he seem any too pleased with me. 'You're running short, kid,' he told me as I came off stage to polite applause from maybe thirty people. 'Throw in a couple more impressions, see if you can stretch it to twenty minutes.'

Then I watched Skinny's face as he watched Randall sing. It wasn't a pretty sight.

And then, one cool July morning, as a fog bank rolled in off the Atlantic, Jack Randall came down with laryngitis.

On one hand, Skinny was overjoyed. On the other, he was out one-third of his show. When I heard him bitching about it to Wolfie, I couldn't help piping up. 'Excuse me, Mr. D'Amato, Mr. Wolf,' I said. 'But how about Dean Martin?'

Skinny winced. 'Another crooner?' he said. 'Christ, I need that like I need a third ball.'

'Oh no, Mr. D'Amato,' I said. 'Dean doesn't just sing. We worked together lots of times — he and I did all kinds of funny stuff together.'

I was tap-dancing, but fast, for two reasons: One, I was worried about my own spot on the show. I knew that Skinny's partner, Wolfie — a sharp-eyed, heavyset fellow who would just as soon have your thumbs broken as look at you — was not my biggest fan. In fact, *Skinny* wasn't my biggest fan, but at least he chuckled now and then at my record act. Wolfie didn't chuckle. As I stood on stage in my fright wig, he kept shooting me looks that said he wouldn't mind breaking me like a stick.

But the other reason I was pushing for Dean was that I missed him. I was telling the truth about the funny stuff. We'd had *fun* together. You

29

didn't see that too often in show business. People tried hard, performed skillfully, but fun was for the audience.

Maybe Skinny read this in my eyes. After thinking a minute, he nodded. 'Okay, okay, I'll book your buddy,' he said. 'But only 'cause I'm over a barrel. And I better see some sparks fly.'

Now that things had turned serious, I had to send Patti and Gary back to Newark. I had a tear in my eye as I put my wife and baby on the bus . . .

★   ★   ★

I was waiting at the terminal on Washington Street, Downtown Atlantic City, and then I saw the bus. As it pulled into the inner drive, I rushed over and watched the passengers unload. First a lady, then a kid, then another lady . . . and there he was!

'Hey, Dean! Over here!' I called. I was standing by a bench with my foot resting nonchalantly on the seat. Dean looked and smiled, because (it occurred to me later on) at that moment he remembered the milk shakes I always drank . . . When I'd first called him about the gig, there had been a bad moment on the phone when he thought I was Jerry Lester (Buddy Lester's brother, and, like Buddy, another excellent comic).

Now he knew for sure it was Jerry *Lewis*.

Still growing at nineteen, but with a pompadour that added another six inches, easy, thanks to about three and a half pounds of orange pomade . . . and the flies liked settling in that pomade! My pants were so pegged that they choked the blood flow to my ankles, and I was wearing my Irvington High School sweater — all wool and a little hot for Atlantic City in July at three in the afternoon. The truth was, I had no clothes to speak of, just my blue stage suit that already had a mirror shine on the ass from too much pressing. Until your suit shone in the back, you were not quite a veteran.

I went to help Dean with his bag, grabbing it in my right hand — but then Dean extended his hand to shake, so I had to switch hands . . . except that as I switched, he went for the left hand with his left, banging into the bag. He smiled and said, 'Oh, we're gonna be all right.' I proceeded toward our transportation (Skinny had lent me the house car, a 1945 Chrysler station wagon with wood on the doors), and Dean stopped.

'Hold on, pally, Poppa's got another little chestnut coming.'

And he strolled over to the bus driver, who was taking luggage out of the bus's belly, and waited till the driver handed him his golf clubs. Dean whipped out a buck and handed it to the driver. Wow! Was he cool! A buck! I shlepped his bags to the back of the wagon and put them in.

In the car, Dean was quite talkative. 'When did you open here?' he asked. 'What's the joint like? Any broads? And what time is rehearsal? And where do I lay my curly head?'

But here we were. I jumped out of the car, got his bag and golf clubs, and started for the lobby.

31

Dean looked skeptically at the entrance awning, which read, 'Princess Hotel and Spa.'

★ ★ ★

The Princess was near the beach, where everything was damp. After one night of hanging in a closet at this (un-air-conditioned) palace, your clothes looked like someone had sat in them during a Greyhound bus ride from Fresno to Hartford. They didn't have hot and cold running chambermaids, you did the bed yourself. Every other day, you found linens outside your door. I think they felt it was costly if they knocked. The bathroom (down the hall) was a delight. You only prayed that all your normal bodily functions would lock up until you checked out of this facility.

Dean looked at the hotel lobby, then at me.

'Is this the best we can do?' he asked.

'No,' I said. 'We can do better at the Ritz-Carlton, but their suites run a little more than the twelve dollars a night we'll be paying here.'

Resigned to our surroundings, we decided to save a little money by splitting the tab. 'Do you have anything in a double for us?' I asked the desk clerk (the same man selling cotton candy outside the hotel lobby).

'Yeah, about thirty-five rooms,' he answered. 'Take your pick. But the twelve-dollar price is only from the eighth floor up.'

'How many floors are there?' Dean asked.

'Eight,' the clerk said.

'We'll take it,' Dean said. 'Can someone carry our bags up?'

The desk clerk looked at me and said, 'Sure, him.'

After walking up the eight flights (the elevator was broken), I was perspiring pretty good into my wool sweater. I reached down and took the key out of my sneaker ('Are you sure your valuables shouldn't be in the hotel safe?' Dean asked) and unlocked the door . . .

Which swung open and hit a bedpost. Dean looked at the room, then looked at me. 'What are we paying here a week?' he asked.

I told him $84, forty-two bucks apiece.

He plopped himself on the edge of one of the beds and lit a Camel. And began to giggle. No one on the planet giggled like he did, and it was catching.

'You wanna share with me what's making you chuckle?' I asked.

'Yeah, sure. That little card on the dresser from 'The Princess Management.' Towels every *other* day?'

'Sometimes they're still damp!' I assured him.

He laughed, so I laughed. While I had him in the mood, I told him: 'Dean, so you aren't disappointed — when we go to the club, our dressing room is a folding chair.'

Our hotel room was so small, the mice had to go out to change their minds. (Credit: Henny Youngman.) But we were together, and that made me very happy. Loneliness was not my strong suit.

* * *

33

We arrived at the 500 Club at a quarter to five, walked in, and went straight to the band. A really nice bunch of guys . . . a small bunch, but nice. In fact, the music complement was as follows: piano, trumpet, bass, and drums. The drummer was Bernie, and he had a big nose that everyone teased him about, so he and I became compadres — his nose and my entire being up for grabs. Bernie was the first one to tell a funny story about his beak. It seems he'd been drinking at a party and his girl aroused him while they were dancing. Well, he got an erection, walked into the wall, and broke his nose. Pete Miller was the bandleader. A very nice man and a terrific pianist (I was so jealous).

Dean put his bag down, opened it, and took out the sheets for his four musical numbers. These weren't arrangements, like stars have, but just straight sheet music, for piano only, purchased at Woolworth's music counter. 'That's it?' Pete asked.

'Just play and let the guys fill in,' Dean told him. 'I've done it before. It always works.'

It appeared that Dean was trying to comfort the band, yet deep down, I sensed that he was the one who really needed comforting. But would he ever show it? Not even close. It was my first experience with the bravado that would amaze me for the next ten years. Dean was always working, not just when he was performing but throughout his life and times. He made me understand that your life is your own — work it, nurture it, protect it. He said to me one day, 'You know, the day you're born, you get the pink

How'd they get rid of the numbers?

slip on you — outright ownership. You must only share that life with those that you, and only you, choose. We are not brought on this earth as an object of sacrifice.'

Often, Dean would speak philosophically, saying things that I believe had been inside him for a long, long time — things that, over the following ten years, he would tell me and very few others. No, he wasn't a drunk or a buffoon, as many thought. He was as sharp as a shit-house rat, and he understood every move he ever made (and every move everybody else made). But he loved playacting. That's how he became the actor he was in films like *Some Came Running* and *Rio Bravo*. I learned a great shtick from Dean early on: If you make believe you've had a few, or you look like you've misplaced your wallet, usually people will stay away. And he did it like a champ . . .

★   ★   ★

One hour to showtime, we're waiting in the alley outside the club, and my stomach is doing the aria from *Figaro*. Dean shows such nerves . . . as he yawns and lights up another Camel.

Who could have thought — as we stood in that alley with the smells from the kitchen, the cats going up and down, the one folding chair between us — who could have thought that in four and a half hours, we would have changed the face of American show business? Certainly not us.

Restless, we walked around to the club's main entrance and went inside for a drink. The 500 Club's bar was huge, running from the front of the house all the way back to the maître d's desk at the entry to the showroom. In order to sit down, you had to grease some palms. Once again, the bills came out of Dean's pocket, and we sat.

'Give me a Chivas Regal, water back,' Dean told the bartender.

What the hell is that, I wondered — *a dog?* Meanwhile, the bartender was looking at me, waiting. I finally decided . . . here goes nothing. 'Give me the same, Coke back,' I said.

Dean watched me as I got the drink. I picked up the Coke first.

'Have you ever done this before?' he asked.

'Done?' I said, sipping my Coke.

'Imbibing. Boozing. Drinking. Ever do it before?'

'Well, not exactly . . . Well, on Passover . . . '

Dean smiled and said, 'Okay, just take it easy.'

A half hour to showtime. We went outside the showroom, and I showed Dean where we were supposed to dress. He put his hands on his hips. 'It *is* a fuckin' folding chair!' he said.

I paced back and forth for a few minutes, then walked into the showroom to see what was up. My heart sank. It was worse than it had been the other night, when I'd played to seven people. Now there were six. I decided not to tell Dean. I walked over to the lighting guy and said, 'Please keep the brights down — we'd be better off not seeing who we're playing to!'

I ran back to our folding chair and got my blue suit on. Dean was sitting on the chair, napping. I had to wake him to remind him that once I went on, he had only seventeen minutes to get ready.

I was the opening act. I went out and did my pantomimicry, and came off to polite applause from the audience, which had now swelled to maybe eleven people. (As usual, there were two or three customers doubled over with laughter; the rest smiled now and then.) Dean went on next. He did his four numbers — I remember 'Where or When,' 'Pennies from Heaven,' 'I've Got the Sun in the Morning (and the Moon at Night),' and 'Oh, Marie.'

I stood in the wings, mesmerized, as he

performed. He really was an amazing singer, warm and direct, with a way around a romantic tune that got to women where they lived. But the funny thing was, Dean didn't seem to understand his own power. Some part of him was always standing back, making fun of what he did. He wasn't yet at the point where he would stop a number to make a wisecrack (and very often, get lost in the process — that's where the drunk act eventually came in handy), but occasionally you could see in his eyes, as he sang, that he just couldn't take the song seriously. And he had a way of making little self-deprecating remarks between songs, almost under his breath, remarks that if you listened — and I sure did — were killer-funny. But they were throwaway, as much of his singing itself was. There was something about how ridiculously handsome Dean was — about the way he could practically get away with just standing there and being admired — that made trying hard seem almost laughable to him.

Impressed by him but slightly confused by his attitude, the small audience gave him a reasonably warm hand. Jayne Manners, our head-liner, closed the show in her inimitable fashion. Unlike Dean, she made sure the people understood exactly what her act was about. She spelled it right out for them: Big boobs — funny. A big-breasted blonde singing badly — funny. A big-breasted blonde making off-color remarks — that's entertainment!

Back at our folding chair, Dean and I were starving — between rehearsing and worrying, neither of us had eaten a bite since that morning. The 500 Club had what they called a runner: a Jewish kid named Morris. So Dean and I slipped Morris a couple of bucks and sent him out to score us some of the food that's killed more of my people than Hitler: hot pastrami on rye, don't trim the fat.

But as Morris walked out, Skinny and Wolfie stalked in. A double visit did not seem like a good sign, and the look in both men's eyes wasn't promising.

'Where's the funny shit?' Skinny asked.

'Excuse me?' I said.

'The funny shit you said the two of you were gonna do together — where is it?'

All the while, Wolfie is glaring at us like we'd propositioned his sister. I looked at Skinny. I looked at Dean. (Dean looked puzzled.) I cleared my throat. 'Ah, actually, we were just going to discuss that, Mr. D'Amato. And Mr. Wolf,' I added weakly.

This time it was Wolfie who spoke up. 'You better,' he grunted.

His meaning couldn't have been clearer. Skinny was the good cop, the nice guy, the guy who'd bend over backwards to make everyone happy. Wolfie wasn't. The word on the Boardwalk was that Irvin Wolf had some serious muscle behind him and didn't hesitate to use it. He didn't say the words 'cement overshoes' — he didn't have to.

Meanwhile, I was shaking in my Florsheims. The fact is, when I'd told Skinny about the funny stuff Dean and I did together, funny stuff had been the last thing on my mind. Staying employed was the first thing on my mind, with the side benefit of getting a gig for (and seeing) Dean.

Who, now that Skinny and Wolfie had stalked back out, was looking askance at me. 'What in Christ's name did you sell them?' Dean asked.

The words came out in a rush. 'I knew you had no gig, they asked me to suggest someone, I suggested you, and they said no, not another singer, so I said, 'But we do things together.' '

'Why did you do that?' Dean asked.

'Because I wanted you to be here and work and be a friend and pay half of a double room, and I was lonely,' I said.

'Get a dog!' Dean said.

Just then, Skinny leaned back through the door, making me jump. 'P.S. — I suggest you guys get something going for the next show,' he said. 'I suggest this only because I told a number of my best customers, who will be here for the next show, that you fellas did other shit besides crooning and miming. Capeesh?'

'Yes sir, Mr. D'Amato,' I said.

No pressure!

As Skinny turned to leave, he almost collided with Morris the runner. I took the greasy brown bag and told Morris to keep the change. He gave the fourteen cents in his hand a fishy look, shook his head, and left. Dean and I were alone, with two hours until the midnight show.

I opened the bag, took a pastrami sandwich, and held one out to Dean. 'Hungry?' I said.

He grabbed the sandwich. 'Gimme that!' he

40

barked. 'Of course I'm hungry — hungry and scared shitless. What the hell are we gonna do here?'

'Relax,' I said around a mouthful of pastrami and rye. 'I have a plan.'

⋆ ⋆ ⋆

While Dean watched, I took a makeup pencil from my table, ripped the greasy bag open to make a flat sheet, and began to write, avoiding the grease spots.

I wrote 'Filler.'

I wrote 'Busboy.'

I wrote 'That Old Gang of Mine.'

I wrote 'Italian Lumberjack.'

I wrote 'April Showers.'

'What the hell are you doing?' Dean asked.

'Okay.' I told him. 'This is material. I'm writing down bits I remember from my dad, from burlesque, from all over. 'Filler' is how we get from your intro to the Busboy bit, which I think you remember . . . '

'What's that say?' he asked, pointing at the bag. 'What's the — what's that say? The Italian Lumberjack?'

'A variation on a theme,' I explained. 'Whatever we do, I'm the kid and you're the big brother. I'm the busboy, you're the captain. You're the organ-grinder, I'm the monkey. You're the playboy, I'm the putz. Follow?'

He was smiling. 'Sure, putz,' he said. Smiling.

'In the Italian Lumberjack, you're the lumberjack,' I told him.

He grinned. 'Naturally.'

'And I'm the kid brother. I say, 'What do you do for a living?' You say, in a nice, old-country accent, 'I cut down the trees.''

He gave it a whirl in his best Italian accent. 'I cut-a down the trees.'

I pitched my voice up a couple of octaves so I sounded maybe eight, nine years old. 'Yeah? And what do you do after that?'

Dean narrowed his eyes menacingly at me. 'Then . . . then I cut 'em up,' he said.

'Bingo!' I told him. 'We're on fire!'

Dean, eating, looked at me as though he knew we'd be OK. I liked that.

★   ★   ★

Okay: twelve midnight, that night.

The joint is jammed, maybe twenty-four people. My God, they must have been giving something away. Anyway, the orchestra plays its timid overture — the orchestra being the aforementioned piano, trumpet, bass, and drums. Once they started playing, it didn't take long to realize they sounded just like a piano, trumpet, bass, and drums.

And I was on. I did my seventeen minutes of miming to recordings, and heard what sounded like some applause. They also could have been calling for a waiter.

Then Dean came on.

He took center stage and sang Song One: 'Oh, Marie.' Nice! Then he began Song Two: 'Pennies from Heaven.'

I'd combed my hair straight and parted it dead center, put on my street jacket, and sat at one of the ringside tables. As Dean finished the number, I caught his eye and nodded at him. *Don't do anything yet* was what that nod was saying. He read me, started to introduce his next song.

'I got a special request,' he told the audience. 'But I'm gonna sing anyhow.'

A couple of laughs from out in the dark.

As Dean sang the first few notes of 'Where or When' — that nice, quiet, romantic tune — I suddenly banged my table as hard as I could. The china and silverware danced. 'Waiter!' I yelled in my Idiot voice. 'Where's my Chateaubriand for two, for Chrissakes?'

Dean stopped the band. 'Hold it,' he said. And to me: 'Hey, I'm tryin' to make a living up here.'

'Doing that?! Hah-hah-huh-huh!'

'You think it's easy?' he asked me.

'It's a piece of cake — you're stealing the money!' I yelled.

He motioned me to come up to the stage. I looked around — me? — then stood and went up there. Did some shtick with squinting into the lights. Got a laugh, did it some more. Dean went over to the piano, took some sheet music, handed it to me.

'You sing it,' he said.

'Me?'

'You.'

I looked at the sheet, the piano went into the intro, I opened my mouth — and out came Yiddish. Double-talk. 'Vay-meen o soy needle

43

rachmon-eetz . . . ' Dean gave me a look. The laughs were coming stronger now.

'Oh, I only sing in Jewish,' I said. 'Is that okay?'

'Jewish?' he said. I nodded. 'I'm Italian,' Dean said. 'You're Jewish?'

I nodded again, with the Idiot face. Dean was smiling. The people were laughing. Hard. Christ, what a sweet sound! More intoxicating than any booze. 'Someone told me you had your nose fixed,' I said in my nine-year-old voice.

'Yeah,' Dean said, pointing to his cheek. 'It used to be here.'

This got a roar of laughter. And I blinked. Something had happened in that instant, something only I had seen, and it was giving me goose bumps. Dean's ad lib had been not just fast but instantaneous. I'd already been in the business long enough to know how incredibly rare that was. Over the next sixty years, I would come to understand it better and better. The vast majority of comedians with good rhythm use beats — small hesitations, often with some comic business or other — to set up their jokes. Dean didn't use beats.

I was in the presence of magic.

I can't tell you what this looks like to somebody whose life is predicated on rhythm. Once we became a team, after we'd been together four or five years, there would be shows where I'd look at Dean and go, 'Holy fuck.' It was like being in a lab, watching this magnificent experiment come to life. Nobody, I swear, ever had it in his bones like Dean had. My dad used to agree with me. Danny Lewis worked with straight men all through his career. Good ones. But nobody could touch Dean.

George Burns saw us at the Sands in the mid-fifties, and said to me over dinner one night, 'He's the greatest straight man I've ever seen.'

George Burns! Who lived through all the two-acts — Smith and Dale. Olsen and Johnson. Gallagher and Shean.

Not to mention Burns and Allen.

George used to tell the classic self-deprecating joke about straight men — namely, that all you really had to do to hold up your end was repeat what the comic said. If the comic says, 'I lost my shoes,' you say, 'You lost your shoes?' George joked, 'It's terrible, because I was at the beach, and there was a kid in the water yelling 'help-help-help,' and I yelled 'help-help-help?' And by the time I got to him, he drowned.'

George was so much better than that, of course. And George thought that Dean was the greatest of them all.

Who knew this on July 24, 1946?

July 25, actually — midnight had passed, and we had the twenty-four audience members of the second show at the 500 Club in the palm of our hands. The people roared as I ran over tables in my busboy jacket, smashing dishes and snipping neckties with a scissors. Our pastrami-bag cue sheet sat on the piano where we'd left it, just in case, but we'd abandoned our plan long before. We were in some different territory, some previously unexplored zone — way out on a limb, streaked with stardust. By the time I glanced at my Timex, I realized we'd been on for close to an hour and a half.

And they still wanted more.

By the time we finally were able to get off, we'd been on for over two hours. And this time, it was just Skinny who ducked into our dressing room — the Wolf had stayed away from our door. Skinny was all smiles.

'Now, that's what I call lightning in a bottle!' he said. It was the first time I'd heard the expression. It wouldn't be the last. 'How come you guys didn't tell me what you could do together?' Skinny asked.

'Because,' I answered, 'we didn't know it ourselves.'

★ ★ ★

Atlantic City had a split personality in those days. On the beach side of the Boardwalk, it was all family sun and fun. The inland side was all grown-up pleasures, 24/7. But AC, on both sides of the Boardwalk, was a tightly knit place, the type of place where, if anything out of the ordinary happened, word got around fast.

The following night, there were 200 people at the first show, out of a possible 240 seats. And they loved everything we threw at them — they went ballistic as they watched us trip and fumble through our wares, knowing full well that they were in on something special.

We were on fire. Not only did we remember the stuff from the first night (and do it better),

With Gary Lewis, Atlantic City, 1946.
Thank God for Tums.

we pulled new things out of the air. The second-night crowd was as enthusiastic as the people the night before — except that 200 people are so much louder than twenty-four! They bellowed with laughter, they didn't want us to stop. After two hours and twenty minutes, we finally had to.

Soon there were lines around the block for all three shows at the 500 Club, including the 2.30 a.m. Dean and I couldn't walk on the beach without people stopping us to say, 'Bravo.'

But we weren't leaving anything to chance, either. Forty years earlier, when the great W.C. Fields had played Atlantic City as a young juggler, he'd come up with a publicity stunt known as 'the drowning gag.' My dad told me about it, I told Dean, and we brought it back. When the beach was good and crowded, I'd wade out into the surf up to my chest, then suddenly start waving my arms and yelling in distress. Dean would splash out, drag me back to shore, throw me down on the sand, apparently comatose, and act like he was about to administer mouth-to-mouth resuscitation. By this time, we'd have a nice crowd around us. But before he'd begin, I'd sit bolt upright and say, 'I'd rather have a malted, sir!'

'We're fresh out,' Dean would say, smooth as silk. Then: 'Hey, don't I know you?'

'I'm Jerry Lewis!'

'And I'm Dean Martin!'

'I know that — I'm at the 500 Club with you, first show is at eight o'clock!'

And we'd jump up and run like madmen, all the way back to the Princess Hotel.

★ ★ ★

The bit was corny as hell, but it piqued the curiosity of a showbiz legend named Sophie Tucker, who happened to be walking along the beach one day and caught one of our 'drownings.' Sophie was a contemporary of Fields — she probably remembered that publicity stunt from when he first pulled it — who billed herself as 'The Last of the Red-Hot Mamas.' She was playing the 400 Club, on the Boardwalk, that July. After her last show, she'd come to see our last show.

She liked what she saw. A lot. She told the

48

local paper, 'These two crazy kids are a combination of the Keystone Kops, the Marx Brothers, and Abbott and Costello. They will leave their mark on the whole profession.'

★ ★ ★

There was a little vest-pocket park down Missouri Avenue from the 500 Club. Before shows and in between, Dean and I would hang out there, sitting around on a park bench and shooting the breeze, reminiscing about the past but mostly dreaming about the future.

Our future was closing in on us fast. One night, Skinny came up to the bench, a little out of breath. 'I been looking for you turkeys everywhere,' he said. 'I got a surprise for you.'

I went into the nine-year-old voice. 'Tell us, oh tell us, oh please, Mr. D'Amato,' I screeched. 'We love surprises!'

'Wolfie and I decided we want to hold you for the rest of the summer,' he said. 'Four more weeks. Seven hundred fifty a week.' He gave us a look, dead serious. 'Apiece.'

We went nuts. We kissed Skinny, kissed each other, kissed our lucky park bench. As soon as we really hit it big — and it wouldn't be long — Skinny had that bench put in the club, bolted to the floor, with a plaque on it. The plaque read: 'Here, on the stage of the 500 Club, Dean Martin and Jerry Lewis became a team in the summer of 1946.'

Oh — by the way. I still have that brown-paper

pastrami-sandwich bag. (I keep it in my safety-deposit box.) Sixty years on, the grease spots are still there. Apparently, great comedy, and pastrami grease, are forever.

3

From the beginning of show business, it's been understood that you're only as good as your billing. You're on top, you're on the bottom, or you're in the middle. If you're just starting out, your name goes anywhere. When you knew you'd arrived, there was only one place to look — on top. Billing matters. A lot.

In late August of 1946, Dean and I knew we were on our way (only five weeks after we'd begun!), and we were discussing that very interesting and always somewhat sensitive matter. We both knew 'Crocetti and Levitch' wasn't going to make it ... that was a no-brainer. Because I'd brought Dean into the mix, the 500 Club had made up early posters that read, 'Lewis & Martin.' I knew that was wrong. Why? I'll never know, but it was wrong. So we talked.

'What about alphabetical order?' Dean said.

'Then we're back to Lewis and Martin,' I said.

'Not if you go by first names.'

'Just 'Dean and Jerry'?' I asked.

'No, idiot — 'Martin and Lewis,' but we use the first names, too, so it's 'Dean Martin and Jerry Lewis,' and we make that contractual. We demand that it can't ever appear otherwise.'

I thought about it. I reminded Dean that it was never 'Bud Abbott and Lou Costello'; it was always just 'Abbott and Costello.'

51

'But they had alphabetical working both ways!' Dean exclaimed.

'Yeah, and L is before M,' I said.

And Dean said, 'You wanna call this act 'Dean Lewis and Jerry Martin'?'

We both laughed at that, and I still laugh thinking about how sharp Dean's mind was. We ultimately agreed that 'Martin and Lewis' sounded great, but that 'Dean Martin and Jerry Lewis' sounded better. So it was written into all contracts and agreements, and the billing could not ever be compromised.

★   ★   ★

We went back to the Havana-Madrid that fall and scored big-time with our nonsense. And it was nonsense — just the same tomfoolery I described earlier, with improvements and variations: The maître d' and the busboy. The drill sergeant and the recruit. Don Juan and the monkey. The playboy and the putz.

Dean was always the suave one, the cool one, the one in charge. I was the wacked-out, terminally insecure (but dangerously uninhibited) nine-year-old.

What he did, his singing and comedy, could have worked without me — if he'd had the self-confidence. But what I did would never have worked without him.

Because everything that I did, I did off Dean. Every move I made was because he went, 'Ah, ah.' No one understood what 'Ah, ah' did. It stopped the body of a wildcat.

For Christ's sake, if he wasn't there, you'd have had a loose cannon! They'd have had me living in a rubber room!

He watched me breathe. He knew my breath. He was so intent, always watching for the exact right second to come in. He knew that there were a couple of breaths coming after this one; he knew to lay back until just the right moment.

I could time *anything*. Never once, in ten years, did he ever get in the way. Never once stepped on a line, spoiled a joke.

He was, quite simply, impeccable at what he did.

He was yin to my yang. Bedrock to my wildfire. His own natural comic instincts dovetailed perfectly with mine and made the sum of one and one into two million.

The more successful we got, the bolder we got. We'd squirt seltzer on each other (and the audience); we'd dump pitchers of water on each other — and the audience. The audience howled.

Please realize that these were very uncertain times. No matter how many images you conjure of the triumphant armies marching home, the sailor kissing the girl in Times Square, the years just after the war were dark and uncertain ones. Millions had been killed and maimed. Russian communism was looking like a very bad thing. Nuclear weapons were being tested. The Red Scares were beginning.

Meanwhile, our G.I.s, back from the war, were encouraged to embrace peace and prosperity. Everybody was supposed to get into harness and turn the U.S.A. into paradise on earth. There was a lot of unease and rebellion just under the country's placid surface.

And so the sight of two grown men in a nightclub squirting water at each other and making silly jokes was a very welcome one. But our appeal went way beyond that.

What audiences saw, in a time of people hating each other, was the look in Dean's eyes as he watched me wreak havoc. It was the look in my eyes as I watched him sing and be so perfect. You can't fake that, nor was there any need to disguise it.

And people got it. Instantly, on a gut level. Our audiences had grown up with great comedy teams: Laurel and Hardy. Abbott and Costello. Hope and Crosby. Bob and Bing were the most modern team of the bunch, and in a way, even when we were just starting out, Dean and I were going up against them. But from the word go — in my mind — there was no contest.

Bob Hope was a great monologist and Bing Crosby was a great singer. Their 'Road' pictures for Paramount were a huge success. (And an accidental one: Paramount had thrown that first script at them, *Road to Singapore*, in 1940, because the studio had nothing else to give them.) But everything they did together was totally scripted, even the live performances, and I don't think the two men particularly liked each other, and I believe that deep down, it showed. The audiences laughed because the material was funny and the performers were skilled. But Hope and Crosby never generated anything like the hysteria that Dean and I did, and that was because we had that X factor, the powerful feeling between us.

And it really was an X factor, a kind of mystery.

The world of show business was so much smaller then than it is today. Word of mouth didn't just shoot up and down the Boardwalk in Atlantic City, but up and down the Eastern Seaboard. So as soon as Dean and I hit big at the 500 Club, word about the new hot guys traveled at lightning speed to New York City, and agents and managers and performers hustled down to catch our act.

They realized we were a hit, but they all left scratching their heads: What is it that these guys *do*?

The news, and the mystery, got around fast. So fast that when we actually arrived in Manhattan for the first time as Martin and Lewis, we were instant celebrities. There was a ton of curiosity about us — and a ton of confusion.

You remember I mentioned Sunday nights, Celebrity Nights, at Leon and Eddie's, the Fifty-second Street club? Only a few months earlier, Dean and I had gone there to star-gaze; now we figured it was our time to step up. So one night after our second show at the Havana-Madrid, we strolled across town.

The celebrity show at Leon and Eddie's usually began about 3:15 a.m.; Dean and I walked in around 3:20 — and immediately found ourselves in the midst of Showbiz Central. Milton Berle was on stage, getting heckled by Red Buttons, Jack Carter, Henny Youngman,

*With Sophie Tucker. She wasn't sure
who she'd go home with.*

Morey Amsterdam, Buddy and Jerry Lester, Alan King, Sonny King, the Ritz Brothers, Danny Kaye, Harvey Stone, Pupi Campo, Shecky Greene, Buddy Hackett, Joey Bishop, Tony Martin . . . More names than I've got type for.

It was an incredible, once-in-a-lifetime experience. Somewhere around 4:55 a.m. Milton decided to introduce us. We hoped he would, but we kept making out like 'Oh no, not us, please . . . we couldn't, really. Call someone else, please.'

We spoke those last few words as we got on stage, and there in front of us was *all* of show business . . . still not clear about what, exactly, we did! Dean started a song that the piano player didn't know all that well, and the pianist hit a few clams. Well, that was all we needed. While

Dean took out his pocket handkerchief and busily cleaned the piano's keys, I lifted the lid, then dropped it with a huge bang.

I then proceeded to half-undress the piano player.

The audience was beside itself.

As the pianist sat there beet-red and bare-chested, Dean asked, 'Would you like to try it again?'

The pianist hit the same clam.

And we both yelled, 'Perfect!'

When we got off, Berle looked at the crowd and said, 'I still don't know what they do!'

★　★　★

The reason Dean and I had such fun ad-libbing and going completely crazy on stage is that we both knew we had a great act — something we didn't ever stray too far from, no matter how wild I got. And believe me, I had to get pretty wild to top myself. One time I'd gone so far that Dean and I found ourselves literally standing nose to nose, with maybe an eighth of an inch of air between us. And he said, with genuine anger in his voice, 'I have finally come to the point in our relationship where I am going to have to tell you, if you do that again, it's *over*. Do you understand that? O-V-U-R!'

I planted my mouth on his, gave him a big kiss, and said, 'I understand *perfectly*.'

Now, I have to tell you — the first time I ever did that, Dean had absolutely no idea it was coming! None! Ninety-nine out of a hundred guys in the business would have blanched, would have flinched and killed the gag. Not my partner. He didn't *budge*. Meanwhile, people in the audience were crying with laughter.

The act might have looked like chaos, but we could always get back to where we needed to get on a moment's notice. We had musicians (that we carried) always at the ready. Cues, lights, sound, all knowing, '*They will steer this machine — just be aware and ready!*' We had that down to a gnat's ass.

Either Dean and I, together, would save us, or Dean would save me, or I would save him. It was a brilliant concept. One that we never sat down and discussed. And once you recognize that the magic is there, you sooner or later become fearless and do just about anything that comes to you . . . always making it look like it has been totally planned. As I write it, it scares me a little to think of the guts we had.

★ ★ ★

After the Havana-Madrid, we played the Latin Casino in Philly, Loew's State Theater back in Manhattan, the Rio Cabana in Chicago, the Stanley Theater in Camden, New Jersey, the Earl Theater in Philadelphia, return gigs at Loew's State and the 500 Club, and Ben Marden's fabulous, glass-roofed Riviera, overlooking Manhattan on the Jersey side of the George Washington Bridge. These were all prime venues of the day (although the venue of venues — which I'll tell you about in a moment — still eluded us), and Dean and I were building momentum as we went, getting better and better known — and, in the process, getting to know each other, and the foundations of our act, ever more deeply.

Three little (but really not so little) things happened along the way, things that made us more *us*. One night while we were playing Chicago, Dean took a look at my pompadour and said, 'What do you do, get your hair cut from the inside?'

It was clearly time for a change.

A little-known fact is that Dean, whose dad was a barber in Steubenville, was a deft hand with the scissors himself. He told me about it that very night — then sat me down in the hotel room, put a sheet over me, took out the snippers he always carried to trim his own curly locks, and made my pompadour history. I was a little shocked when I saw the result — 'Where's the rest of me?' I said, stealing Ronnie Reagan's line from *King's Row* — but I understood the wisdom of Dean's move in our very next show, when I suddenly found myself getting bigger laughs than I'd ever gotten before. With my crew cut, I looked much younger — which sure helps if you're acting like a nine-year-old — and more monkeylike — which sure helps if you're acting like a monkey. With one haircut, my partner had given my stage persona an unforgettable stamp: Nobody had ever mistaken either of us for the other before, but now? Impossible!

And one unintended side benefit: I suddenly looked two inches shorter! Another little-known fact is that (once my adolescent growth had topped out) Dean and I were the exact same height, six feet tall on the button. The fact is little-known because we didn't *play* that way. If Dean was the older brother and I was the kid, it had to look like that on stage. The crew cut helped, and so did the fact that I went into a kind of crouch when I was standing next to him. But I decided to give nature a helping hand (and return the favor for the haircut). I took Dean's show shoes to a shoemaker and had a quarter-inch added to the heels.

Suddenly, he was towering over me on stage. The effect was perfect.

But there was still something missing.

It came to me as we were about to open at the Chez Paree in Chicago — a place that would come to have a big part in our professional lives, and in Dean's after we broke up. 'We've got to work in tuxes,' I told my partner.

I might as well have told him we had to work naked. 'Tuxes??' he said. 'Why?'

Up to that point, we'd been performing in gray street suits with matching four-in-hand ties. We could have been borrowed from Florsheim and no one would have noticed. 'Because,' I said, 'if we don't, then we'll look like the act that opened in Atlantic City — two stumble-bums getting paid a load of cash. We're getting a bundle, and we have to look like we deserve it. An audience can see anybody on the Bowery wearing a gray suit — and lying in the gutter, yet. But when a comic takes a fall in a thousand-dollar tux . . . that's funny! Don't ask me why, but I know what I'm talking about.'

I'd said the magic words: Dean knew I knew. When Mike Fritzel and Joey Jacobsen, Chez Paree's owners and two great guys, heard what we had planned, they called us into their office. Joey said, 'I've just made arrangements for both of you to be fitted for high-class tuxes made by Pucci on Michigan Boulevard — only the top-of-the-line tailor in the country!'

When the fittings were done, we were convinced that when these tuxes were finished, we were going to see work like we had never seen before. And since we were booked into the Chez Paree for twelve weeks, it was certain the great Pucci would take his time getting the tuxes made. Meanwhile, Dean and I continued to work in our gray street suits, at the same time reporting back to Pucci every week for further fittings.

This went on for seven weeks, and — not wanting to insult Mike and Joey, who were paying the $2,000-plus for each tux (big bucks in those days) — neither Dean nor I ever uttered a peep of protest. When we finally got the tuxes, we decided to wear them the same night.

We did, and we were awful.

Not only did our work feel stiff and strained, but we both felt like we were appearing at a funny farm and we were two of the inmates. The only good part was that everyone that saw us that night said, 'Now the act has class.' So Mike and Joey were right! Gradually, we started to get comfortable — but not as comfortable as we would be when we eventually had our tuxes made by our tailor, Sy Devore, in Hollywood. When that happened, we really looked great, and we felt as strong as we looked.

From that night at Chez Paree, and not only for the rest of the ten years that we were together, but for the thirty years thereafter, Dean would never work without a tux. It became part of his persona, and he always looked smashing in it, as well. There were dates when my wardrobe didn't show on time, and I would rather rent a cheap tux than work in a $1,500 suit. Dean and I both recognized that looking like big-time brought big-time.

★ ★ ★

That venue of venues I mentioned a moment ago was, of course, the Copa. The crème de la crème of nightclubs, the top spot in the country, and the big one that had eluded us so far. In early 1947, when Martin and Lewis were really starting to pick up momentum, the club's bookers approached our agent, Abner Greshler (Dean had fired Lou Perry, and all his other agents and managers, by this time) and offered us $750 a week, less than half of what we were earning elsewhere by then. Abby turned them down flat — and we almost fired him. 'It's the *Copa*, for Chrissakes!' we yelled. 'How could you do that?'

'You can't sell yourselves short — it sets a bad precedent,' Greshler told us. 'They'll be back with a proper offer.'

He turned out to be right. After we'd finished

our swing around the East and Chicago, establishing ourselves as *the* hot new act, our agent was able to book us at the Copacabana, starting in April 1948, at $2,500 a week.

We were in!

With the following large caveat: If we hit big, we'd be the toast of the town — of *the* town. But if we fucked up, we'd just be toast.

No pressure!

★   ★   ★

Like almost every important nightclub of the 1940s — all right, like *every* important nightclub of the 1940s — the Copacabana was owned by the Mob. In this case, the proprietor was New York boss Frank Costello, although for appearance' sake he had a front man, Jules Podell, a former bootlegger with a prison record. Julie, a would-be tough guy with a raspy basso voice and a huge star-sapphire pinky ring, was not renowned for his tolerance or sensitivity. Once, when Sammy Davis Jr.'s act ran long, Podell yelled, 'Get off my stage, nigger!'

The Copa was the summit. The epitome of glamour and unstuffy sophistication. The gorgeous, scantily clad Copa chorus line was legendary. As were the audiences packed with every boldface name in the gossip columns — along with all of New York's top mobsters and their girlfriends on Saturday nights. (Those same mobsters would bring back their wives and children on Sunday!)

And Dean and I were petrified that opening

night. Or, I should say, *I* was petrified. Dean was his usual serene self — and as always, the calmer he looked, the more certain I was that something was cooking. I didn't want to think too hard about that, though. I desperately needed that cool of his to keep a lid on my own anxiety.

The Copa was so big-time — and, even after our big first year and a half, we were so fresh on the New York scene — that we weren't even the top-billed act. That honor went to a Broadway singing star named Vivian Blaine, who'd conquered Manhattan, gone out to Hollywood to make movies for 20th Century Fox, then returned to the Big Apple in triumph. Vivian was a lovely and very talented actress and singer, a sweet and vivacious woman whose hair was a remarkable color that the creative publicity department at Fox called 'cherry blonde.' She would go on to have a very successful career, most notably starring as Miss Adelaide in both the Broadway and film versions of *Guys and Dolls*.

Which makes me feel a little less bad about what Dean and I did to her.

Vivian Blaine or no Vivian Blaine, second billing or no second billing, Dean and I knew only one way to go out onto the stage of the Copacabana, and that was with a big bang.

It was Thursday night, April 8, 1948. First show, 8:30 p.m. After the Copa Girls and the house singer had performed, I stepped out on stage, my heart in my mouth. I scanned that super-glamorous audience and saw my mother and father, Patti, and Dean's wife, Betty. Not to

You're all wrong!

mention every heavy hitter in show business. There wasn't a nobody in the joint — it was all somebodies. I saw Billy Rose, Walter Winchell, Milton Berle — all of them (except, of course, our families) there to see Vivian Blaine. And I stepped up to the mike and spoke.

'My father always said, 'When you play the Copa, son, you'll be playing to the cream of show business,'' I told the audience.

My dad smiled. I looked out over the crowd, made a face, and shifted into a Yiddish accent: 'Dis is *krim*?'

The crowd went nuts.

I did a few bits, then introduced my partner. Dean came up on my right and said, 'How long we been on?'

When the laughter faded a little, he asked me, 'Are you gonna be out here for a while?'

'No, I've got something to rinse out,' I said. 'Sing something, why don't you? They're waiting!'

Then Dean sang 'San Fernando Valley' and 'Oh, Marie' and 'Where or When' — and he sang wonderfully. Smooth, funny, sexy: The ladies, feeling as though they'd just discovered him and had him all to themselves, swooned. And then I stuck fake buckteeth in my mouth and careened around the Copa like a bat out of hell, knocking over busboys' trays right and left, destroying crockery like I owned stock in Wedgwood china. It was the same act we'd been doing since the 500 Club, but this was the *Copa*. Our pandemonium worked like gangbusters (literally!) in these classy but mobbed-up surroundings.

We'd hit it just right. The Copa was the High Temple of nightclubs, but then and now, New York has always loved chutzpah. We were having a little fun with the Holy of Holies, getting right in its face.

But remember this: An audience is like a jungle animal — it smells fear. It will turn in a second. What Dean and I did on that all-important night wouldn't have worked nearly so well if the crowd hadn't caught on, immediately, to our self-assurance (the tuxes helped) and the fun we were having together. This ultrasophisticated audience had never seen a two-act enjoy themselves, and each other, so much. It was like nothing these smart-ass New Yorkers expected, including the critics. (Cough!)

We were supposed to do twenty-five minutes — and we were well aware of Podell's ugly temper if you ran long — but we finally left the stage after fifty minutes, exhausted, with the crowd yelling for more.

We walked off that stage as if we had wings. We flew to our dressing room, and had to come back for three encores, doing fresh shtick each time. In the dressing room, we had the stage monitor turned up so we could hear the applause.

When it finally subsided, we heard the strains of the headliner's music as the announcer introduced 'the star of our show, Miss Vivian Blaine!' Almost sixty years later, people who were there still recall the eerie silence that followed that announcement. You know *A Night to Remember*, the movie about the *Titanic*? Well, this was a night to remember, and Vivian Blaine was the *Titanic*.

We were still listening on the monitor in our dressing room, changing our clothes as she began her opening number, a typical special-lyric song about how 'I finally made it to the Copa' (probably written by Sammy Cahn, the special lyricist to the Hollywood heavyweights). At the finish of her number, the applause was something like what a white act, with no rhythm and singing off-key, might get at the Apollo Theater on amateur night. Vivian halfheartedly sang one more song, then left the stage in tears.

There were at least a hundred people jammed in the hall outside our dressing-room door, waiting to tell us how we'd conquered New York. People were hugging us, kissing us, just wanting to touch us. Every once in a while, Dean and I would glance at each other, shaking our heads.

Then Monte Proser, Julie Podell's partner, stuck his head in the door with a grim look on his face. He was a short, balding, very natty fellow, always dressed to the nines — cuff links, stickpin, velvet-collared jacket, black-and-white shoes at the wrong time of year. *Very* natty. He whispered something in Greshler's ear.

'What was that all about?' Dean asked.

'We have to be in Proser's office as soon as the crowd clears out,' our agent said.

★　★　★

Proser was sitting at his desk, shaking his head. 'I'd be a damned fool if I did nothing about this show,' he told us. 'It's all wrong.'

Greshler instantly went on the defensive. 'Wrong? They took three encores, got a standing ovation — where the hell did you see wrong?'

'It's not them I'm talking about,' Proser said. 'Vivian Blaine is the problem. After what happened tonight, there's no way for her to headline. So I'm going with Martin and Lewis. I'm putting her in the opening slot.'

I glanced over at Dean. He had a pipe stuck in his mouth, and he was doing Eddie Cantor banjo eyes. Leave it to my partner to cut up at the most important moment in our career. But that was Dean's way of handling big moments.

Poor Vivian quit the next morning. What else could she do?

And Podell and Proser extended our engagement at the Copa for twelve weeks, at $5,000 a week.

*   *   *

It was like stepping onto a merry-go-round spinning at a thousand miles an hour. Between the Copa and a one-show-a-night gig at the newly renovated Roxy Theater, we were pulling down $7,500 a week. Each. As a point of comparison, the apartment Patti and I were renting in Newark cost sixty bucks a month.

And it wasn't just the money. Suddenly, it seemed as if everyone in New York City wanted

69

to meet us. A lot of them were female people.

Dean, of course, had never had any trouble in that department. I was a little slower to come to the party. At twenty-two years old, I'd never been what you'd call a ladies' man — all the more so since I had married at nineteen. But I'd paid careful attention to Dean's words during our late-night bull session; I'd been impressed by his free and easy way of drawing the line between his fun and his domestic life. A super-handsome man, I knew, could always have it both ways. But now, I was learning, success and fame were just as much of an aphrodisiac as good looks.

Two encounters during our first few weeks at the Copa would have a huge effect on us, both as a team and as individuals. The first, like something out of a fairy tale, was good and evil at the same time. It would take us to enormous wealth and fame — and would lead, ultimately, to our breakup.

The second would join us forever to the biggest star in the world, and would continue to reverberate for both of us, individually, long past the split.

The first meeting was with the legendary Hollywood producer Hal Wallis. As production chief at Warner Brothers, he'd made *Little Caesar, I Am a Fugitive from a Chain Gang, The Charge of the Light Brigade, Casablanca,* and *Yankee Doodle Dandy.* He'd left Warner's in the midforties and hung out his shingle as an independent producer. Now he and his partner, Joe Hazen, had a distribution deal with Paramount Pictures. We both knew Wallis's name, and we were pretty damned impressed when he stopped by.

But then Hal B. Wallis seemed pretty damned impressed with himself. He was a stocky, well-dressed fellow with a big, suntanned bullethead like one of those stone statues on Easter Island. Wallis squinted at you, sized you up, and made you feel like it was a privilege just to shake his hand. He also didn't appear to have a sense of humor — especially when he told us he thought our act was 'terrific fun.' In fact, you'd have had trouble finding many comedies in his résumé, which should have told us something right then, but we weren't thinking about that when he said he wanted to sign the two of us, then and there, to a Hollywood contract.

'Where's a pen?' I yelled. Funny guy. Dean looked pretty excited, too. But once again Greshler, who was standing by, prevailed.

'The boys are booked at Slapsy Maxie's' — a famous Los Angeles nightclub — 'in late August,' our agent told Wallis. 'We'd love to sit down and talk with you then.'

Wallis smiled politely — looking not especially pleased that he hadn't gotten his way on the spot — and said he looked forward to it.

'What were you thinking?' we wailed to Greshler after Wallis left. 'Hollywood comes calling, and you send it packing?'

'You think he's the only fish in the sea?'

71

Greshler said. 'You watch — they'll all come courting.'

Once again, he turned out to be right. And though what resulted wasn't a shotgun marriage, in the end it might as well have been.

4

The day we arrived in Los Angeles — August 9, 1948 — our new press agent, Jack Keller, took us to George Raft's house for our first Hollywood party. George *Raft*! My eyes were practically falling out of my head. My God, Raft was the biggest movie star in the world (or at least the biggest one I'd ever met), and here he was in his cabana, telling me to pick out a pair of brand-new swim trunks and go jump into his gorgeous backyard pool. I suited up and ran out to Dean — who was standing poolside, cool as could be, with Loretta Young, Sonny Tufts, Edward G. Robinson, Veronica Lake, Mona Freeman, William Holden, William Demarest, and Dorothy Lamour . . . All big, big names of the day. I tapped my partner on the shoulder and — I couldn't help myself — screamed, 'Now, *this* is show business!' Despite his blasé appearance, I knew Dean couldn't have agreed with me more. He idolized Raft, who'd had a rough background similar to his own. As a kid, he'd seen every movie the tough-guy actor ever made.

As the sun set, Keller came by Raft's house to pick us up for our press conference at the Brown Derby. When we got there, we met the queen of gossip columnists, Louella Parsons, aka The Headhunter from Hearst. She spoke like a Muppet without a hand up her back. As she interviewed us, she wrote on a little pad given to her by the Shah of Iran during a polo match at the Will Rogers estate in Pacific Palisades on a hot summer day when Clark Gable was sitting on a horse but couldn't get a game . . . We found all this out because we asked, 'Where did you get the cute pad?'

Lolly Parsons may have sounded like Betty Boop, but she wielded a lot of power. She was the Big Mamoo, the Chief, the Ultimate Journalist. Give me a break. She was an old, fat has-been who couldn't make it in Hollywood, so she made it with everyone she could, including William Randolph Hearst. She'd tried acting and flunked, and Mr. Hearst needed a spy to live in the underbrush of Hollywood and tell him all the stuff that eccentric old men need to hear, so poof! She was a columnist.

At the press conference, Lolly tried to take us down a peg. Sure, we'd been a hit in New York, but Hollywood was a very different place, she told us. From the outset, though, I made it clear that I wasn't about to kneel before her. 'We'll be an even bigger hit here,' I predicted flatly. Lolly made a face like she'd bitten a lemon. I was always outspoken and honest with her, and would eventually get in deep trouble because of it. Later Keller said, 'If you think of the cosmos, we are but sand on a world of beaches . . . we almost mean nothing when you count it all. What are you trying to be? The conscience of the world of show business? Wise up, sonny. They won't hear you, but I love that you try!'

At the Brown Derby, Dean whispered to me, 'Please, don't flag wave. We're lucky we're here!'

I said, 'We're not lucky! We're good at what we do, and don't ever forget that.' Then I made the face of a little kid who has just spoken out of turn . . .

★   ★   ★

That night we opened at Slapsy Maxie's, on the Miracle Mile — Wilshire Boulevard between Fairfax and La Brea. After all the publicity about these two crazy people, the Crooner and the Monkey, every big shot in town had come to watch.

It was an era when all the stars went out at night — to dance and dine, to see and be seen. Los Angeles was a city of fabulous nightclubs: Ciro's, Mocambo, Trocadero. But the biggest, poshest, most fashionable club in L.A. was Slapsy Maxie's. The ringside was huge — it looked like 180 degrees when you were standing at the center of that great stage. And at the tables were (get a load of this): Barbara Stanwyck, Humphrey Bogart, Lauren Bacall, Jane Wyman, Ronald Reagan, James Cagney, Joan Crawford, Clark Gable, Donald O'Connor, Debbie Reynolds, Gene Kelly, Fred Astaire, Rita Hayworth, Orson Welles, The Marx Brothers (the important ones: Harpo and Chico), Edward G. Robinson, Bob Hope, Bing Crosby, Carmen Miranda, Al Jolson, Mel Tormé, Count Basie, the whole 'Metro' group, including Judy Garland and Mickey Rooney, not to mention Greer Garson, Spencer Tracy, William Powell, Billy Wilder, June Allyson, and

Gloria De Haven (more about these last two soon) . . .

Keller was outside our dressing room, announcing every name as they entered the club — names that could not only excite but make you shake with fear . . . And we were about to go out there in front of all those people and do our stuff.

I looked at Dean a moment, and he saw the question in my eyes. I never said a word, though I wanted to ask, 'Are we good enough?'

And he smiled at me as only he could smile, and in his eyes I saw my answer: 'We're fine! We'll be a smash!'

And we were. Oh, were we a smash. We tore that goddamn place down.

★ ★ ★

The day after our opening at Slapsy Maxie's, the studios came calling.

We had an initial meeting with Jack Warner, who delighted in doing his own stand-up and clearly would rather have gotten a laugh with a joke he'd heard from a grip or an electrician than sign a new twenty-year deal with Bette Davis.

Then we got a call asking us to meet with the great Louis B. Mayer himself, at Metro-Goldwyn-Mayer Studios in Culver City. After taking the famous Long Walk — everyone in Hollywood knew about that intimidating corridor that led to Mayer's office — we were ushered in by two security guards, one on Dean and one on me. The office was known as Mayer's Folly, and when I saw the layout, I understood why.

We were asked to sit in two chairs carefully placed before Mr. Mayer's desk — close enough for him to shake our hands. Although he wasn't a tall man, he was looking down on us, as if we were two street urchins. I kept staring around the huge office, and it soon became evident to me that Mayer was sitting on a platform. It was subtle, but he was definitely sitting higher up than the two of us — an ingenious device that made him the prophet and all those sitting before him the disciples. A great device for him and his need to dominate . . . But as young as I was, I could still smell a rat.

We sat and listened politely as he told us his life story: how he'd started from nothing, come west, and built this studio . . . and now he was L. B. Mayer! When he took his first breath from the dissertation and made us an offer for forty thousand dollars a picture — with MGM's ironclad control over all our outside work — I wanted so much to say, 'And you're still nothing.' But because I was afraid Dean might slash my throat, instead I said, 'Mr. Mayer, we would like to sleep on your offer and get back to you.'

Mayer didn't look happy. 'No one out there will better my deal!' he shouted.

Both Dean and I half-smiled. We got up, made that interminable walk to the door, and, as if we had rehearsed it, both turned and waved heartily . . .

(We later found out that after we'd left, Mayer had delivered the immortal pronouncement:

'The guinea's not bad, but what do I do with the monkey?')

When we arrived back at our hotel, there was a message to call our agent. Dean made the call. I made a malted — the only true sustenance I gave my body in those days. I was just too excited about everything that was happening to us to eat anything else. My partner, on the other hand, had a six-course dinner every night, without fail. I'd say to him, 'Eat, my boy, build yourself up so you can continue to carry the Jew.'

Dean, on the phone with Greshler, was doing all the listening. I heard nothing after the first hello. He finally said, 'Okay, Abby, I'll tell Jerry. He'll like that a lot.' Then he hung up and, to drive me crazy, stuck a cigarette in his mouth and proceeded to look all over the suite for a match.

I knew what he was up to, but I bit anyway. 'Tell me already, you lousy fink,' I said. 'And use the goddamn lighter in your pants pocket.'

He sat on the edge of the bed, grinning. 'Abby says he's not really interested in the Mayer meeting,' he told me. 'He says we can do better.'

* * *

When we sat down with Greshler, he told us that Universal had offered us thirty thousand dollars a picture. Twentieth Century Fox offered a little less, but for a six-picture deal. Sam Goldwyn wanted us as a team, but with the option to split us up when a project called for either a handsome leading man or a crazy Jewish

78

First tux: Chicago was never handsomer.

monkey. Republic wanted to make a film with us, but basically wanted to shoot our act in a nightclub. (An interesting idea — in hindsight!) United Artists thought we'd be good in a remake of *Of Mice and Men*. Columbia, in the person of the notorious Harry Cohn, told Abby Greshler we were nothing more than The Three Stooges, minus one. Warner Brothers offered us the most money — but only if we signed for a seven-year deal.

Finally, our agent mentioned the one studio I'd silently prayed we would hear from — Paramount.

Hal Wallis, the producer who'd come on so strong in our dressing room at the Copa, was back with a serious offer: fifty thousand a picture to start with, working up to a ceiling of $1.25 million a film over the next five years. The money sounded good. But I told Dean and Greshler that for me there was a lot more to it than money.

For about a year, when I was seventeen and eighteen, I'd worked as an usher at the Paramount Theater in New York, the site of Frank Sinatra's first great triumph in the early forties. And so I had a sentimental feeling about Paramount, but it was more than sentiment. While I was ushering, I had the chance to see the studio's in-house promotional films, which showed the stars on the lot, the sound stages, the art department, the camera department, the wardrobe and makeup departments, the stars' dressing rooms, the commissary, and — most fascinating to me — the editing room. Wow! I thought Paramount was just the greatest studio of them all, the best of the best. That name! Those stars . . . W.C. Fields, Gary Cooper, The Marx Brothers, Mae West, Claudette Colbert, William Powell . . .

'A lot of people have serious money on the table,' Greshler reminded us. 'I can go back to Mayer . . . '

'Let's go with Paramount,' Dean said.

Greshler said, 'You're sure?'

'My partner's sure,' Dean told him.

★   ★   ★

When Dean and I signed to make movies with Hal Wallis and Paramount, I thought all our troubles were over. Little did I know they were only beginning.

After all, becoming a movie star is the American dream, right? Sign on the dotted line; fame and riches follow! Well, the movies would bring us a ton more money; they would spread our fame around the world. But they would never take us to the artistic heights we achieved in live performance: in clubs, theaters, and on television (much of early TV was broadcast live).

Why was that?

When my partner and I got up in front of an audience, any audience, we and they knew that at any minute absolutely anything could happen. Our wildness, our unpredictability, were a big part of the package. It was thrilling to an audience that we could do all the mischievous things they might imagine but would never really do.

This was only half of it, though.

The other half was that indefinable something I've talked about: our obvious pleasure in performing together. Audiences have a great desire to *feel along with* their favorite performers. Dean and I had an uncanny ability to get an audience to not just be viewers but to participate in our fun.

In films it wasn't as easy to generate those feelings. In fact, it was damn near impossible. After all, the pleasure of movies is not in spontaneity but in story. Boy meets girl, boy loses girl, boy and girl get back together. Three acts — that structure is as old as the hills. But there are parts of the human spirit that three acts can leave out.

For his first project with Martin and Lewis,

Hal Wallis had decided to try a low-risk proposition: plugging us into a low-budget movie project he'd already started. The picture, called *My Friend Irma*, was to be based on a popular radio series of the same name, about a ditzy Manhattan career girl, Irma (played by Marie Wilson), her best friend Jane (played by Diana Lynn), and their adventures. The series had been created by Cy Howard, who had also written the screenplay. With a little revision, Wallis thought, Dean and I could be plugged into the script as Irma and Jane's boyfriends.

So he thought.

It felt like Fantasyland when the two of us were ushered onto the Paramount lot for our initial meetings with studio brass and our director-to-be, George Marshall. Mr. Marshall, who had directed W. C. Fields in *You Can't Cheat an Honest Man* and Bob Hope in *Monsieur Beaucaire*, was not only a terrific filmmaker but a wonderful person (and, ultimately, a dear friend and confidant). He was to direct us in our screen test first thing the next morning.

The 5:30 a.m. wake-up call came as something of a shock: Normally, that hour was one my partner and I only saw when we were turning in! For the first time, we began to realize what moviemaking held in store for us. Shooting generally begins around nine in the morning, but with travel, breakfast, makeup, and wardrobe, you'd better get rolling at half past five or you'll have a couple of dozen people understandably pissed. So we learned right away that being on time was a top priority.

We sat down in canvas director's chairs, and a crafts-service gentleman gave us coffee. At about five after nine, George Marshall and his assistant director walked onto Stage 9, along with Marie Wilson and Diana Lynn. Introductions all around — matter-of-fact for Marie and Diana, not so for Dean and me. My God, we had seen them on the huge screen at the Paramount in New York, and here we were standing next to them, getting ready to *act*. To be *directed*. Two little things we'd never done before.

Neither Dean nor I knew anything about Mr. Marshall's career. And 'Mr. Marshall' was what everyone called him — until you knew him much, much better, and then it was 'Bones.' That was the nickname for anyone who had *funny bones*: a deep-down, world-class sense of humor, the kind you're born with, the kind that can never be learned. George Marshall had the funny bones of Laurel and Hardy — in fact, he had directed some of their earliest work, which I didn't learn until much later. Had I known that morning, I'd have died from fear.

The set was Irma's apartment. Dean was up first, to play a scene with Diana Lynn as Jane's boyfriend Steve, an aspiring singer. Paramount had signed Diana to replace the woman who'd played Irma's sidekick on the radio, feeling that as a known box-office quantity, she might sell a few more tickets. The studio was certainly still unsure that Martin and Lewis would mean anything on the big screen. This test was supposed to give them a clue.

In Dean's scene, he was to ask Diana's character to please understand that he couldn't just get a job — that he loved singing, that was his life. She was to ask him why he couldn't do both: 'Sing *and* work like a regular person.'

The scene went very well: Dean was terrific for his first time. In fact, most of the crew and people around the set that morning were a bit surprised, as was I, at how comfortable he looked doing the scene, how relaxed. The camera doesn't lie. It takes what you give it — no more, and very often a little less. Dean was my hero that morning: He was giving me a leg up (I thought) on being a movie star. Everybody was ecstatic, and before we knew it, it was time for lunch.

I was to do my test after we ate. I've never been less hungry in my life.

Oh, well — off to the Paramount commissary. Pauline Kessinger, head of the commissary and a power broker in her own right (imagine the world's most exclusive restaurant — seating is everything), gave us a big greeting at the door and steered us toward a good table. Herb Steinberg, head of the P.R. department, had publicity stills taken of us as we entered. Then we sat down. If you craned your neck, you could see Cecil B. DeMille and his entourage at his huge table in the back. As Dean and I ordered our lunch, we stared around the place, trying to see everyone. (A couple of weeks in, after we got comfortable at the studio, we'd be treating the place the same way we treated any nightclub we played — breaking up the joint.) We spotted

Bing Crosby, Dorothy Lamour, Marlene Dietrich, Alan Ladd, William Bendix, Bill Holden, Rosemary Clooney, Barbara Stanwyck, Gary Cooper, Burt Lancaster, and Kirk Douglas — all in the same place at once! Some of the biggest stars ate in the private dining room, a privilege we, too, would be allowed once we became box-office hits — and not a second before.

Then lunch was over, and it was back to Stage 9, where I would shoot my screen test with Marie Wilson.

Mr. Marshall explained the scene to me: I was to play Al, Irma's loser boyfriend. Al was a schemer, a leech; Irma basically worked to support him. He was brash, he was pushy — Hal Wallis must have thought that role was created for the Jerry Lewises of the world. Since the movie was, after all, a comedy, Al was supposed to come off as funny, with a kind of Damon Runyon edge to him. Remember Jack Carson in all those B pictures of the forties? But I wasn't Jack Carson. It was hard for me to think of a way to make this character sympathetic.

Marie and I did the scene. She was cute, she was bubbly — but she was thirty-two years old to my twenty-two, ten years that really made a difference. And I, having never acted before, was trying hard to pretend to be someone I profoundly was not.

Neither my partner nor I could figure out why Dean was essentially playing himself and I was supposed to play someone else altogether. What had Hal Wallis seen at the Copa that made him want to sign us? Where were the two guys he saw that night?

Good questions!

I had a sinking feeling the next afternoon when we sat down in the executive screening room. Dean's screen test with Diana was wonderful, as we all knew it would be. Cy Howard was thrilled. George Marshall was ecstatic. Hal Wallis and the Paramount executives in the room were slapping him on the back.

Then came the scene with Marie and me.

It limped onto the screen, and finished even limper. When it was over, it was so quiet in that room, you could have heard a mouse piss on a blotter.

Wallis suggested we meet in his office. We all gathered there — Dean and I, our agent, press agent, and lawyer; Wallis and his minions — around twenty people in all, and the atmosphere was not lighthearted. 'Gentlemen, I think we all agree we have a problem on our hands,' Wallis said. 'I think we must move ahead with great care, given the very significant commitment we've made to Paramount on Martin and Lewis. We have to deliver on that commitment. Now, my suggestion is that we all sleep on this, and reconvene at the end of the workday tomorrow to begin to formulate a plan.'

My heart sank even further. I was a sharp kid, and I knew what Wallis was up to: He wanted to spend the early part of the day on the phone conferring with Paramount executives in New York, seeing what his options were. Maybe cut the Monkey loose and make the Crooner a star?

I had to think that was on somebody's mind. Nobody but Dean would really look me in the eye.

The driver took us back to our hotel. 'Sleep on it,' I muttered. 'Sleep on what? Sleep on the fact that they *took what we were and changed us!*'

In our suite, Dean and I sat in silence. Finally, he said, 'Hey, who the hell wants to live in Los Angeles, anyway?'

Oops, I thought. *Here we go. He's gonna do it. He's about to make the grand gesture.*

'Listen,' Dean said. 'If they just put the camera on what we did at the Copa, it would've been great!'

'But that's not what movies are about,' I said. 'Movies are about personalities playing characters. Movies are about story.'

'Well, I say bullshit,' Dean said. 'I say it's Martin and Lewis or nothing.'

I loved him for it, and I was torn. There was no way in hell I could watch my partner throw away what might be his chance of a lifetime; at the same time, I agreed totally with what he was saying. There was no way in hell I could watch Hal Wallis throw away Dean Martin and Jerry Lewis.

★   ★   ★

We decided to forget our worries and go see what the Hollywood nightlife was all about. We called a Paramount car and told the driver to take us to Ciro's. He smiled . . . and drove us straight across Sunset Boulevard, about sixty-five feet. Who knew?

Jack Keller had set us up with a couple of terrific chicks, and we spent the evening drinking, dancing, smooching . . . having a great time pretending we were having a great time.

I don't remember exactly how we got back to the hotel, having been at the chicks' respective apartments, drinking champagne, and doing all the things two guys on the town do . . . Married or not, you do them — certainly at that age you do.

Dawn came through the curtains of our suite like a lightning bolt. Our schedule for the morning was to meet with the Paramount photo department to have official studio photographs taken of Martin and Lewis — the team that, until that screen test, had been a hot item. Was our photo shoot even still on? While Dean slept, I phoned Herb Steinberg. He confirmed that we were still on, then I summoned up my courage and popped the question.

'Herb, could we possibly arrange for the shoot to be later in the day, so I can make an appointment to meet with Mr. Wallis?'

Herb, a nice man, agreed to postpone the session to three-thirty in the afternoon.

I wrote Dean a note. 'Paul, couldn't sleep,' it read. 'Going to Beverly Hills to shop a little. Photo shoot has been moved to 3:30 this afternoon. Just relax till I get back. Love, the Jew.'

Then I went down to the lobby and called Abby Greshler on the house phone.

I told our agent I needed to meet with Wallis, alone, that morning if at all possible, and I told him why. I asked if he could set it up. Greshler said he'd do his best. I told him to call me back in the lobby, explaining that I didn't want Dean to know about any of this yet.

Then I hung up and counted the seconds.

Imagine you've gone in for root canal, and the doctor is delayed, and you're sitting in the waiting room, not wanting him to show up but desperately wanting the torment to be over. That's about how I felt.

After six long minutes, Greshler called back. Wallis would see me at 11 a.m.

★ ★ ★

'Sit down, Jerry,' Mr. Wallis said kindly. We were in his big office at Paramount, and my heart was pounding. He gave me a look, and I gave him a look back. It was a tense moment, and we both knew why.

He pushed a button on his intercom. 'Evelyn, hold my calls,' he said. 'Thank you.' Then he looked at me again. 'What's on your mind?' he asked.

'Mr. Wallis,' I said, 'this Martin and Lewis thing is my baby. I put it together, and I'll be damned if I let it go down in defeat without trying to correct the situation. I know what went wrong here.' I actually hadn't the slightest idea of what I was about to say — except that my feelings were so strong, I knew they'd take me in the right direction.

'I'd love to know that myself,' Wallis said.

'Okay, then. If you loved what you saw Dean

and me do on the stage at the Copa, why not film the essence of what you loved?'

'Which is what, precisely?'

'The handsome guy with the monkey.'

'Go on,' he said, looking intrigued but puzzled.

'Dean, as the straight man, can be any straight character,' I said. 'But Jerry cannot be anyone or anything other than Jerry. If you take that away, or separate the two of them, you've lost the essence of the act.'

All at once, Wallis seemed excited. 'Will you sit down with Cy Howard and try to get a handle on this?' he asked.

*   *   *

And that was how Seymour was born. After I told Dean some terrible lie about the terrific chick I'd met shopping in Beverly Hills, I spent the evening — and then the rest of the night — at Cy Howard's house, hammering out the idea for a less-than-bright pal for Dean's character Steve. (Dean managed to entertain himself while I was away — believe me, he was not lonely.)

'Why Seymour?' Cy asked, making a face. It was his real name, and he hated it.

'Because that's what Jerry is,' I told him. 'He is Seymour, Marvin, Melvin, Norman, and Bernie, and so on. He's Mr. Everyone in the World That Gets Shit On. He is *not* Al. Al needs an actor. Jerry needs to be Seymour. Make him Steve's pal and we hit pay dirt!'

Cy and I met with Wallis first thing the next morning, while Dean slept off a wonderful hangover. The producer glanced back and forth at the two of us while we bubbled over with excitement. We went on and on about the need to have the team be just that — a *team*. Dean could still sing, be the leading man, the romantic interest, but with a sidekick — the busboy, the waiter, the parking attendant, the usher, the American Everyman.

We had him. Wallis was sold. He called the Paramount production department and ordered another screen test.

I ran into our room at the Sunset Towers and jumped on Dean's bed, waking him from a deep sleep. 'We've got it!' I yelled. 'We've got it!'

'You and the chick?' Dean asked.

'What chick?' I said.

'What are you talking about? What's happening?' he asked — but I could see he realized something big had changed since he tied that last one on.

I told him the whole story. And then, after he had slapped me on the back and gone to shower, I finally gave in to the emotions that had been building up over the past five roller-coaster days.

A few hours later, we were once again on Stage 9, for 'Martin and Lewis Screen Test 2.' Instead of Irma's apartment, we were standing by the orange-juice stand that Steve and Seymour operated — Steve out front, selling, Seymour in back, squeezing. Within minutes, we would develop the business about Seymour's occupational injury, the hand that became a claw from so much orange-squeezing . . .

But what we had already developed, in the time it took to make that second test, was the Martin and Lewis we all grew up with — including me.

The act that would work not only for Paramount but also for companies like RCA, Liggett & Myers Tobacco, Famous Music Corporation, Kodak Corporation, Technicolor Corporation, Chapman Boom Corporation, Mitchell Camera Corporation, Panavision Corporation . . .

This chain of companies, entities, and individuals would never have come together if it hadn't been for that second screen test —

The same screen test that led (it could be argued) along a winding but certain path to our breakup eight years later.

5

While waiting to shoot, we got busy in other ways.

We might have passed on MGM, but we didn't overlook two of that studio's loveliest young stars, June Allyson and Gloria De Haven. June was the same age as Dean, an established screen presence, a sweet woman who specialized in wholesome, girl-next-door parts. The beautiful Gloria was, like me, in her early twenties, and (unlike me) playing mainly ingenue roles.

Dean and June found each other almost as soon as we arrived in L.A. There was never any stopping my partner, and there was no stopping women once they'd set eyes on him! And since June and Gloria were best pals, it made sense — by the peculiar rules of Hollywood, and of up-and-coming young performers — that Ms. De Haven and I would get together.

What made a little less sense was that all four players in this little roundelay were married . . . to other people.

June's husband was the movie star Dick Powell (*42nd Street*). They had a little boy and a young daughter. Gloria was married to the movie star John Payne (*Miracle on 34th Street*). They had a little girl and a baby boy. Dean and I, of course, were married to Betty and Patti, with four children between us.

Were we nuts?

Sure we were, but try to understand. My partner had established his ground rules well before we met: A real man has a wife and kids — and whatever he can get on the side. And Dean could get plenty.

He was handsome and suave and funny beyond compare, and I wanted to be just like him — to the extent that anatomy allowed. Dean could get women before he had a dime in his pocket. I had to wait. But not any longer.

When fame and money come all at once, even the strongest men will get their heads turned around. I had plenty of strengths, but avoiding temptation was not one of them. Imagine — just months before Dean and I played the Copa and Slapsy Maxie's, I was lucky to have fifty bucks to my name.

Now I was walking down Fifth Avenue (we were back in New York, to plan the upcoming year) with three grand in hundred-dollar bills in my pocket. And plenty more where that came from.

Same with my partner.

Can you blame us for going a little hog wild?

Dean and I booked two suites at the Hampshire House on Central Park South. Previous to this, we'd usually shared a hotel suite. But with all the action we were about to show New York, we needed space!

Now, imagine our surprise and delight when the very same two young ladies we had been squiring in Hollywood suddenly showed up in Manhattan and checked into the Hampshire House . . .

June and Gloria had come to New York, without husbands, to go on a shopping spree. It was the kind of thing that young actresses did then — a chance to kick up their heels and get some publicity at the same time. The MGM publicity department underwrote the whole trip, even their shopping bills. It was all stage-managed to the nth degree. Little did MGM imagine the kind of publicity their two young stars would actually generate.

Dean and I happened to be in the lobby when their limo pulled up and dropped them off. We watched the girls check in. We made some small talk, and then the desk clerk called for a bellman to take the young ladies and their bags to their suite. Another bellman took care of us.

We all rode up on the elevator together: Martin and Lewis, Allyson and De Haven, two bellmen, and twenty-seven suitcases. The four of us had some giggles, while the bellmen pretended not to notice. It was as if we were all in on a big, delicious secret. Some secret it would turn out to be.

June and Gloria were dressed to the nines in Lord & Taylor clothes and mink stoles. (While Dean and I, wearing the first civilian suits that we owned outright, were undressing them in our minds.) For the five days they were staying in New York, the girls had ten or fifteen changes of clothes: dresses, skirts, blouses, ball gowns, riding habits — all of it provided by the humongous Metro wardrobe department, the use of said garments approved by L. B. Mayer himself.

He was a pure showman, always demanding that his contract players carry themselves with grace, charm, and manners, as well as expensive attire. When the actor or actress didn't personally own the appropriate clothes, it was SOP that the studio would step in and provide what was needed to maintain the glamour and glitz — and protect its investment, which was considerable.

The star system was big business. The studios would find talent and nurture it with everything from acting to voice and piano lessons. The stars-to-be would learn to move their bodies gracefully enough to pass muster in the world's biggest and most demanding fishbowl. Hollywood was always watching, alert to every step, every gesture — and every slipup.

And so when two of Metro's newest, most sought-after female stars decided to fly off to New York and unwind — and encountered the new comedy team of Martin and Lewis, both Hollywood (though 3,000 miles away) and New York sat up and took notice.

Dean had a suite on the twenty-third floor, and mine was on the twenty-fourth floor, with but one flight of stairs between us. The girls were staying together in a suite on the twenty-fifth floor ... *By God*, I thought, *what a swell arrangement*.

The four of us were so totally wrapped up in one another that we never gave a thought to how things would look. So we played and played, and didn't give a gnat's ass about anything but having a good time. Wine, women, and song up the kazoo . . . We had it all — and then some.

But you always have to pay the fiddler.

The first night at the hotel, we had a champagne toast and, full of anticipation, prepared to go to the theater. Did we think about the fact that, in the winter of 1948, Broadway had an oversized media apparatus and thousands of gossipmongers — not to mention everyone who worked at the hotel and at the shops and restaurants we patronized?

We did not.

And so we, the Fun Foursome, strolled delightedly and without the slightest compunction into the St. James Theater to see that season's hot new musical, Frank Loesser's *Where's Charley?*

Everyone that was anyone had seats for that performance, and we became an added attraction. Until the houselights went down, we were the show. We loved the play — Ray Bolger was awesome — and after the final curtain we were off to a quiet dinner at one of New York's most laidback spots, where being noticed wasn't something we had to be concerned about . . . El Morocco!

We arrived at the fabulous nightclub on East Fifty-fourth Street — where, if you were a celebrity, trying to be unobtrusive was like being Mark Spitz calling for help in a pool. After we squeezed into one of the zebra-striped banquettes, we had to sit cozily, without being able to get a waiter so we could order drinks and dinner, for forty-five minutes — and that was after the fifty-dollar bill we handed the leech at the door! Later, we learned that the El Morocco staff did not share in one another's gratuities; the tradition there was dog-eat-dog.

So Dean got up, walked over to the door captain, and insisted on getting the fifty back. Which, even in front of a lot of people, didn't faze my partner at all.

Not so amazingly, we got a waiter right away. Whereupon Dean strolled back to the door captain and gave him the fifty all over again — plus another fifty. He grinned all the way back to the table.

Once he was back, we asked the girls to dance. There we were out on the dance floor, which was lit by a hundred baby spotlights: It was a little bit like a night game at Chavez Ravine.

We danced with complete abandon — in hog heaven — until we were spotted by Radie Harris, a monkey-faced little gossip columnist who wrote 'Broadway Ballyhoo' for the *Hollywood Reporter*.

If the cat hadn't come out of the bag before, it sure did now . . .

For the next week, all anyone in Manhattan talked about was the 'Fearsome Foursome,' dining, dancing, making the city our very own. We went to more Broadway shows and sat together. We strolled arm in arm through Central Park. We made reservations at the best restaurants, and we had some pretty heavy-duty parties in the three suites at the Hampshire House. Meanwhile, all the bellmen and telephone operators who were on the arm to Winchell and the rest of the newspapermen in

Gotham made sure we stayed the talk of the town.

Oh, we had a ball. We didn't even find time to see our attorneys and agents — the reason we'd come to New York in the first place . . . or so we said. The girls extended their stay another week. I must have lost five pounds, and I was only 124 to start with. Dean just basked in it all, looking like a cat with a mouth full of canary.

Then came the telephone call.

It would be sunrise in an hour or two, and I had just drifted off into some badly needed shut-eye: We had a date to go horseback riding in Central Park at 8 a.m. — the girls had to use those riding habits!

The phone sounded like a jackhammer in the middle of my brain. I grabbed at it just to make it stop.

'Hey, Jer, this is important,' I heard my partner saying.

'What time is it?' I croaked.

'It's 4 a.m. and I just had a great hour on the phone with Betty!' Dean said.

'Oops,' I said, and I knew in my heart — I'm next!

'Maybe we better cut back a little,' Dean said. 'There are more eyes on us than I ever could've imagined.'

A fact that was borne out to me when my phone rang again twenty minutes later. It was — of course — Patti. Two hours later, with the Manhattan sky turning gray, I was still trying to explain to my wife.

'Listen, you schmuck,' she said. 'If you have to

get your rocks off, why do it in Madison Square Garden?'

'What do you mean?' I asked innocently.

'It's all over the papers about you, Dean, and the two chippies you're with,' she said. 'Didn't you know that what you were up to would have consequences?'

Patti was a band singer, a show-business veteran who'd been around the block a few times. She knew how men — especially successful men in show business — acted. She just didn't want me humiliating her, and of course she was completely right. I pacified her as best I could.

But Dean and I had a date to go riding in Central Park, and we both meant to be there, and so we were at 8 a.m., like pointers in the hunt, ready and willing! The four of us rode all over the park, having fun — as were the reporters following us on horseback.

Our public-relations guys, George Evans and Jack Keller, had both handled Sinatra; they were used to this kind of thing. But that didn't mean they liked it. 'Do you guys realize,' George said, 'that your anonymity is gone? That you are now public property? That you cannot do whatever you want anymore? Don't you realize that you, you Italian idiot, are married with three children, *and* you're Catholic? Which is just a tad more serious than it is for the Jew with the one kid? Your people still go to confession!'

★   ★   ★

Did the four of us have any concerns about what effect this conduct might have on our careers, not to mention our marriages? Professionally, the girls had much more to lose than we did. In effect, they were the property of Metro-Goldwyn-Mayer, the studio giant that could snatch your stardom back as easily as they'd conferred it and send you straight back to where you'd come from. Dean and I were independent contractors, with only Hal Wallis to answer to — and how I loved giving him all the wrong answers! (Another story, for later.)

Professionally, we would all recover. How our little playtime would affect the four of us personally was another question.

★   ★   ★

Stars have always played around, but in those days most were a bit more discreet than they are now — as was the press. Even Frank Sinatra kept up his reputation as a family man until the end of the forties, when his P.R. people could no longer keep the lid on his affair with Ava Gardner. But in April 1946, Frank's image was still relatively unsullied, and his fame at its zenith. And that month, not long after Dean and I had first met, Sinatra was about to open at the Paramount — *in person*, for Christ's sake! Dean and I had just begun hanging around together, and one thing we discovered we had in common was a huge admiration — and believe me, that's not putting it quite strongly enough — for Sinatra.

101

We thought we might get in and see the best singer around do his thing, but the crowds of fans were so great we couldn't get near that theater, much less get tickets.

Then the proverbial lightbulb flashed on over my head.

Stella Ardis, a nice lady who worked in the administration office at the Belmont Plaza, was my very first all-out fan. She would come down to the Glass Hat to see my show at least three times a week; she told me she thought I could be a big star one day. I would smile and nod, thinking: *Mouthing to records? I don't think so, honey* . . . .Still, it was nice to hear.

When you're on the lower rungs of show business, you're constantly around people who aspire upward — hangers-on, wannabes, and (sad but true) mostly never-will-bes. But everybody seems to have an angle, a connection. So when Stella, the nice lady in the administration office, said, 'You know, Jerry, I'm kind of in show business myself,' I responded politely.

'Oh, really, Stella?' I said. 'How so?'

'Well,' Stella said proudly, 'my cousin, Mark Leon, is the head usher at the Paramount Theater.'

Needless to say, this conversation came back to me in full force when Dean and I found we couldn't get near the Sinatra show.

Did I want to see Sinatra? You bet. Did I want to impress the hell out of Dean? You bet. I made a beeline for the administration office at the Belmont Plaza and told Stella I had a little favor — oh, hell, a big favor — to ask her.

She smiled. 'For my brilliant Jerry? Anything.'

Two hours later, Dean and I were standing at the employees' entrance of the Paramount with a watchman who told us to stay right where we were, since Mr. Leon had to come back from a meeting through the very door we were standing by. Long minutes afterward, the door opened and an important-looking fellow emerged. 'Mr. Leon,' the watchman said, 'these two young fellows were looking for you.'

I was worried for a second, but as soon as I mentioned Stella, the head usher beamed. 'My cousin says you're a very talented young man.'

Pay dirt! We were not only going to get in, we were going to get in for *free*. We were like little kids being given a treat. A very big treat.

Soon Mr. Leon was whisking us to a spot — standing room, of course — in an alcove on the first mezzanine. Naturally, there wasn't a seat in the house, since most of the audience had been there all day anyway.

And so we waited. Through the coming attractions, some announcements about social events of the season to be held at the Paramount, and then, of course, the newsreel. MacArthur in Japan ... President Truman creates Atomic Energy Commission ...

Then the houselights came up, and a roar from the audience told us, 'Here he comes!'

The lights slowly dimmed, and we heard the strains of 'I'll Never Smile Again.' The big band headed by Axel Stordahl blew all the notes that made your heart stop.

The opening act was Phil Silvers, the

comedian. Phil was in fine form, telling a series of jokes about Sinatra and his thin frame. The crowd loved him, but only for about eight minutes.

Then the lights came all the way down.

The band hit 'Put Your Dreams Away,' and out he came! No announcement . . . no nothing. Just Frank in a dark-blue suit, cuff links, a flower handkerchief in his breast pocket . . . He reeked of California — sunshine, bucks, style. And he started to sing the moment the crowd stopped screaming. They settled in and just listened for a while, but screamed at the end of every song.

Frank did forty-five or fifty minutes, and the theater exploded once again as he thanked the audience, shouting to make himself heard above the tremendous uproar. Then he went off, and the stage descended into the gigantic pit and out of sight, to the last strains of 'I'll Never Smile Again.'

Dean and I didn't say a word all the way back across town, a pretty long walk from Times Square back to the Belmont Plaza. (Cabs weren't that expensive, but they were definitely over our budget.) When we got to the hotel, Dean said, 'You wanna get coffee?' It was the first time either of us had spoken in half an hour.

We went into the drugstore next door and sat in a booth. The waitress brought his coffee (and my usual, a vanilla milk shake), and I thought about what we had just seen. It was all so perfect: the band uniforms; the light cues; Sinatra's newly shined loafers; the way his bow tie flopped loosely, with studied carelessness, under that bobbing Adam's apple . . .

Dean shook his head. 'Man, I couldn't believe the way that guy phrases a lyric,' he said.

'Yeah,' I said. 'It makes you feel — '

'Jealous!' Dean said. 'That's what it makes you feel!'

'Yeah — I guess you're right,' I sighed. 'I kept seeing myself up there in front of four thousand screaming fans.'

'It's great to live in a country where a kid from Hoboken, New Jersey, can have the world in the palm of his hand,' Dean said.

'Well, I guess we can dream,' I said.

Dean banged the table with his palm, making me jump. 'Dreaming is for loafers who never do anything. I don't have time for dreams,' he said. 'I want action. I want a car and a home and all the things you get when you get there. If you don't push through the crowd, you'll be stuck here your whole life.'

I had never heard him talk this way. I didn't know how to respond. 'Well,' I finally said. 'I bet my impression of Sinatra will be better tonight than it ever was before.'

But Dean was barely listening. His gaze had drifted to some far-off place . . .

★ ★ ★

By our fourth week at the Copa, we'd introduced so many celebrities from the stage that it was getting ridiculous. 'Ladies and gentlemen, we're thrilled and honored to have in our audience tonight . . . Mr. Yul Brynner! Miss Ethel

105

Merman! Mr. Lee J. Cobb!'

But there was one celebrity we hoped for beyond all others: Frank Sinatra. It was right around then that Frank was beginning to get in some very public hot water about Ava Gardner, as well as his supposed Mob associations. As to the latter, I'll maintain till the end of my days — which of course will be a long, long time from now — that in the 1940s and '50s, before the Mob lost its hold on nightclubs and Vegas, it was literally impossible for an entertainer, any entertainer, not to deal with them. I also maintain that they were a class of men who could, under their own particular set of rules, be very honorable. Dean and I had our own strategies for handling the wiseguys. As for Frank, maybe he romanticized them a little. Maybe he hobnobbed a bit too much. But ultimately, he was always his own man.

The next five years wouldn't be good to Frank. But just then no one was a bigger or brighter star, and one night there he was, ringside at our show at the Copacabana!

Everyone in the place knew that Sinatra was sitting dead center. I was starting to give my 'Ladies and gentlemen' speech when he popped up and said, 'They know I'm here!' That got a big laugh. He strolled to the mike, looking ultra-natty in a dark suit and tie, and said, 'Ladies and gentlemen, in case you're just occasional visitors to the world of nightclubs, I want to tell you a little something about what you've seen up here tonight. Now, I've been around the block once or twice' — he smiled as he got his laugh — 'but I have to tell you that in terms of sheer showmanship, I've never seen the likes of the performance these two guys have done for you.' This got a big round of applause, and after a minute, Frank smiled and said, 'All right. All right, already.'

The clapping died down. 'Anyway,' Frank said, 'I just want to tell you that these guys are going straight off into the stratosphere. They will be the biggest stars in our business.'

As the Copa Girl photographer snapped a picture of the three of us, the applause began again. I was thrilled at Frank's graceful speech — all the more since I had never met him at that point. Dean had talked to him once, briefly, after he'd filled in for Sinatra at the Riobamba. But the moment that Frank came up, I could see something strange happen, just for a second, to my normally unflappable partner: He got rattled. It was only for a second, and only the man who was closer to Dean Martin than anyone else would be capable of seeing it, but it happened. The moment was so big that for a split second Dean simply couldn't get his mind around it.

★　★　★

Fifteen years later, and long after our breakup, I snuck into the Sands with a few pals to watch the Rat Pack perform.

Frank, Dean, Sammy, Joey Bishop, and Peter Lawford were headlining the midnight show. And I was at a table a discreet distance from the stage, along with Buddy Lester, Harold J. Stone,

Three friends for half a century.

and my bandleader, Dick Stabile. I didn't want Dean to know I was there . . . only because I knew how I'd have felt if the shoe had been on the other foot: nervous and uncertain. Why do that to one another?

Well, we had a ball. Frank, Dean, and the guys were absolutely fabulous. My pals and I snuck out, went back to our hotel (the Frontier), ordered room service, and sat around my suite discussing the show. Frank was looser than I had ever seen him. Peter was Peter (he would have been a *Star Search* loser). Joey was always terrific, and Sammy was in his own orbit standing next to Frank (his first hero; I didn't mind that I was his second).

But the spine of the Rat Pack was my partner.

Dean gave what was happening a sense of mischief, and his glib, laid-back air undercut any idea that these great entertainers were being self-important. He never lost his suave manner, but he enjoyed himself like a kid on the town. He was the heart and soul of that act.

Frank looked to Dean for bits and extras that only a comic force like Dean could supply. Sammy played off Dean as well as I did — and that's a compliment to both of us. One of the great things about the Rat Pack was that they all knew, instinctively, that Dean was the real power on that stage — a different kind of power from Sammy, who was always so strong on his own as well as with those guys.

I think that what Dean brought to that group was his half of Martin and Lewis — he just replaced Jerry with four other guys. And he made it work, big-time, for all of them. In the past, in his own act, Frank would rarely talk: He would just sing and, from time to time, announce the composer of the song. That was it.

Dean showed Frank how to play on stage. How to make a party. The secret to Martin and Lewis's success was that we had *fun* together. People who hated their jobs, and even people who didn't, loved seeing that.

Dean brought that same quality to the Rat Pack. He even brought along many of the bits and lines that he and I had done, and they worked again for the same reason they had worked for us: fun!

And here I sit in the early years of the twenty-first century, listening to the CD of the Rat Pack at the Sands — a recording probably made at that very date — and marveling at its timelessness. Marveling, too, at the way Frank felt about Martin and Lewis.

Frank was always very gung ho about the team, and he had tremendous respect for both of us as individuals. Where Dean was concerned, I'll say this: Frank Sinatra idolized very few men — but Dean was certainly one of them. It was complicated. Frank was a softie under a brass exterior, a mama's boy who never felt, despite his many conquests, that he was manly enough. Dean was a man's man, a big jungle cat, totally easy in his skin — or at least very, very good at convincing the world that he was.

The reality was, this was his way of keeping the world at arm's length.

The truth behind the spaghetti-and-meatballs

Steubenville myth was (I learned as I got to know my partner better) that Dean came from a cold, calculating, insensitive Italian family. Doesn't match up with the cliché, right? Well, there are all kinds of Italians — scientists, statesmen, artists . . . and killers.

His mother and his father told him the following: One: 'You're going out into the real world; there is no one there that will care for you.' Two: 'Be sure that the money you have in your hand goes in your pocket.' Three: 'You cry, you're a fag. You show people any kind of warmth, and they will get closer to you. If you show them that you have your own persona and you're happy with it, they *will* stay away.'

Dean got squat from his mother, father, brother, aunts, uncles. He was lonely, unhappy, and felt totally unloved. Throughout his previous career as a casino dealer, small-time boxer, and semi-successful singer, he was always *alone*.

And so was I. Even though I had the love of my Grandma Sarah, who kept me weekends . . . my Aunt Rose, who kept me Mondays and Tuesdays . . . my Aunt Betty, who kept me Wednesdays and Thursdays, and my fat Aunt Jean, who kept me Fridays only, because she had Saturday-night poker parties with six Jewish ladies. I was known as the Pony Express kid, shipped from one place to another — always traveling, because my mom and dad were always on the road, to burlesque, vaudeville, concert dates, the Borscht Circuit; to Lakewood, New Jersey, in the winter months.

And so Dean and I understood each other.

111

Deeply. He maintained that distance from everybody except me. Our closeness worked for us, bonding us in the way that audiences loved, and — over time — against us.

But where Frank was concerned, Dean could never totally let down his guard. And — in a not totally healthy way — Frank was drawn to that reserve. It made Dean more manly and fascinating in Frank's eyes. When Frank saw the way Dean handled the Mob, he was amazed. Dean never gave them the time of day; he played dumb or drunk, or he was just off playing golf. He referred all business decisions to 'the Jew,' anyway. Frank, on the other hand, was drawn to the wiseguys' mystique because it made him feel tougher. But he was also a very smart man, smart enough to know that it was a crutch, one that Dean didn't need.

With Frank and me, it was different. We shared a huge regard for each other's talent, and a deep personal affection: Our personalities dovetailed. Very often he and I would be alone, on a plane trip to a benefit somewhere, or at Paramount, in my office or dressing room, while Dean was playing golf. Frank was always very open about his love affair with Martin and Lewis, and when we split as a team, he had to make a choice. It had to be one or the other. Dean and I were not talking, and Frank knew that Dean needed a friendship with substance.

For a while after July 24, 1956, people thought I would be just fine (even if I didn't always know it myself). But they worried about Dean.

6

In terms of ownership, backing, and patronage, organized crime played a central role in the nighttime world of cabaret entertainment in the 1940s and '50s. Inevitably, Dean and I came to know, usually on quite friendly terms, every major figure in the Mob, from Bugsy Siegel in Vegas to the Fischetti brothers, Tony Accardo, and Sam Giancana of Chicago, to Frank Costello and Lucky Luciano in New York. And while it may not be politically correct to say so, I found the great majority of these guys to be men of their word, far less hypocritical about their business than most of the politicians of the day. (As a young comic still wet behind the ears, I racked up a huge gambling debt at Bugsy Siegel's Flamingo in Vegas — but paid it off, to the penny, over the next two years, forever earning the respect of the Organization. And the word came down: *Anytime we can do something for you, just let us know.*)

It was usually the lackeys who made trouble.

Take the time that Dean got into a slightly sticky situation with the wrong guy's girlfriend. This was in Miami in 1950, and the guy was . . . Wait, I'm getting ahead of myself.

Dean Martin in real life was much the way everyone perceived him: cool, relaxed, unfazed by most anything. The guy who could take a nap during a gang war. But beneath that unflappable exterior was a different man, a man I began to understand over our ten years together.

Dean had a number of chinks in his armor, as we all have. And one of them almost led to a disaster. He loved the ladies (as we all do and did and always will), but he didn't care about the where or when. In fact, I constantly teased him that 'Where or When' was the one lyric he had committed to memory.

We were playing a Miami nightclub that shall go nameless (I don't know who might still be around and reading this!), when Dean spotted a lovely young lady sitting ringside with her grumpy-looking boyfriend, and proceeded to do what he always did when he spotted a pretty woman in the audience: He performed entirely to her. Sang and flirted, as if he were all alone with her.

When the show was over, I went into the men's room — and saw Dean standing face-to-face with the grumpy-looking boyfriend, who was pointing a .38 Special directly at Dean's stomach, about one inch away from the pasta he had eaten before the show.

The gun scared me all the more because I knew exactly who this man was, and what Dean and I were dealing with. The man — call him Harold Francis — was a low-level hood, a peripheral associate of Meyer Lansky's, but more to the point, he was one of the crazy gangsters, a guy very much like the one Joe Pesci played in *Goodfellas*, only taller. A hood with a hair-trigger temper, for whom knocking someone off, especially someone who had pissed him off, would mean less than nothing.

And so without thinking, I stepped between my partner and the man's gun (the gun that was now pointed into my stomach) and proceeded to do the verbal tap dance of my life.

I knew he was a mobster, and I knew what a handshake meant. I said, 'Harold, you have to understand something. People make mistakes — that's why they have erasers on pencils. Now, I'm going to admit to you that my partner made a mistake. I know Dean did what you said he did, but I'm going to offer you my hand, to give you my word of honor that I know my partner, and I know that out of respect for you, out of the same respect I have for you, he would never have done this if he had known who this young lady was.'

I was lying through my teeth. But I had no alternative, because Harold Francis was very serious. And as I stood there with my hand extended, I saw something in his eyes change, and I exhaled for the first time since I'd walked into that men's room.

Harold lowered the pistol. He was still angry, but he had inched back from the boiling point. 'This one time,' he said. 'This one time. But if he ever — '

'He will never,' I said.

'Ever,' he repeated.

'Won't happen,' I swore.

Harold gave Dean one last dirty look and exited the men's room, leaving us to stare at each other for a second. Dean was white, and I was whiter. The quiet was deafening.

Then Dean said, 'I've never seen a more stupid son of a bitch — you could've been killed!'

★　★　★

Flashback to the beginning of my Mob education: The time was 1947, and the place — what better place? — was Chicago. The Chez Paree was one of the great nightclubs, and the club's owners, Mike Fritzel and Joey Jacobsen, were very nice guys who were also, let's just say, very nicely connected, in a town that prized such connections above all else. The Chez Paree was a beautifully maintained operation, both in its main public room and its private Key Club, and in those days, it was the home base to the most important wiseguys in Chicago.

I, being a mere babe in the woods at the time, didn't fully appreciate this fact. Dean had played Chicago as a single, so he knew the score. (He also came from Steubenville!)

Talk about Chicago and a thousand stories float around my brain. Like the night — it was our second time at the Chez Paree — when a bulky gentleman with a hoarse voice poked his head into our dressing room and invited us to come sit at Joe Fischetti's table.

Now, for me, the name Fischetti rang no bell — hadn't I seen it on a bakery somewhere? But as Dean put his arm around my waist and led me very assertively toward the Key Club, he explained that in Chicago, the name meant three brothers — Joe, Rocky, and Charlie — who were

116

forces to be reckoned with.

The brothers were cousins of Al Capone, Dean said. Charlie Fischetti, who had been Capone's chief lieutenant in the twenties, now ruled Chicago, along with Capone's old accountant, Jake Guzik, and Tony 'Joe Batters' Accardo. Rocky and Joe worked closely with their big brother — they were one big happy Family.

And now they were at their table with almost twenty guests. One of the men stood and introduced himself as Joe Fischetti, then proceeded to introduce everybody else to us. We met Rocky and Charlie, and their wives. Mr. and Mrs. Tony Aiuppa, the Cheech Pitashes, the Johnny Ambrosias, and Mr. and Mrs. Arnold Feldman. (Arnold grabbed my lapel and said, 'One of your people, Jerry.')

'And there in the back,' Joe continued, 'are Anthony Verlatti, Jake Cleveland, and' — he smiled — 'the notorious Carmine, the cop.'

'Is he really a cop?' I asked Dean. He gave me a nudge that told me I'd better save the Idiot for the act.

We sat. 'You two are absolutely terrific,' Joe told us. 'We had a ball watching the two of yiz put on your skits.'

Dean and I smiled, and there were murmurs of agreement and raised glasses all around the table.

'Hold on a second,' Joe said. 'How rude could this be?' He turned to us. 'What will you fellas have to drink?' A waiter materialized instantly.

'Jack Daniel's rocks for me, and a . . . ' He

masked his mouth with his hand and lowered his voice, so I listened even harder. 'A Shirley Temple for my partner,' Dean said. To the general merriment of the table.

I shot him a look. He shot me one right back: We still had a second show to do. Once, in Los Angeles, I'd had a hard drink before we went on — another social situation — and Dean might as well have been working with Johnny Puleo, the harmonica player. So no more hard drinks.

We sat and made casual conversation. The men all loved Dean, and the women even more — and they looked at me like they wanted to burp me. Not the worst situation, as I was in the process of discovering! It was great for my partner to be unbelievably handsome and charming (and famous), but it wasn't hurting me one bit to be young and funny (and famous).

It seemed that Carmine was the clown of the group. He told us jokes, and he told them poorly . . . jokes that we had heard in gym class many years earlier. Dean and I laughed politely, but where the others were concerned, it was quickly apparent that Carmine told the same dirty jokes whenever the group was gathered. The women were rolling their eyes, as if to say, *Dear God, not again . . .*

We sat for around forty-five minutes, smiles frozen on our faces, and then we had to excuse ourselves to get ready for the second show. Everyone at the table said they'd be staying to see it.

'You know, we don't change our material from show one to show two,' Dean said.

Joe Fischetti gave us a look, from heavy-lidded eyes, that would have frozen running water. 'You change anything . . . ,' he said in a low, raspy voice. Then one corner of his mouth turned up in a faint semblance of a smile. ' . . . and I want my money back.'

★　★　★

The phone in our suite at the Palmer House rang promptly at nine the next morning. Since we had turned in at close to 6 a.m. and told the desk to hold all our calls, I assumed it was an emergency.

Not quite, but close. It was Johnny Ambrosia, telling us we were going to play golf that afternoon with Charlie Fischetti at the Bryn Mawr Country Club, one of Chicago's premier courses.

Dean told Johnny, 'Jerry doesn't even know how to hold a caddy. He doesn't play at all!'

Johnny: 'If Charlie Fischetti invites him to play, he *just learned*.'

He said a car would pick us up at noon. We were to go to the club, eat lunch, have a couple of drinks (again with the drinking!), and play a round of golf. Dean was excited about the prospect of playing this famous course, but I could also tell he was nervous about what, exactly, his partner was going to do out there.

We decided to just go and have fun, if possible. Our first show was at eight o'clock that night, and we had to get back to prepare for that, so it would be tight. We figured a noon pickup

119

would get us to the club around one, and, what with meeting and greeting and having a couple of drinks and lunch, we wouldn't be able to tee off until at least 4 p.m. It was early April and the sun set around six, but maybe with Charlie Fischetti, it set later! Who knew? We'd go, we'd see . . .

We did the meeting and greeting in the men's grill — a magnificent replica of an English golf-club bar, with everything in it imported from Scotland and the English countryside, plus general golf memorabilia collected since the turn of the century.

We order lunch while waiting for the booze. The drinks come. It's one o'clock in the afternoon and I'm drinking what the big boys are drinking . . . boilermakers: shots of twelve-year-old Haig & Haig whiskey followed by Budweiser chasers.

Oy vey, as my Grandma Sarah used to say.

All I can think about is the 8 p.m. showtime that we have to make . . . sober!

Dean has a couple and I have a couple, and bit by bit, we're starting not to care so much about the 8 p.m. show . . . And suddenly Charlie says, 'Okay, let's eat.'

The waiters start to bring platters of food. And more platters of food. And more platters of food. It looks like we're in ancient Rome, for Christ's sake! Charlie and his pals dig in, laughing and having a great time. Then come coffee and dessert, and that runs another half hour. Finally, it's tee time.

Dean is all excited about the game. I don't

know what to think. The foursome is Charlie, Dean, me, and Jake Friedland, a Chicago lawyer. But there are also two extra carts for some very intimate friends of Charlie's who will be following us on the course — just in case we need to move a tree.

Charlie tees up his ball, saying, 'I have the honor.' We hadn't hit a ball yet, and he has the honor? On the other hand, who was going to tell him he didn't have it? Not me!

He hits the ball and it makes the fairway, about sixty yards out. Nobody laughs. Charlie decides to take a mulligan, which I later learned meant a second swing. He hits a pretty decent shot this time, then Jake gets up and, without a glance at where he's aiming, hits a beauty — not so far, but down the middle. Dean's up next. He blasts that drive at least 240 yards down the fairway, dead center, and he looks terrific doing it.

Then Charlie says, 'Okay, kid — let's see if you really never played before.'

This actually makes me feel a little better, because I literally don't even know how to hold the driver. (I'm using Dean's club.) Dean whispers, 'Just swing easy, keep your eye on the ball, keep your head down, don't sway too much, and be sure you follow through.'

'Is that all?!' I scream.

As in life, I proceed to make funny from what I fear. I look like Ray Bolger as The Scarecrow in *The Wizard of Oz* . . . no spine to speak of, and certainly not standing upright. I sway like a weed in the wind, look out at the fairway, sway some

more . . . hold the club too low . . . then too high
. . . then sway some more. Dean and the guys are
hysterical at my antics. *Good God*, I think. *I may
get through this yet.*

After doing all the body English I know (and
more), I finally strike the ball.

It soars back over my head and lands about
forty yards behind the tee box. The laughter is
deafening. Then they all head down the fairway
to make their second shots. Dean can't wait to
get to his ball: He hit such a great drive that he's
thinking maybe this could be one of those days.

I go pick up my ball. 'What do I do now?' I
implore. Dean waves me over to him, and we
watch as the others hit their shots. Charlie,
farthest from the green, goes first. He sets up,
swings at the ball, and hits it hard. The ball sails
. . . and sails . . . and lands in the trees, out of
bounds.

'Let's get another drink at the clubhouse!'
Charlie yells.

Charlie and Jake's cart turns and starts back
up the path; the two carts full of bodyguards
follow. Dean and I stand dumbfounded. We later
learn that if Charlie doesn't like the way he's
playing, he has a drink, then goes home. In fact,
Charlie Fischetti has played only about thirty
holes in the twenty years he's been a member at
Bryn Mawr.

As all the carts go up the path to the
clubhouse, Dean says, 'Look at this shot. I
could've hit an easy eight-iron and putted for a
bird.' Fuming, he takes out his eight-iron and
hits the ball stiff to the pin, maybe two feet from

the cup. Then he turns and gets in the cart. 'Let's go, Jer — it looks like this ain't gonna be our day,' he says. We go back to the clubhouse and make nice with the guys, just like nothing ever happened.

After a bit, Dean and I are getting hammered again. We catch each other glancing at our watches. Then Charlie notices. Thank God, he looks sympathetic. With an eight-o'clock show-time and an hour-and-a-half ride back to Chicago, we are officially excused. We stand and make our apologies, but as we head to the door, Charlie calls, 'You better hurry — I got my regular table for the eight-o'clock show!'

I felt bad for Dean: Though I wasn't a golfer, I understood his disappointment. For someone who knows and loves the game, a great golf course is like a beautiful, slightly unattainable woman — full of challenges, surprises, difficulties, and delights. Dean was like a man who'd been stood up. It was a long, quiet ride back to the hotel, not a time for humor. A good time to get unhammered.

In the dressing room at the Chez, I was drying my hair while Dean shaved and muttered to himself. 'Lloyd Mangrum played that course and won the Tam O'Shanter there. Jeez, I probably would've done terrific if I had half a chance.'

I had a brainstorm.

That night I phoned Johnny Ambrosia and asked him the name of the pro at the Bryn Mawr Country Club. The next morning, I pried my eyes open at eight sharp and phoned that pro, who was a hell of a nice guy and very excited to hear from me. I explained what had happened with Dean the day before, how frustrated he was that he couldn't finish his game.

'Where can I reach Dean now?' the pro asked.

'At 8 a.m.?' I said. 'In his room, I hope.'

The pro called Dean and told him he was a big fan (true), told him he'd heard he was in town (also true) and was a big golfer, and asked if Dean would accept his personal invitation to play eighteen holes with him on the coming weekend.

When Dean rushed into my room, he looked like a kid who'd found out Santa was coming. He jumped up and down on my bed, yelling, 'I'm gonna play with the pro at Bryn Mawr! I'm gonna play with the pro at Bryn Mawr!' For the next two days, he whistled, hummed, and sang around the suite and our dressing room at the club. I'd never seen him like this before.

Saturday morning came, and out he rolled at 6:30 a.m., fresh as a daisy on one hour's sleep. I stayed at the hotel all morning, taking pictures (my big new hobby, which I could finally afford) and silently praying that Dean would play well. That was stupid of me — he always played well.

Around two in the afternoon, there's a bang on the door like only Dean banged on the door. I open it and Dean's standing there with his bag of clubs standing next to him and his scorecard stuck to his forehead, covering his face. (You just wet the card and stick it to your forehead — works every time.)

I take the card from his head, and behind that scorecard is the face of the happiest man I ever saw in my life. I look at the card. The pro shot a 71, and Dean shot a 74 — three strokes' difference! I jump into his arms, yelling, 'I knew it! I knew it!' and the clubs fall to the floor with a big clatter — which, since it's 1:55 in the afternoon, shouldn't be a big deal, except that some people might still be asleep, especially the ones who were at our club the night before till 5:30 a.m.

Maybe it was my imagination, but I swear Dean sang better that night. He built a nice relationship with that club pro and played there, over the years, every time we were in Chicago.

When Dean was happy, the work was better. The same with me. When either of us was sad, the work broke down a little bit — not always so the outside world could see, but we knew. For now, though, we were happy.

7

It's a story as old as time: People meet, fall in love, have babies, fall out of love. The process is especially severe if one's life changes radically while the other's doesn't.

When Dean first met Betty McDonald, she was a reach for him — a fresh-faced, lacrosse-playing Swarthmore girl, the adored youngest daughter of a successful liquor distributor. Who the hell was Dean Martin in 1941? A tough Italian kid fresh out of Steubenville who had made it as far as Cleveland. A band singer with a handsome face (and as yet unfixed nose), a smooth manner, and a sixty-five-dollar-a-week contract with Sammy Watkins and His Orchestra.

An upstart and a social climber, in the eyes of Betty's family, when the two of them courted and married.

And a national star when they came to grief and parted.

Betty was as bowled over by Dean as he was by her. She dropped out of college and married him at eighteen, had their first child when she was nineteen. Three more babies came in quick succession, and with them, Betty's bitterness. It's hard in the best circumstances for a woman to be married to a traveling performer, and the best circumstances rarely exist. Four small children and an absent husband with a wandering eye are very far from ideal conditions. Betty began to drink. She tried using guilt and anger to hold on to Dean, failing to keep in mind the two keystones of my partner's character: First, he hated confrontation of any kind, and would go to great lengths to avoid it. And second, he devoted all his energy to living his life exactly as he wanted. He literally walked away from anything and anybody that got in the way of that principle.

Maybe Patti and I stayed together as long as we did (thirty-six years) because she let me know, at the beginning, that she knew I'd face temptations on the road, and, being a man, I'd give in to them. She just didn't want me to humiliate her. She called me on the carpet when I did that, and I did my best to be more discreet afterward.

I don't know what agreement — if any — Betty and Dean had. She knew how handsome he was, she knew what a magnet that was for so many women, and she knew his ways. What she — and he — had never counted on was his falling in love.

It was the last thing Dean expected: He never liked being tied down. It happened in Miami, where we were playing a four-week run at the Beachcomber Club at the end of 1948. This was the first time Dick Stabile ever worked with us, the first time we could afford our own conductor — the Beachcomber was paying us $12,000 a week. We were on stage on New Year's Eve when Dean looked over at a ringside table and saw the Orange Bowl Queen and her ladies-in-waiting, one of whom was a pert, gorgeous, twenty-one-year-old blonde named Jeanne Biegger.

It was (as they say) as if he'd been struck by the thunderbolt.

I was thrilled to see my partner so happy, but I also understood his dilemma. It's no small deal to be a Catholic father of four who wants — who needs — to get out of a marriage. Selfishly, I wanted Dean to be able to find a way. Betty represented all the pain of his young manhood. She brought back memories of what he was and where he came from, and Jeannie brought him thoughts of what he could be. And a performer needs to feel free in his mind to do his best work.

I've seen the other side of that so many times in my career. When Jackie Gleason wanted to marry Marilyn Taylor, his wife, a devout Catholic, didn't want to give him a divorce. For a while, Jackie's work in *The Honeymooners* became stilted and uneven — but then, when his wife finally agreed to the split, he was a new man on and off the screen.

I needed — the act needed — Dean's best work. From day one, I understood that even though I'd been born funny, my partner's magic was to bring it out of me in a way that looked effortless. I knew, selfishly, that if Dean wasn't there, I'd be in trouble.

Dean agonized about leaving Betty, and — freely admitting my personal stake in it — I advised him to follow his heart. He did. He moved Jeannie to a rented house in West Hollywood in early 1949, and Betty, back east

128

with the kids but up on all the developments, served him with divorce papers.

★   ★   ★

When a lot happens to you all at once, you learn fast. In the months after Dean and I first hit Hollywood, we learned plenty about the town, its workings, and its players. The two greenhorn kids who didn't even know where Ciro's was quickly became pals with its owner, Herman Hover.

Ciro's was the ritziest nightclub on Sunset Strip, and Herman was quite a power in the Hollywood of the late forties. Short, gruff, always impeccably tailored, he was the same height and build as Edward G. Robinson, with the same hairline — except that instead of looking like a gangster, Herman resembled a textile salesman. He wore expensive hand-painted ties and custom-made shirts: Whenever he extended an arm, you saw his monogram, 'H.H.,' right there on the cuff. The first time I got a load of that, I said, 'Wow! Harry Horseshit!' Dean made an Oliver Hardy face at me, and I never did it again.

Herman Hover spent money exactly the way you'd think a guy who looked like Herman Hover would spend money. He lived in a mansion on North Bedford in Beverly Hills that had once belonged to Mary Pickford: Howard Hughes, another pal of Hover's, conducted most of his business there. Herman's home had a $40,000 supply of liquor on hand at all times — he skimmed pretty good from Ciro's. Oh, he was a piece of work. (I'm sorry to say he wound up broke.)

It was in Herman's mansion, on September 1, 1949, that Dean married Jeannie. It was quite an affair, small and private but lavish. Herman footed the bill (of course), including ten grand worth of white gardenias. I was best man. Patti was present, under protest — she still felt bad for Betty. And Dean, in a separate room from Jeannie so they wouldn't have the bad luck of seeing each other before the ceremony, was nervous as a cat. My partner and I were alone together, as he paced and lit cigarette after cigarette. You'd have thought he was going to the chair! Soon all the pacing and smoking began to get to me. When he said, 'Christ, I need a drink!' I was thrilled.

'You're gonna be all right if I leave for a minute, right?' I asked him.

'Of course!' he bellowed. 'Get the drink!'

I dashed out to the pantry, swung open the door, and got my first eyeful of Herman's fabulous liquor collection. Jesus, there was enough booze in there to get all of Pasadena loaded. I took out a bottle of Dean's favorite (at the time), Johnnie Walker Black Label, and filled a huge tumbler — at least sixteen ounces' worth. There were smaller glasses, but whenever there was a chance for a laugh, I always went for it. Then I strolled back into the room and handed the tumbler — it had to be at least nine inches tall — to Dean. He took one look at it and fell apart, just thought it was the funniest thing he had ever seen. It really wasn't, it just happened to be the perfect time for that kind of a sight gag. He sipped some of it, put it on the table, and lit another cigarette.

'Can I ask you a personal question?' I said.

Dean looked at me like I was nuts. When, before, had I ever *asked* if I could ask? Not my style, especially where he was concerned! But on this one, I genuinely felt a little timid. I cleared my throat. 'You just got out of one marriage.' I said. 'What the fuck are you rushing into another one for?'

He just stared at me, shocked that I had hit the issue on the button. I hurried to explain myself. 'Forgive me, Paul,' I said. 'Jeannie's a great girl, and I think she would follow you to the ends of the earth. I know she would wait until you were ready. And there are four kids to think about.'

Dean thought for a moment. 'Listen, Jer,' he said. 'You know me better than anyone, so what I say is between us. I do worry about my kids. But this feels so *right*. So *strong*.'

I nodded, finally understanding that he was really in love, and probably for the first time. 'It's your life, pal,' I told him. 'And you have to do what's best for you. You've always taken care of your kids; now it's your turn to take care of yourself. Everything'll fall into place.'

He threw his arms around me in a bear hug and whispered into my ear: 'Thanks, Jer.'

As it turned out, Jeannie was the best thing that ever happened to Dean. Unfortunately, she and I never really hit it off.

Both of us were jealous of Dean's deep

feelings for the other, both of us wished we could have him all to ourselves. But I repeat: Jeannie was the best thing (next to me) that ever happened to Dean. They had a loving, strong, and enduring relationship. A complicated relationship, yes — it was impossible to have any other kind with Dean. Though he and Jeannie would eventually divorce (twenty years later), I always felt that that was just legal paperwork. They never stopped caring for each other. I guess I loved her, too, in my own way. Someday I *may* tell her.

★　★　★

In the annals of marriage counseling, I know there is the following sentence: The couple that laughs together, stays together. I'm totally convinced of the wisdom of that, and I'm positive the same holds true for partners of all sorts, because as long as Dean and I were laughing with each other, we stuck like glue.

When two guys perform and travel together ten months out of the year, they form a unique attachment. Staying in the same hotels, sharing a two-bedroom suite at the beginning, Dean and I found out almost everything there was to know about each other — sometimes secrets you wouldn't want to share with anyone.

There was the time we played a gig at the Presidente Hotel in Acapulco. We'd only been a team for eleven months, and suddenly we were being offered big bucks to do a show in sunny Mexico, including everything else that came with the package: water-skiing, frolicking on the beach, frolicking off the beach.

We went, we played, we rehearsed, we did the show, and then we played some more. All night, in fact: from around 12:30 till 8:30 a.m. We stumbled back to the hotel for a couple hours' sleep, then staggered to the airport for the flight back to L.A.

After grabbing some rest in our Los Angeles hotel (this was around a year before we both moved to the West Coast), we had to get ready for the evening's show. Dean came into my bathroom to borrow some toothpaste and saw me examining myself in the mirror, trying to figure out where the itching was coming from.

'Having trouble, Mr. Lucas?' he said. (I don't think, in ten years, that he said 'Lewis' *even once*. His favorites were: Lucas, Loomis, Lousy, and Looseleaf.)

'Yeah, I'm having trouble,' I answered. 'What the hell is happening to me?'

It was apparent that my partner had been there before. (I was only twenty-one, and hadn't.) He took my arm. 'Step up here for a minute,' Dean says, pointing to the toilet-seat cover. I stand up there as he instructs. His head is right in line with my penis.

'I didn't know about this perk, pal!' I say.

Dean tilts his head ever so slightly and says, 'The day that becomes a possibility is the day I go back to doing a single.'

By now I'm getting annoyed with his survey of my pubic stuff. 'What the hell are you doing?' I ask. 'And what's going on down there, anyway?'

Dean says, 'Hold on for just a second.' He leans over to the medicine cabinet and retrieves a small tweezer I had in my toiletries case. He looks like he's scrubbed in for the operation and ready to begin the incision.

He plucks something off me and opens the tweezer over the white porcelain sink, and I go ballistic. 'It's moving!' I scream. 'It's a moving thing! What do I do, Dean? There's animals climbing on my bones! What do I do?'

Dean begins to laugh, and I wonder what the hell he thinks is so funny. 'What is it?' I say. 'Will you please tell me?'

'Jerry,' he says, 'you got crabs.'

'What the hell am I doing, ordering seafood?' I yell. 'What the hell do you mean? And what the hell do we do?'

Jack Eigen, Al Jolson, Dean and Jerry: Copa, 1948. No we were not the King Family.

'I have to get us some alcohol and sand,' Dean says.

He's lost it, I think. 'Alcohol and sand?' I say. 'Then what?'

'We throw the sand on them,' Dean says, casually, 'then the alcohol. They get loaded and kill one another throwing rocks!'

(Thank God he knew to send for Campho-Phenique. The morning came and the itching went.)

You might also be interested to hear that my partner loved to read comic books.

You heard me, comic books! *Captain Marvel, Superman, Batman*. (Once when we got to meet Bob Kane, the creator of *Batman*, Dean was more knocked out than I'd ever seen him about meeting anyone — except perhaps Frank.) I don't remember ever seeing him buying a newspaper; he'd only look at a paper if I bought one. But I *had* to buy his comic books. Why? Because he was embarrassed, that's why. He was always sensitive about his lack of education.

He also loved — and I mean loved — to watch Westerns on television. I remember third shows at the Copa where he'd speed up so as not to miss the 3 a.m. showing of John Wayne in *Red River* or *Stagecoach*. In fact, I'll swear: As much as Dean loved the ladies, when the fun was done, he preferred being left alone to watch his Westerns or read his comic books. Women always seemed to need the kind of attention he wasn't much interested in giving.

But God, did they pay attention to *him*. And I have to admit: When I was an impressionable

135

young man, one of the first things that fascinated me about Dean was the way he smelled.

The postwar years were a great era for men's colognes, especially after Leo Durocher, the tough-guy manager of the Brooklyn Dodgers (who would become a pal of ours) let it slip that he liked to slap on something nice-smelling after he showered and shaved, and he didn't care who knew it. Dean's cologne was the provocatively named Woodhue (say it out loud and it sounds like the kind of question Dean might ask a beautiful young woman — or that beautiful young women would ask him), by Fabergé. The minute I first sniffed it, I associated it with the almost incredible voodoo my partner exerted on the opposite sex. I wanted some of that, too!

I began paying close attention to Dean's postshower ritual: He would take his bottle of Woodhue, pour some into one cupped palm, then put the bottle down and slap his palms together. Then he'd rub the cologne all over his body — as far as I could see, anyway. At this point he was always in the bathroom, the door just slightly ajar to let out the steam. After a couple of minutes, he'd emerge in his robe, smiling with complete satisfaction: He looked, felt, and smelled great!

I'll never forget what happened one day in Detroit.

We had done six shows at the Fox Theater, were dog-tired, and were back in our suite at the Book-Cadillac Hotel. Dean was lying on his bed, reading a comic and drinking a beer, and I was ready to take a nice, long shower. I sauntered into the elegant bathroom, turned the radio on, and stepped into the shower, ready to spend twenty minutes just letting the warm water hit my body. The music was nice, we had done six terrific shows, and I felt swell.

When I stepped out of the shower, I yelled out to Dean: 'Hey, Paul — can I use some of your Woodhue?'

'Sure, use what you like!'

I took the bottle, unscrewed the top, and, just for a moment, admired my twenty-three-year-old body in the full-length mirror. Then I started to splash the cologne on — under my arms, on my chest, on my legs, even down my back . . .

Then I poured some of the liquid into my hand, put the bottle on the sink, and proceeded to anoint Little Jerry and the entire surrounding region.

It might have been about fifteen seconds before the burning sensation began — and did it ever. I bounced out of the bathroom Indian-style, whooping and dancing in pain. I went through both bedrooms into the kitchenette, then the sitting area, until finally, deciding I needed air, I flung open the door of the suite and dashed down the long hall, hoping I could create a little wind on my crotch.

I passed the elevators — naturally, they opened with women in them, who screamed louder than I did. Down the hallway, doors began to open as people emerged to investigate the noise . . . men laughing . . . women aghast . . . and at our door, there was Dean, leaning against the jamb, laughing hysterically.

I finally ran into a room-service waiter and his cart — rolls, knives, forks, and steaks flew from one wall to the other — and picked up two silver plate covers, using them like Gypsy Rose Lee used her boas. I limped back to the suite, where Dean was still laughing. I crawled off to my bed and lay down with a pillow between my legs, waiting for the pain to quit, and swearing to myself I would never use the smelly stuff again.

I just couldn't seem to keep away from Dean's Woodhue, though.

Practical jokes were an important part of our life on the road, and I worked overtime to tease my hero, my big brother: When the devil got into me, I would stop at nothing. Once, back in Atlantic City, I found a duplicate of his pin-striped performing suit (these were the pretux days) in a pawnshop, and made razor cuts along the stripes. The incisions were impossible to see until Dean put the suit on — at which point it fell apart. Another time I took his prized bottle of Woodhue, dumped it out, and put in Coca-Cola that I mixed with water to achieve an identical light-brown shade.

It was a perfect match. I put the bottle back in place, cleaned up my tracks, and couldn't wait until he got home from golf, showered, and went for his 'Woodhue.'

Some hours passed, and I took a nap. When I awoke, I heard Dean in his bathroom, taking a shower. *Yeah*, I said to myself. *The beaver's in the hopper.*

I waited . . . and waited. Finally, I decided it was time to shower and get ready for our shows.

When I was done, we met for a drink in the living room of our suite, and Dean said nothing to me. I didn't understand. I walked by him . . . His Woodhue aroma was in place — he smelled like always, and I didn't get it. I said nothing, we just made some idle chatter, and off to work we went.

We did our two shows, had a ball, and headed back to the suite. But I didn't have great success with sleeping that night, because when you do a practical joke, it isn't sweet until you got the mark and it's done. Well, this one wasn't done, and I had no mark!

This went on for another two or three nights. Dean would shower, shave, use his 'Woodhue.' (I tried sneaking into the bathroom to reexamine the bottle, but Dean was always around, for some reason!)

Soon I was starting to feel an itching in my scalp . . . and the jumpies. If anyone spoke a little louder than usual, I'd jump. All symptoms of an unfulfilled gag.

After a while, the symptoms wore off and I started to forget the whole thing.

We were doing the second show on our next-to-closing-night performance, and as I began to leave the stage (a planned point in the act when I walked off so Dean could do a song), he stopped me, turned to the audience, and said, 'If you'll excuse me for just a second, I need to confer with my partner about something.'

A little ripple of laughter started up in the audience — I'm sure they thought we were setting them up. And Dean turned to me and whispered in my ear, 'I didn't want you to suffer any longer, pally — I know what you did with my aftershave. I dumped it and got a new bottle.'

He looked at me and laughed hysterically, which made me laugh hysterically — and the audience was still waiting for the joke! We recovered, Dean sang, and the 'Woodhue' became history.

We loved the sheer nonsense of it all, having as much fun off the stage as we did on.

I don't think, early on, that we really knew the difference.

A little while later, though, I came up with a scheme I thought might be foolproof. It was 1952, we had just completed two weeks at the Chicago Theater — seven shows a day, forty-nine a week — and we were as exhausted as a groom on his wedding night. Especially my partner. When we finished the last show of the engagement, I heard Dean say something I'd never heard from him before: 'Jer, I'm outta gas. I'm really very tired.'

'Let's go back to the hotel, order room service, catch a Western on TV, and hit the pad early,' I said. (Early for us was before 3 a.m.)

We got into the limo and rode back to the Ambassador Hotel. We were both so beat we didn't speak for the whole twenty-five-minute drive, but I had time to think about a scenario I'd been developing for years. All I needed was for my partner to give me ten minutes in the suite before he came up. So I suggested we have a nightcap in the Pump Room, and to my delight, Dean accepted.

140

As soon as we ordered, I excused myself, telling Dean I had to go to the men's room. Off I went — not to the men's room, of course, but to the elevator and up to our suite. It took me no more than three minutes to short-sheet his bed, and when I was done, I just had to spend another moment or two admiring my work.

I rushed back down to the bar, and Dean gave me a look. 'Did everything come out all right?' he asked.

'It must've been all the Cokes I had today,' I said.

We finished our drinks and headed up to the suite, both of us so fatigued that our feet were literally dragging. When we got inside, Dean went straight to his bedroom.

I stood just outside his door, pretending to be busy doing something, but really listening carefully. I heard his shoes falling, the bedcovers being pulled down, and finally his last sound — the sigh of a dead man. I waited, eager to hear the roar of laughter or the roar of the jungle beast. Nothing. It was as quiet as a zipper in the men's room. I waited a little longer, completely stumped: What had happened?

Finally, I sneaked into his room to take a look. Dean was sleeping like a baby, snoring a little, his legs tucked into the fetal position. He was so exhausted that he'd never even felt the short sheets — he slept all through the night that way.

I sighed. *Oh well*, I thought. *Maybe I'll get him next time.*

★ ★ ★

Some of the best times we had were hanging out with other performers. Both of us were crazy about Jackie Gleason, who in addition to being a comic genius was the greatest party animal alive. He loved teasing Dean about his wussy drinking. It finally got to be too much for Dean. 'Let's have a contest and see who's standing at the finish!' he told Gleason.

It was February 1950, at Toots Shor's restaurant on Fifty-second Street in Manhattan. The three of us were standing at the bar, and everyone heard the challenge. We now had at least forty people surrounding us, watching to see how this episode played out. Jackie ordered for both of them: 'Let's have two boilermakers!' Dean called out, 'Give us both a Pink Lady!' This got a great laugh — ordering a Pink Lady at Toots's would be like ordering a condom at a convent.

The drinks got served, and down they went. First Jackie, then Dean. Jackie said, 'What a joy! Round One is completed.' He then remembered that no bet had been mentioned. Jackie said to Dean, 'How much are we wagering on this little sojourn?' Dean, of course, had to play this out. 'Make it easy on yourself,' he said.

Without a second thought, Jackie said, 'How about a grand?'

Without taking a breath, Dean agreed. 'You got it!' he said. I rolled my eyes, with visions of this all winding up in *Hollywood Confidential* (the *National Enquirer*'s ancestor). I thought Dean wouldn't be sober till Labor Day!

Just as things were getting interesting, Leo

142

Durocher walked in with the most gorgeous goddamn woman ever seen on earth! Legs up to her ears, breasts (if they were real) far out enough to ring her own doorbell! Every man in that joint had a community erection. Then Dean hit on her. Jackie Gleason hit on her. Leo loved to laugh (guess he liked comedy better than sex), because he forgot she was with him the minute he saw Gleason. So she became fair game, and most everyone there that night was trying to get her attention.

Guess who left Toots Shor's with her?

About 4:15 a.m., Dean strolled into our suite and entered his room. I heard him moving about while I was still busily engaged in explaining to this lovely lady how my wife didn't understand me. There was a knock on the door. I continued sipping Dom Pérignon along with my new friend, and I heard, 'Hey, Jer, you in there?'

I didn't answer. I told her to be very quiet.

'Come on, Jer, I know you're in there!'

We let Dean knock and knock, and I finally yelled out, 'What do you want?'

'I want sharesies!' he said. 'Don't we always share everything?'

'Yeah,' I said. 'We share sandwiches, makeup, towels, tux ties, but we never share ladies. I would never let you near mine, and you would never let me near yours.'

'Did you ever hear of an amendment?' Dean laughed.

George Burns understood the depth of my partner's comic genius. Danny Lewis understood it. Millions of people — including some otherwise quite intelligent people — had no clue. 'In the bones' funny is a gift: You're either born with it or you're not. Gleason had it. Milton Berle had it. Sid Caesar and Stan Laurel had it. Charlie Chaplin had more of it than anyone else. Discussing Chaplin's genius would be like measuring the ocean with a cup.

Dean had it, too, yet he never understood the depth of his own skill. He was insecure about it; at the same time, he was never one to betray his insecurities. So he was stuck in kind of a hard place — one that became progressively harder as the press wrote about the comic brilliance of 'the funny one.' And that was how our reviews went: 'The handsome one comes out and sings pretty nicely — although he's no Bing Crosby. Then the kid comes out, and the act really catches fire.' Time after time after time, Dean had to read those words.

And you wonder why he never bought a newspaper?

It got worse when we began making our movies. After *My Friend Irma*, the august Bosley Crowther (you think he made that name up?) of the august *New York Times* opined as follows: 'We could go along with the laughs which were fetched by a new mad comedian, Jerry Lewis . . . the swift eccentricity of his movements, the harrowing features of his face and the squeak of his vocal protestations . . . have flair. His idiocy constitutes the burlesque of an idiot, which is something else again. He's the funniest thing in it. Indeed, he's the only thing in it that we can expressly propose for seeing the picture.'

Crowther, that sniffy bastard, called Dean my 'collar ad partner.'

Meaning: Handsome but empty. A mannequin. A prop.

Meanwhile, the *Los Angeles Examiner* said Dean would 'undoubtedly be more at home on the screen with added experience,' but 'he shouldn't oughta listen to any more Bing Crosby records.'

Cruel, cruel, cruel. And what was my partner's reaction? He didn't react, not at first. You have to understand: Even though Dean had saved me from a lifetime of lip-synching, even though he had in many ways made me into what I became, he didn't have a speak of ego about it. He didn't have enough ego, really. There was a big part of him that felt supremely lucky to have made it to where he had. The money, the broads, the life — why should he give a shit about what some pointy-headed schmucks wrote about him in the papers?

If the shoe had been on the other foot, if I had been the kind of target for the press that Dean was, I wouldn't have lasted anywhere close to ten years. I'd have been out of there by the third year, at the latest — and I would have made it that far only because the loot was so good. If I had to go back and pull all the written material on Martin and Lewis, it would read like a bunch of writers had gotten together and decided, 'Let's kill the singing part of that team.'

Did they actually decide to do that? I doubt it, but if you read what I have in the files, you'd wonder, too. And I think the critics refused to change their minds because Dean never let them know he even read what they wrote. He carried himself like a champ, and they hated him for it.

★ ★ ★

On the morning of October 6,1950, a golden fall Friday, Dean and I and Jeannie and Patti took a picturesque, hour-long drive: west from Pittsburgh (where we were playing a show at the Stanley Theater), across the state line and through a dog-poor sliver of West Virginia, then over a big iron bridge straddling the Ohio River and into Steubenville. The occasion was to be a weekend-long celebration of the town's Local Boy Made Good: Steubenville had declared that Friday Dean Martin Day.

The parade began at noon. Fifty cars and several marching bands snaked slowly around narrow streets lined with thousands of locals, every other one of whom seemed to know Dean personally. Finally, we wound up at the Municipal Building, where the mayor presented Dean with the key to the city.

Dean thanked him and said, 'I love getting the key to the city. When I lived here, my folks wouldn't give me a key to the house!'

After giving a performance at the very high school my partner had dropped out of seventeen eventful years earlier, we were ushered around town, stopping in at all of Dean's old haunts: the poolroom where he hung out, the steel mill where he worked, the after-hours club where he sang, the back rooms where he dealt poker and blackjack.

And we met his old friends. Oy, did we meet his old friends! Coming out of the woodwork were: Mindy, Ross, Jiggs, Smuggs, Ape-Head, Cheech, Vigo, Teeth, Harry the Spoon, Doggy, Spongie, Locust, Brains, Meat-Jaw, Meathead, Teeth Mancini, Breathless Andriano, Choker DiStefani, and Apples (*she* married Boneyard Carbieri). They could have cast *The Godfather 1, 2,* and *3* from this crowd.

The only Jew who lived in Steubenville didn't show up, because he didn't particularly care for our act.

Never before had either Dean or I had our cheeks pinched, our backs slapped as much as we did that weekend. I loved it. But Dean hated it.

He smiled, he ate, he made the small talk — but I could see that he was unhappy. He never said anything, but I know what he was feeling: He had *left* Steubenville. It was a gray, sooty steel town, where the best any of his old friends could hope for was a sixty-bucks-a-week job in the mill. He was the one who got away. He didn't *want* to go back, not on Dean Martin Day or any other day.

And here's the thing: My partner had made it out of Steubenville on a smile and a shoeshine and the sheer force of his personality.

And a lot of what we'd done was just about luck and moonshine and having a good time.

Dean: 'Did you take a bath this morning?'

Jerry: 'Why, is there one missing?'

Milton Berle: 'I still don't know what they do!'

We believed in our skill, our funniness, our chemistry — but at the same time, nobody understood how incredibly lucky we'd been. I think Dean was superstitious about our luck. Didn't want to be reminded of it; didn't want to think about how fragile it all was.

We were flying high, the two of us — high above the earth, with its steel mills and factories and offices, its nine-to-five, grocery-buying, bill-paying concerns. Why should we ever come down?

8

By the end of 1950, Dean and I had released three movies — *My Friend Irma, My Friend Irma Goes West,* and *At War with the Army* — and had another, *That's My Boy,* just about in the can. That September we'd begun our new Sunday-night television show, *The Colgate Comedy Hour,* on NBC. Our national radio show (also on NBC) was chugging along merrily. Much of the reason we were so successful was that in a tense and conformist time, the country needed wildness, needed nonsense. Elvis and rock and roll would provide a different kind of outlet in the mid-fifties, but Martin and Lewis awoke the country to the sound of its own laughter.

In July 1951, we played the Paramount Theater on Broadway for the first time. On an unseasonably cool and rainy Thursday morning, our taxicab crept through the traffic toward Times Square, as Dean and I gawked out the window at an amazing sight: our faces on a sign as large as the building, reading, 'Martin and Lewis on Stage, in Person and on the Screen.'

Then we were stopped by an incredible spectacle: a huge mob of fans filling Times Square, waiting to get into the Paramount. Most of them, we later learned, had been there since 6 a.m. I knew there'd be pandemonium when we got out of the cab, but there was nothing to be done — we had to get as close to the backstage door as possible, as quickly as possible. The driver edged through the crowds, up to the curb, and we started to scramble. We were recognized before we even left the cab.

'It's them!'

Dean's prized Aquascutum trench coat sticks in the cab door as the screaming fans grab the side of his coat; the driver isn't sure he's going to get his fare . . .

'Leave the coat, for Christ's sake!' I yell to Dean. 'We're making enough to buy the company!'

The coat frees itself into the hands of a happy fan — leaving Dean free to dash into the theater. We rush backstage and into the elevator, which runs us up to the sixth-floor dressing rooms — which, at the Paramount Theater, are shoe boxes instead of a nail.

Dean and I have one room on the sixth floor, and our bandleader, Dick Stabile, has another . . . and that's it. All the rest of the company are on seven, eight, and nine; the band is on ten, and their horns and music stands are in the basement.

We get dressed as quickly as possible, because the movie is just about done. The audience is primed and ready for us. We finish getting into our tuxes (at 9:45 a.m.!) and hit the stairs. Why the stairs? Because the goddamn elevator *always* gets stuck. And we have four thousand people out there, waiting . . .

The band hits the Dick Stabile theme song, 'Blue Nocturne,' as the hydraulic platform they're sitting on starts its mighty rise from the bowels of the orchestra pit to its triumphant high finish. They wind up the theme just as the platform stops moving. Then Dick steps downstage and introduces our opening act: 'And here they are, Barr and Estes!'

Their official billing was Barr & Estes, Eccentric Dancers, and their official reason for being there was that Leonard Barr was Dean's uncle. That was it, pure and simple: Leonard was Dean's mother's brother (Barra was the original family name). Barr & Estes were our insurance. Both Dean and I felt that if anyone was going to get rotten tomatoes, it might as well be the opening act!

Dean's Uncle Leonard was a very big-nosed, funny-looking guy, skinny and crazy-limbed. His partner, Marie Estes, was a contortionist. They danced around the stage, twisting their bodies to the sound of 'Song of India' — and light titters and coughing.

Well, Barr & Estes finished their twelve minutes, and Dick, as always, introduced me: 'The first half of this great comedy team, please welcome Jerry Lewis!' The band played me on with a jazz riff, to enthusiastic screaming.

'Ladies and gentlemen,' I finally said when the noise died down. 'I'm the first half you'll see tonight of the team of Dean and Jerry, and I have to clarify one thing — I'm Jerry.'

This got the reaction I was looking for, allowing me to peer around the theater with a hurt face. 'Because a lot of people mistake me for Dean,' I insisted — and then I gave them the

Idiot laugh, which got a big laugh from them.

'But,' I said at last, 'but my partner *will* come out here, and, God willing, he *will* sing.' And then I had to wait another couple of minutes until the cheers died down before I finally introduced my partner.

You wanna talk loud? You wanna talk electric? You wanna talk pandemonium? It was all of that when he walked onto the stage. Then, when we finally got them back in their seats, we did a routine together, finishing with a bit of business where I begged Dean to sing.

Dick hit the downbeat, I wandered into the wings, and Dean sang — as well as he could over the screaming. I looked on in wonder from stage left: *My God. It's Sinatra at the Paramount all over again.*

Then I bounced back on stage and Dean and I did our forty-five-minute routine of singing, dancing, leading the band, playing our instruments — trumpet for me, trombone for Dean. Dean played the trombone about as well as I played the trumpet, but no one cared.

After we finished, our latest movie came on — *That's My Boy.* When the first credit came up on the screen, the audience exploded again.

The band platform sat back at the bottom of the great orchestra pit, and the musicians hustled off to grab some breakfast. After all, it was almost 10:40 a.m.! Dean and I hurried back to our dressing room, where we would literally be prisoners until the next show, in precisely two hours.

Prisoners because six stories down, outside the

Paramount's stage door on Forty-fourth Street, was a crowd of at least 20,000 people, waiting to catch a glimpse of us. To clear the theater between shows, the Paramount management had told each audience that Dean and I would be giving out pictures backstage.

It was a little white lie, but it got them all out of the theater. (Had we not done it, they'd have stayed there for six shows.) Up in our dressing room, we'd throw up the sash, sit on the ledge, and bask in the excitement. We would yell jokes, sing (both of us!), play our horns, throw stuff down to the crowd: T-shirts, hats, handkerchiefs. And thousands upon thousands of black-and-white, five-by-seven publicity photos.

The crowds were backed down Forty-fourth Street and around the corner onto Broadway. The mayor himself, the honorable Vincent Impellitteri, came to personally welcome us to New York — and to personally plead with us to cut out the dressing-room shows. His cops couldn't handle the traffic!

And the musicians couldn't get out the door to get breakfast. We had to begin bringing in food for the crew, the band, the acts. Dean and I would have deli sent in from the Stage Delicatessen (naturally, we patronized the restaurant that named a sandwich after us: tongue and ham!).

We had contracted to do six shows a day. But at the conclusion of our sixth show on opening day, Bob Weitman, the shrewd, stingy managing director of the Paramount, came up to our dressing room with a bottle of champagne and some glasses and said, 'Today, you guys smashed every record held at the Paramount! Now, here's my problem — we have 4,000 seats in this house. With the Fire Department's blessing, we can stand 800 in the orchestra and 600 in the balcony. So for all intents and purposes you played to just about 30,000 people today. But we turned away more than 50,000 people! Now, what do I do, pray tell? I have to get a seventh show tomorrow!'

Cross-eyed at the concept of trying to work a seventh show into an already very full day, we left Bob Weitman at the backstage door and shoved our way through to our car. Twenty police officers were on hand to help. When we finally got into the car, our chauffeur said, 'Hey, guys, I can make five hundred bucks if you give me the used blades you shaved with this morning!'

And Dean and I, in unison, said, 'Take us home, please!'

We were staying in our favorite hotel, the Hampshire House, in two adjoining penthouse suites. Around eighteen people in our entourage were staying on the floor just below us, and we rented a huge storage room in the hotel basement for stage props, music cases, and cartons and cartons of those publicity photos.

The next day, after seven shows, it was back to the hotel to try and get some rest. But needing rest and getting it, in those days, were two very different things. We were on such a rush after performing that we had to come down before trying to sleep. So we played, and we played hard! Drinking, women, fun, parties — the whole 'we're rich and famous' bit. One night the managing director of the Hampshire House came up to inquire respectfully if we might consider using their basement ballroom for our after-theater parties so we wouldn't be keeping the other guests awake half the night!

We said we'd be more careful. That night we cut the crowd visiting us in the penthouse down to forty.

At around 4 a.m. we would crash — only to remember that we had a 6:30 a.m. wake-up call so we could get to the Paramount by 8:00 and have a half hour in the dressing room before the first show . . .

And that's how it went for two solid weeks — to the tune of around $150,000. That was just our end. We let the Paramount Theater have the rest, and it was substantial.

★ ★ ★

Back in the fall of 1948, when we first went out to Hollywood, Capitol Records approached us. Their idea was to put our act on disk, meaning that Dean would sing straight, then I would chime in in a few of my 897 different voices. Our first Capitol recording was a novelty number, cha-cha-style, called 'The Money Song,' and the chorus went:

Funny, funny, funny what money can do . . .

And the funny thing about that song was what money was doing to us, and for us, even as we

155

sang it — and what it would continue to do, only much, much more so.

Three years later, September of '51, we were doing five shows a day at the Roxy Theater in New York and two shows a night at Ben Marden's Riviera, in Fort Lee, New Jersey. We were taking vitamin C and B12 shots to try to enlist some energy from our exhausted bodies . . . Believe it or not, we didn't look at a girl for the entire two weeks!

We called those two gigs our Bataan Death March. The first four shows, at the Roxy, were at 10 a.m., noon, 3:45 p.m., and 8 p.m. The eight-o'clock show was a problem. We went on at 8:05 and finished at 9:15 — then jumped into a car with a police escort to drive across the George Washington Bridge to the Riviera.

We'd get there around 9:40, then go on for the dinner show, from 9:50 to 10:50 — then drive back to the Roxy for the 11:20 show!

Then, when we finished *that* show, at 12:40 a.m., we drove back to the Riviera for the 1:15 show, which went until around 2:30 in the morning.

And over again the next day. And the next day . . . For two weeks of fun and hell.

For this ordeal, the Roxy was paying us $100,000 a week, plus a percentage of the receipts — which brought our end up to around a quarter-million dollars. The Riviera was paying us a flat fee of $125,000 a week. So for almost four hundred grand a week, we did the best we could, groaning all the way to the bank.

All the driving back and forth could get a little

hairy. One of the first times we were heading back over the Hudson from the Riviera, we ran out of the club and into the car in our tuxes. Big mistake. For one thing, riding in a limo in a tux just isn't comfortable. For another, it ruins the crease! (Since then, I've made a practice of never sitting in my tux, to protect it for the performance.)

So Dean took off his jacket, then his pants. I did the same. Meanwhile, the driver was peeking into his rearview mirror, not so sure about his customers . . .

Both of us began to giggle. Then laugh out loud. Then we got stuck in bridge traffic. Then Dean had to pee. Then — Jesus, it was catching — so did I!

The driver edged through the lines of cars over to the side of the road — and there, right in front of us, miracle of miracles, was a convenience store. Never has a convenience store been so convenient. We both got out of the car.

In shorts and shirt only.

I was wearing leather boots with my tux, and Dean had on patent-leather loafers: We looked ridiculous! As we walked into the store, there were six or seven customers browsing the aisles. They recognized us right away and wanted autographs. Then someone found a camera. (We politely declined to be photographed.)

Dean went to the john, then so did I. We bought some candy and headed back to the limo — where two of the largest highway patrol officers I've ever seen were waiting for us, glaring. 'You're disturbing the peace!' one of them said.

'Please, Officer, give us a break,' Dean said. 'I'm his lawyer and he's on parole. This could go very badly for him.'

At which point both officers burst into laughter, shook our hands, and asked for autographs.

'Watch Martin and Lewis Sunday night on the *Colgate Comedy Hour!*' we yelled to the cars that had slowed down at the sight of us. '8 p.m., Eastern Standard Time!'

The cops escorted us back onto the highway, and we made our show at the Roxy with tuxes uncreased.

★   ★   ★

One night back in our first year at the Copa — June of '48, to be exact — we'd finished our first show, then rushed from the stage door to yet another waiting limo. We popped in with Louie (our pianist) and Ray (our drummer), and headed off for the Essex House in glorious Newark, New Jersey.

Why Newark? Because a New Jersey boy was about to give his daughter away in marriage to another Jersey boy. Actually, the boy doing the giving away was a nice Italian man named Willie Moretti, and he was quite a character.

Willie, aka Willie Moore, was a longtime friend and associate of Frank Costello's who was probably most well-known for giving Frank Sinatra a big boost back at the very start of his career. In the late 1930s, just as the Sinatra phenomenon was beginning, Frank was under contract to the bandleader Tommy Dorsey at $125 a week. It wasn't a bad salary at the time, but it was chump change compared to what he could make if his fate was in his own hands. Frank wanted to get out of the contract, but Dorsey wouldn't budge. Now, the story goes — I wasn't there, so I can't confirm it — that Mr. Moretti put a gun in Mr. Dorsey's mouth and politely asked him to release Mr. Sinatra from his contract. Which (the legend goes) Dorsey promptly sold to Willie for one dollar.

This was Willie Moretti.

Dean and I had gotten to know Willie and his closest New Jersey associate, Longy Zwillman, at the Riviera nightclub. Like many of the major nightclubs of the day, the Riviera had a private gambling club on the premises: The Riviera's was called the Marine Room, and whatever Willie and Longy's business arrangement was with Ben Marden, Willie and Longy paid very close attention to the Marine Room's operations — as they did to the operations of the Riviera as a whole. And because my partner and I were very big business for the Riviera, Willie and Longy extended us every courtesy, including, most especially, their friendship.

Dean was of two minds about wiseguys. On the one hand, unlike Frank, he never went out of his way to cultivate them. Believe me, Dean could have found any number of such gentlemen who would have been tickled pink to help him with his career early on. But he elected not to, because it was never his way to cozy up to anyone.

On the other hand, my partner always felt that you treated people the way they treated you — no matter what anybody else said about who those people were or what they did. And as I've said, the major Mob figures were, each and every one, all gentlemen to us, so we gave as good as we got.

Longy Zwillman, the longtime boss of New Jersey, was a real gent — quiet, well-dressed, and with beautiful manners. Willie Moretti was a little rougher around the edges, a little louder and funnier. When he appeared on the nationally televised Kefauver hearings on organized crime, he told the esteemed members of the congressional committee next to nothing — but in a very entertaining fashion. He charmed the pants off those congressmen, and when one of them

Somewhere backstage.

thanked Willie at the end of his testimony, Willie invited the whole bunch of them to come visit him at his house on the Jersey shore!

That was Willie Moretti.

He was widely liked in the world of organized crime, but he also had made a powerful enemy of New York boss Vito Genovese, a dark character who didn't have many friends anywhere. Still, we liked Willie, and when he invited Dean and me to his daughter's wedding, we were genuinely touched. Our present to the bride and groom (and the bride's father) was a command performance.

Dean and I were scheduled to appear between our first two shows at the Copa, so Willie knew we had to get on and get out. We arrived as the families were gathering to make their presentations of gifts to the newly married couple. And gift-wise, we're talking very big bucks.

The young couple sat at one of the larger tables in the room, behind a stack of white envelopes, and the line of people with more envelopes extended all the way out into the foyer.

Dean and I made our way to the ballroom. Willie saw us, and had the envelope line shifted into the ballroom so the people would be able to see us. He tapped a water glass and announced, 'We have Martin and Lewis with us for some entertainment.' He wasn't quite Ed McMahon, but we went on, did a few bits, and took our bows to somewhat distracted applause. Willie thanked us, but I knew we hadn't done as well as we could have because — let's face it — we were upstaged by all that money.

But Willie always remembered a favor, and always showed up at our shows at the Copa. And one night three years later, he came backstage, all smiles, and invited us to join him for lunch that coming Thursday at his favorite restaurant, Joe's Elbow Room in Cliffside Park, New Jersey. Sure, we said.

As we walked into our hotel suite very early on Wednesday morning, I suddenly remembered Willie's invitation. We always finished our last Copa show at 4.30 a.m., and I was never able to calm down and fall into bed until around six. As nice a gentleman as Willie Moretti was (to us, anyhow), it made me weary just to think about hauling my behind out to Jersey the next day for lunch. I said, 'Do you think we really need to have lunch with Willie?'

'Sure we do,' Dean said. 'One, you don't offend someone once an invite is made and you've accepted. Two, you don't offend Willie Moretti.' He gave me a look. I got it.

But when I woke up that afternoon, I was dragging. I barely made it through our three shows that night, which is not good if the people are paying to see you bounce off the walls. Sure enough, when I woke up the following morning, I was as sick as a dog, my neck swollen to the dimensions of a medium-size life preserver.

I had the mumps.

The *mumps*, for Christ's sake — that's what children get. 'I'm twenty-fuckin'-five!' I screamed at the doctor who'd just examined me.

Stay in *bed*?!

'We do three shows tonight!' I told him.

'Not tonight,' the doctor said. 'Not this night, and not any night for the next ten days, at least. If you don't respect this illness, it can get away from you and you'll do twenty-one days in bed. You'd better listen to the doctor!'

After he left, I called Dean. 'You've got *what?*' he yelled.

'Are you coming over?'

'Aren't you contagious?'

'No, I'm Jewish!'

Dean laughed, came over. We sat and watched daytime television. In 1951, it was mostly test patterns and cooking shows with Jack Lescoulie. We had a very dull day sitting there, with me depressed and Dean on the phone to Jack Entratter at the Copa, trying to figure out what to do about the next week and a half.

Before long, Dean and Jack got Frank Sinatra to pitch in and work with Dean for a couple of days. Then Joey Bishop agreed to help out. As long as there was another name with Dean, it seemed to soften the blow of Martin without Lewis. But in those days, believe me, neither one of us was prepared to set the world on fire as a single.

After a long afternoon of daytime TV and penny-a-point gin rummy with my partner, I looked at the clock for some reason. Four-twenty-five. All at once, I remembered — our lunch with Willie! Jesus! Dean phoned New Jersey, prepared to give our very legitimate excuse . . . but no one could be reached at Willie's office. This was long before answering

163

machines: There was no way to leave a record of our good intentions. We had officially stood up one of the most powerful wiseguys in the metropolitan area.

The mood in my hotel room got even glummer as we channel-surfed (1951 channel-surfing in New York City: six channels) and stared at the boob tube. Having had our fill of soap operas, we switched to the five-o'clock news — and suddenly a Special Report filled the Philco's twelve-inch screen. There was a flash shot of a man lying in a pool of blood on a white-tile floor, while a deep voice intoned, 'This is mob boss Willie Moretti, killed today in a gangland-style hit while he ate lunch in a restaurant in Cliffside Park, New Jersey . . . '

I looked at Dean. Dean looked at me. Neither of us said a word.

★ ★ ★

'The Money Song' did all right for us, but since it didn't look as though we were going to blaze any trails as a novelty act in the music business, Capitol decided to record Dean alone. Interestingly enough, his first solo disk (this was still in the days of the 78-rpm record, just before the LP format came in) was Frank Loesser's 'Once in Love with Amy,' from *Where's Charley?* — the Broadway hit we'd seen with June Allyson and Gloria De Haven.

From 1948 to 1950, Dean made quite a few records for Capitol, songs like 'Power Your Face with Sunshine (Smile! Smile! Smile!)' and

'Dreamy Old New England Moon' — songs that did not exactly establish him as a solo singer. But then he had a minor hit with a number called 'I'll Always Love You,' from *My Friend Irma Goes West*, followed by another song called 'If,' which Perry Como had recorded earlier and taken to number one.

At the time, it was perfectly fine with Dean to ride Perry Como's coattails: He still felt as lucky as I did to be soaring along on our fabulous comet. It was always a big part of his charm that he refused to take himself seriously as a singer. But the day was swiftly coming when he would have to rethink that position a little bit.

9

Year by year we kept making movies, cranking out two or even three (!) pictures every year. In 1952, we did *Sailor Beware* and *Jumping Jacks*. In 1953 came *The Stooge, Scared Stiff*, and *The Caddy*.

We stuck with the blueprint that I'd finally been able to talk Hal Wallis into on *My Friend Irma*, the formula that was the basis of our act: the Playboy and the Putz. But just as we stuck with that formula, we also *got* stuck with it. We settled into a rut. And if you want to know what kept us from blossoming and finding our highest comic potential onscreen, I can tell you the answer in two words: Hal Wallis.

Ed Simmons, a comedy writer who, along with another young whippersnapper named Norman Lear, wrote *The Colgate Comedy Hour* with Dean and me, once told an interviewer a story about getting hired by Wallis to rewrite *Scared Stiff*. 'We had always liked Dean,' Simmons said, ''cause Dean was very funny, and we felt he wasn't given a chance to do things in pictures . . . So we kept putting in scenes for Dean, and Hal Wallis kept sending them back . . . Finally, he called us up to the office and said, 'Why do you keep sending me this stuff?' And we said, 'Because Dean is funny. And he should be doing this stuff, this is a good scene for him.' And he said, 'Fellows, look. A Martin and Lewis picture

166

costs a half-million, and it's guaranteed to make three million with a simple formula: Jerry's an idiot, Dean is a straight leading man who sings a couple of songs and gets the girl. That's it, don't fuck with it.''

That was Hal Wallis.

As I've said, our producer had had a long and distinguished career in movies — beginning (I kid you not) in 1927 as the publicist for *The Jazz Singer*, the very first talking picture. He'd made all those great dramas — *Casablanca, Sergeant York, I Am a Fugitive from a Chain Gang* — as production chief at Warner's, and, once he'd set up shop as an independent producer at Paramount, had discovered and signed Kirk Douglas, Burt Lancaster, Anna Magnani, and Charlton Heston.

And then Martin and Lewis.

But the thing about Hal Wallis was that while he was great with drama, when it came to comedy, he had a sense of humor like a yeast infection. And I told him so. He said, 'Listen, kid, I've been making films for forty years.'

I said, 'You could've been making them wrong!'

He wasn't crazy about any artist who challenged his concept of a movie, and I challenged him big-time. I never let Wallis alone. I was in his office six times a day questioning the script. Needless to say, he wasn't charmed. His attitude was: Just get Dean and Jerry in front of the cameras and shoot enough footage to make a feature-length movie. 'All the Martin and Lewis movies make money,' he was fond of saying. 'So what's the difference how it turns out?'

Clearly, this wasn't headed in a good direction, especially where Dean was concerned. But Dean played more or less the same game with Wallis that Wallis played with us: He never let the producer know how perceptive he was. I think Wallis thought Dean was a fool . . . playing golf all the time. That's where he made a big mistake.

You see, I was in charge of everything where the act was concerned; Dean played golf. That was our arrangement. That was the way Dean wanted it. He loved golf, pure and simple. He loved that game more than he loved women — and he was very fond of women — and much more than he liked alcohol.

Meanwhile, I was falling in love with every aspect of the movie business. And so I had more and more to do with production. Still, while part of Dean wanted things that way, there was another part of him — aided and abetted by all those people who gathered around him as he grew more successful, the people I called *shit-stirrers* — that began to feel like a second fiddle.

The question might have occurred to you by now: Did *I* go to Wallis and demand more for Dean to do in our pictures? Sometimes I did. What was always front and center in my brain was the team, and the Act: Were Dean and Jerry coming across on the big screen in some close approximation of the way they came across on stage? If Dean was diminished in that equation, we both were diminished.

But — was my ego growing? Was I enthralled, enamored, enraptured by all that I was learning about film? Was I knocked out by the unlimited comic possibilities for the Jerry character onscreen?

Yes, yes, and yes. It all happened silently, the way one week you can see perfectly and the next week you need glasses: I was developing a certain myopia about Dean. And since my partner feared and hated any sort of showdown, he wasn't calling me on it. Yet.

But others were beginning to tell him about it. All his life, Dean was a pretty solitary cat. He never went in for cliques or crowds. But his magnetism was so strong that there were always people around who wanted to get close to him, be on his good side. He was *Dean Martin*, for God's sake! Guys in bars, casinos, golf-course clubhouses — he spent a lot of time in those places — would sidle up to him, tell him how great he was. All by himself.

At the same time, I think Dean was starting to feel that he was ready to stretch as an actor. But in the meantime, he was seeing all those reviews that put him down or just ignored him. He had to listen to *Jerry, Jerry, Jerry,* all the time.

And the shit-stirrers kept stirring . . .

★   ★   ★

We didn't disagree about much for the first half of our decade together, with one exception: his singing. I loved it and thought he could do more with it; he would never take it seriously. Once I

169

asked him, point-blank: 'Just once, would you sing a song straight?'

He gave me a funny look. 'I do,' he said.

'No you don't,' I told him.

When I pressed the issue, things got pretty sticky between us. I'd been thinking, *Hey, maybe he could have a fourth song; it would be great for him.* We were on for two hours. What's the big deal? Another three minutes? It was okay with me.

So I said, 'You know something? You're doing so good in your spot, maybe I'm coming on too early.' He said, 'Fuck you! Whattaya talkin' about? You're gonna spoil what we got. Forget it.'

His mind was made up, but when we played the Fox Theater in San Francisco in 1951, the reviewer in the *Chronicle* wrote a big rave about the show — without mentioning Dean once. That hurt. I saw it in his eyes. And — for both our sakes — I found myself giving him a pep talk.

'You know something?' I said. 'They're always going to like the kid who makes the biggest noise. They're always going to pay attention to the fuckin' monkey. You're going to hear more about him than the straight man. Nobody ever talked about George Burns. It was always Gracie. When Jack Benny and Mary Livingston worked in vaudeville, they didn't know who Jack Benny was.'

I said, 'You have to know that the straight man is never given the kudos that the comic gets. And I just need to know you're okay with that.'

This was really opening a sore. Dean said,

170

'Jerry, look. Your father told you once, Be a hit. With the monkey act, with a couple of broads, with two balls and a watermelon. Whatever — just be a hit. We're a big hit. And you need to know that *I* know when our film is on that screen and I start to sing, the kids go for the popcorn.'

'I don't think that's true,' I argued. 'I don't think little kids go for popcorn at any particular time.'

But in my heart, I knew he was right. Kids go to the movies to laugh and see action, and singing and love scenes slow things down.

What I *should* have said was that the people also went for popcorn during Crosby's songs. And Perry Como's. And every other singer who went into film, including Frank. The songs and the kissing scenes — that was the time for popcorn.

But Bing Crosby was Dean's first idol, and he often felt he was walking in Crosby's shadow. There were too many kids in Steubenville — and too many reviewers later on — who said, 'You're imitating Crosby.' Dean carried that around with him. I'd tell him, 'Crosby has a voice, but he's got no fuckin' heart, you putz. You got heart.'

He also had a thing about Frank. Dean always felt like the guy who had subbed for Sinatra at the Riobamba. Sinatra was so great, why even try to take him on? Even though what Dean did and what Frank did was apples and oranges.

Every once in a while, Dean would make some joke about how he'd had to sing on the radio for free. During the war and just after, several of the stations in the New York area had what they

171

called 'sustaining' — nonsponsored — programs. When there was no sponsor, there was no pay for the talent: It was strictly a showcase.

'It may interest you to know,' I said, 'that Sinatra was on Hoboken radio sustaining.'

'Horseshit,' Dean said.

I said, 'Really?' I went to the phone and called Frank. He confirmed that he'd sung on Hoboken radio for free. He said it was only for three days, but he had! I said, 'Paul, they couldn't afford to pay you. We were coming out of a depression and a war. They were broke.'

After he had a couple of small hits on Capitol in the early fifties, I decided to take matters into my own hands. Was I being overcontrolling? Maybe. But I needed to protect our act. In 1952, we were in preproduction on our new picture, *The Caddy*, and we needed some songs for Dean. So I went to the great Harry Warren, the Oscar-winning writer of such songs as 'Forty-Second Street,' 'You Must Have Been a Beautiful Baby,' and 'Chattanooga Choo-Choo,' and his lyricist Jack Brooks, and paid them $30,000 out of my own pocket. I didn't want Dean to know I hired them, and I never told him. But I knew that Harry Warren could write hits, and I said to Harry, 'I want a hit for Dean.'

And he wrote one. Boy, did he write one.

★   ★   ★

Cut to the following fall, about a month after the release of *The Caddy*. Dean phoned me from his dressing room on the Paramount lot: 'What are you doing?' he said.

'Darning a sock,' I told him. I waited for the laugh, then remembered I had used the line before. 'Why, what's up?'

'Wanna take a ride?' he asked.

Six-year-old voice: 'Ooh, goody, I love rides.' Grown-up voice: 'Where we going?'

'It's a surprise. See you outside.'

We always kept our cars parked right behind the dressing-room area, poised for action. When I opened the door, Dean was sitting at the wheel of his blue Cadillac convertible with the top down, a grin on his deeply tanned face. I think he loved that car more than any he ever had, and he had a few.

I got in and he started her up. We pulled through the studio gates, drove down Melrose, took a right up Vine, and turned left onto Sunset. Quite a few heads turned as we passed by. It was a warm, hazy, Indian-summer day in L.A., and we were at the height of our fame, riding down Sunset Boulevard in an open Cadillac! An open *blue* Cadillac. I was very aware of the impression we made, and I loved every second.

And so did Dean. As I glanced over at my partner, I could feel his total satisfaction. He was at peace with the world: smoking his Camel, driving his great car, his partner at his side. He never said it, but his eyes reflected a happy man.

As we pulled up in front of Music City, Dean stopped the car and pointed to the huge store window, where a double-life-size photo of himself stood, next to a sign announcing his new

173

single, 'That's Amore.'

'Hey,' he said. 'Is that one handsome Italian, or what?'

Neither of us had any idea that day what a monster hit 'That's Amore' would become (it would sell two million platters as a single, and be nominated for an Academy Award) and what kind of effect the song would have on both our lives. It was a number Dean tired of singing after a couple of years, but for the time being, it gave him an identity with the public that he had never had before.

★ ★ ★

In *The Caddy*, Dean played an up-and-coming golfer who leaves the game to become a

She wouldn't leave me alone.

professional comedian. In real life, I don't think he'd have minded doing it the other way around.

As a struggling young singer in the forties, Dean couldn't afford to play very much. But once we hit it big, Dean proceeded to spend every free minute he had on the links — he would have played at night if he could.

With his natural grace and athletic ability, he overcame his late start and got better and better, finally whittling his handicap down to a six. Not bad for a kid from Steubenville, where all the hitting you did was at each other! Once we moved out to the Coast in 1949, he figured he'd found golfing heaven. The second house he and Jeannie bought was right next to the Los Angeles Country Club.

Dean loved golf because it was made for his chemistry: quiet, soft breezes, green grass, no people gawking at him, and a bar at the nineteenth hole. But mainly quiet. The few words you might exchange with your partners as you strolled down the fairway were plenty for him. And he chose his partners carefully. Or so he thought.

When Dean joined the California Country Club, his golfing skills made him the envy of much of the membership. But those same skills also made him a target. The advice his parents had given him about keeping to himself had insulated him from potential friends and annoyances alike. Still, there were times that even he let his guard down. In short order, he fell in with a group of hustlers headed by a character named Bagsy Kerrigan. These were guys who claimed to have a certain handicap, nine or twelve or sixteen, but who in reality could play lightsout, par or subpar golf whenever they wanted.

Dean was flush with our new success. And so as a born gambler, and as a guy who was pretty confident about his skills around a golf course, my partner just had to get some action going. Bagsy and his pals were glad to oblige.

At first they'd just bet a couple of hundred a round, but then the stakes got heavy: four or five grand every game. You do that ten days in a row, and they've got you for $50,000. On the eleventh day, they'd pick you up at your house just to be courteous!

I'm told that Dean played terrific golf with these guys but just missed pay dirt. Bagsy and his pals were so good that if Dean shot a 74, they could throw a 72 (handicap factored in) at him. When he shot a 78, they got a 76. They did whatever was needed, nothing more. And oh, of course — now and then, just to break the monotony (and avoid suspicion), they'd let Dean win. Didn't that make him feel fine!

By the time the year was over, my partner had lost over $300,000 to Bagsy and company. And talk about it was beginning to circulate around Hollywood.

For a long time, Dean never understood what hit him. He was loving the golf, and he was winning now and then. When you're freewheeling and have bucks in your kick, you rarely take inventory . . . After all, he was in the game, and *taking part* was all he really wanted at the time.

Let me be clear about one thing: Dean was not a fool. He was very smart, as long as you were straight. In this one instance, he acted naively because he believed that the handicaps posted in the clubhouse were earned honestly. These guys he was playing with weren't cheating obviously. They weren't moving the ball; they weren't changing the numbers on the scorecard. They were coming to Dean under false pretenses, and — maybe because he spent so much of his life avoiding close relationships — that was one area where my partner was always vulnerable.

★　★　★

Bagsy and his pals built themselves a couple of upscale homes, complete with swimming pools, on the money they won from Dean over the next couple of years. And Hollywood was a tightly knit community. When these guys boasted, 'I'm living in Dean's other house,' or 'Let's take a dip in Dean's pool,' word got around. In fact, after our first four years in Hollywood, rumor was that Dean had lost two or three million in all. A lot of money anytime, but especially in those days, when two or three million was what one of our movies might gross domestically.

Maybe Dean didn't hear the gossip. Maybe he didn't want to. In time he would learn that he'd been had, and he dumped Bagsy and his crowd, leaving that country club for others where such shenanigans didn't take place. But he took the rip-off in stride. He never sought revenge. He just found other partners who pushed him to excellence without taking advantage of him. Ultimately, you play golf against yourself, and money wasn't what it was about for Dean. He just wanted to play the best he could.

Golf remained Dean's great refuge. But no matter how far he ran from people, they continued to surround him. And that was how he — and there's no getting around it, we — got into trouble.

* * *

My partner's self-esteem was a funny business. With looks, talent, and a sense of humor like his, Dean Martin should have been the soul of confidence — but if you knew him well, you could never tell when you might strike a nerve. The problem was, he was so good at covering up his vulnerabilities, you might never realize he was hurt. But I was so good at reading Dean that I almost always did.

Which is not to say that I didn't commit my share of stupidities.

Dean was very proud of his golfing skills, and deservedly so. He took a natural gift and, instead of coasting, the way you might have expected a guy with his laid-back reputation to do, he worked very hard on his game. He might have been a one-take guy when it came to movies, radio, and TV — 'You only have to tell me once' was his favorite saying to directors — but he thought nothing of practicing his putting and driving for hours at a time.

178

The results showed. He had a beautiful swing, and a real sense of command on a golf course. He would joke while he played (he always joked), but he still took the game very seriously. And he got better and better at it over time.

Early on, though, I stepped over the line. Feeling that it might bring us closer to play golf together, I secretly took up the game — and, to my delight, found I had some innate skill. My plan was to surprise Dean: 'Isn't this great?' I would tell him. 'Now we can play together wherever we go!'

And so the day I went to Palm Springs (where Dean was taking some R&R time between films) to join him for lunch, he thought it was just lunch. He had already played nine holes when we met at the club-house. After we ate, Dean said, 'You want to ride around with me for the back nine?'

'I'd love it!' I said. 'Wait here!'

I ran from the clubhouse to my car, popped the trunk, and took out my shiny new golf shoes and my expensive new clubs. Slipped on the shoes, shouldered the bag, and ran back to Dean, who was putting on the practice green. He looked me over and just said, 'I thought it would only be a matter of time before you found out how great this is!'

We both jumped into his cart and rode to the first tee. I was breathless with excitement — couldn't wait to show off for my big brother. We hopped out, and Dean said with a big smile, 'You first, pally.'

I teed the ball up with a silent prayer: *Please*

let me be good for him . . . . Took my driver back — and blasted it straight down the fairway, 200 yards.

Dean blinked. 'When did you learn this?' he asked. 'I thought you were always in the office or the editing room!'

I admitted I'd taken lessons so we could be together more. His look told me: Wrong! But he covered it well, and we went on playing.

After we'd finished the thirteenth hole, Dean was one under and I was two over. *Not bad for a beginner!* I thought. I glanced at my partner's face as he filled out the scorecard. Nothing. Throughout the first four holes (back nine, remember), I'd been looking for some acknowledgment of how well I was doing.

Nothing.

Then Dean said, with a strange smile, 'Why don't we make it interesting and bet the last five holes?' he said. 'Five hundred bucks, winner takes all?'

'Sure!' I said. Naturally, I would have paid the five hundred just for the privilege of playing alongside him . . . But then I birdied the fourteenth, and Dean bogeyed it. All at once it was a shooting match: He was at even par, I was one over.

Dean made par on the fifteenth, and — to my great surprise — I birdied again. Now he's even and I'm even. We both parred the sixteenth, and I scanned his face. No reaction.

A bogey for both of us on seventeen. All tied up.

Then I hit the biggest drive of my life, so did

Dean, and now we're looking at a pretty fancy run for the roses. As I took out a nine-iron for my third shot, he put up a hand. He had a mischievous smile on his face. 'Hold on, Ben Hogan,' he said.

'Of course,' I said.

'Side bet of two hundred you don't par the hole,' he said.

'What about if I birdie?' I asked, all innocence.

He shook his head at my nerve. 'Hey, hotshot, you birdie and I'll pay you a grand!'

I didn't birdie. (Thank God.) I parred the last hole, as did Dean, making us all even — except that he had lost the side bet. He took the bills out of his hip pocket, counted them, and handed them over. He was smiling, but his eyes were cold. 'Boy, talk about beginner's luck,' he said.

I put my hand up. 'That's okay,' I told him. 'I don't want the money.' I was beginning to feel uncomfortable.

'Oh, no,' Dean said. 'A bet's a bet.' And he stuck the bills in my pocket.

I knew in my heart I had made a great mistake. Not simply by winning the money, but just learning how to play.

When I phoned my dad and told him what had happened, you could have heard his scream across the room. 'You fool!' he shouted. 'You young, stupid fool! Why did you do that?'

'I just wanted to spend time together playing his favorite game,' I said sheepishly.

'All they ever write about is the skinny kid,' Dad said. 'Jerry this and Jerry that — he's the funny one, he's the smart one. Don't you see that all Dean ever had to himself was golf — and now you're trying to take that, too?'

My dad was smart. Dean and I never played together again, except for a cancer benefit we did for Bing Crosby. But that was it. I never again talked to my partner about my golf, only his.

10

A number of entertainers stayed out of World War II with questionable physical or psychological conditions, but both Dean and I were genuine 4-Fs. My problem was a heart murmur, a congenital defect; Dean's was a double hernia. Nothing by halves for my partner!

Seriously, though, it had not been fun to be classified 4-F. I had badly wanted to join up, and was devastated to be turned away. (Dean, never a joiner and no fan of uniforms, might not have been as crushed as I was.) But in the mid- and late forties, both Dean and I faced audiences who accused us of draft-dodging — doubtless the same kind of people who had thrown tomatoes at the front of the Paramount Theater when Frank Sinatra, another legitimate 4-F, played there in 1944.

Although the strong emotions stirred up by the war died down by the early fifties, Dean's hernia had gotten worse. Jack Entratter of the Copa recommended a doctor, and the doctor told Dean he would have to operate. The procedure, at the Harlem Hospital Center on 137th Street in Manhattan, went well. So well that two days afterward, my partner was complaining of hunger pains.

'Is this an endurance contest? When can I have some *real* food?' Dean said when I visited him.

'I'll go to Lindy's and get you some nice

chicken soup,' I told him. 'That'll be good for you.' And without giving him a chance to say anything, I dashed out of his room and ran down the stairs. (Hospital elevators always have old men gasping for air in them.)

I hailed a cab and told the driver, 'Take me to Lindy's at Fifty-first Street and Broadway, and step on it!' We were just crossing 121st Street when a roar of thunder and a flash of lightning almost stopped my watch. The rain looked like something out of one of those old Saturday-afternoon King Brothers B movies where the dam breaks.

The traffic moved agonizingly slowly: A half hour later, we were only at Eighty-fourth Street, and it was another half hour before we got to the restaurant. I ran in and ordered hot chicken soup, with lots of noodles, to go. It was only when I stepped outside that I realized I should have kept the cab and let the meter run, because when it rains in New York, every taxi in the city is taken.

I started to walk. From Fifty-first and Broadway I was going to walk to the hospital at 137th and Lenox, assuring myself that I would be able to hail a cab along the way, or at least find one letting someone off. Not in this lifetime!

I am now at Seventy-eighth Street, with only fifty-nine blocks to go, and it feels as if I've been walking for days. I am so wet, my skin is wrinkled. Cabs are still zooming by, keeping their passengers comfy and cozy. All I see are silhouettes of happy people, dry and comfortable, while I am trying to keep my Jewish Boston Marathon going.

The next time I glance up at a street sign, I see Broadway and 112th Street. Christ, only another twenty-five blocks to go! Half the sole of my shoe has come unglued, and the faster I walk, the louder the flapping. I stop . . . it stops. I start, it starts. What am I doing? Just playing, but I really did feel Dean had no one but me, and I couldn't let him down . . .

It was four hours later when I returned to Dean's room. He was watching television, smoking a Lucky, and totally relaxed! I scraped off the remnants of the soggy paper bag and proudly showed him the big jar of *cold* soup.

'No matzo balls?' was all he said.

★   ★   ★

I remembered the chicken-soup fiasco a couple of years later, when I tried to come up with an original present for Dean's thirty-fifth birthday — Saturday, June 7, 1952. A big landmark, it seemed to me, but also a big challenge: What do you get for someone who has everything?

The answer to this particular riddle flashed into my aspiring director's brain like a comic setup from one of our movies. It involved spectacle, excess, absurdity — my favorite elements! — along with a warm personal nod to my partner's greatest passion.

I saw, in my mind's eye, hundreds of bags of golf clubs.

Great. Now, how to make my vision real?

I drove out to the Riviera Country Club in Brentwood and told the pro at the driving range about Dean's big birthday and my big idea. His face lit up as I talked: One of the major perks of fame is that not only does everybody know you, but they all want to do things for you, too. And as it turned out, the driving-range pro at the Riviera Country Club had more than 150 bags of clubs to rent. Now, we're not talking fancy equipment here — this stuff was the equivalent of bowling-alley or bike-shop rentals. But the point was the big picture, not the details.

I next went to the transportation department at Paramount and talked with the head man, a nice guy who loved Dean. I told him of my plan — and another face lit up. He arranged for a studio truck and five guys to go the Riviera Country Club, pick up a hundred bags of golf clubs, and deliver them to Dean's house right smack in the middle of his birthday party!

Patti and I were to arrive promptly at 7 p.m., so I told the transportation head to have his truck and handlers arrive at 9:45 — just about (I calculated) when Dean would be opening his presents.

The party was great, and Dean was his most outgoing. In later years, I've heard, he would often leave a dinner party at his house and go to the den to watch a Western on TV. Sometimes he'd call the cops to complain about the noise at his house! This wasn't one of those nights. He was excited, alive, funny — delighted to be the center of attention. He was always incredible when he performed off the top of his head, and everyone there, including the guest of honor, was half bombed, to boot. Christ, did we laugh . . .

Dean started to unwrap his gifts. Typical for him would be to open a box, throw the contents in the garbage, and thank the giver for the lovely wrapping paper. You had to be there to get it, but nobody could bring off a joke the way Dean could. His performance was effortless, pure grace and charm — not to mention that he was acting a wee bit drunker than he actually was.

Just as he was getting to the bottom of the pile, the doorbell rang. Jeannie (whom I'd let in on the gag) went to answer it. She swung the door open wide, allowing five men to enter the living room, each of them packing about four golf bags apiece.

'This is just for openers,' one of them announced.

They went back and forth from the driveway to the living room, setting bag upon bag upon bag against the wall for nearly thirty minutes. Dean's eyes were bugging out of his head. He had absolutely no idea where all this was coming from, and, just as he was about to collapse with laughter, one of the guys took out a card and read: 'To Dean, my partner and best friend. Here's to never having to be without these. Love, Jerry.'

We hugged. The crowd cheered. And the five guys proceeded to take all the bags of clubs back outside, which took another half hour — while Dean kept asking, 'How'd you *do* that? Where'd they *come* from?'

I just smiled.

★　★　★

What brought these two stories to mind? It just occurred to me, as I sat here writing, that never once in our ten years together did Dean give me a present. Not once, amid the scores of gifts I gave him — the gold-link watch, from Billy Ruser's jewelry store on Rodeo Drive in Beverly Hills, that he always treasured (check out our old *Colgate Comedy Hours*, and you'll find a sketch where water was spurting from a pipe in a wall and Dean was trying, in all seriousness, to protect that watch); the cigarette lighters; the golf clubs; the gorgeous diamond studs for his tux, with diamond cuff links to match; the solid-gold flask, et cetera.

Why was that?

I don't think it was because he thought, *He doesn't deserve it*. I think it was because he was taught that you didn't do that. Men did not give other men presents, period.

I have been charged, now and then, with being a tad lavish in my gift-giving. Cross, Tiffany, Cartier, and Dunhill have done very well by me over the years — as has almost everybody who ever worked with me in television and the movies. But I also recognize that there is a certain selfishness to my gifts.

Here's how it works: I get pleasure from giving to those I love. That's *my* pleasure. But I'm perceptive enough to realize that there are those who have felt oppressed by my generosity. It's not always easy to *get* when you can't give back to the same degree. Once, after I'd given television sets to two of our *Colgate Comedy Hour* writers, Ed Simmons and Norman Lear, they retaliated by presenting me with a gift-wrapped old man — an actual living person whom they'd imprisoned inside a giant box for six hours. The card read, 'For the Man Who Has Everything.'

Dean always used to take me to task for what he called *flag-waving*. In his book, that could mean any number of things. It could mean giving money to the needy. We would walk down the street together, and I literally couldn't pass a man with his hat out. If there was one on every block, I'd hit each and every one. If we walked back the same way and the same guy was still there, I'd hit him again. Dean would say, 'That fucker can get a job! What the fuck are you givin' him money for?'

At the same time, I think he was happy to see me do what he couldn't, even when he wanted to.

Flag-waving was tipping your mitt emotionally, showing your colors. It was loving parades, thinking Sophie Tucker was great, Al Jolson was a genius.

It was, of course, the exact opposite of everything Dean Martin had been taught to feel and — God knows — to show.

Putting it mildly, I knew I could sometimes be a bit much for him. I'd always worn my emotions on my sleeve, but as our career skyrocketed, the sleeve became a size extra large. I was constantly *rewarded* for showing my emotions. Everybody in the country — the critics included — jumped up and down for me. Did I feel bad that Dean was overshadowed?

Sure I did. But did I also feel excited at what was happening? You bet your ass I did.

And so the more I got, the more I tried to give to Dean. But I recognize — now, fifty years later — that being at the receiving end of outrageous generosity isn't the easiest thing in the world.

★ ★ ★

To make matters worse, Dean had claustrophobia. Literally. I mean, he wouldn't ride in elevators if he could possibly avoid it. (He especially hated the backstage elevator at the Paramount, which was the size of a coffin and unreliable, to boot. Whenever we played there, he would walk the six flights from the stage to the dressing room, then back down, seven times a day — a round-trip for each of our shows! And the last time he lived in New York City, in 1948, he and Betty rented a lovely third-floor apartment on Riverside Drive and 106th Street. Dean would walk up the stairs.) We always had to get him two seats on planes, so he wouldn't feel boxed in by another passenger. There were times when our dressing rooms were tight and he would dress at the hotel, then wait in the lobby of the club till showtime. It didn't happen a lot, but enough for me to remember. I also recall that back at the beginning, when we'd dance with our wives in a club or a hotel ballroom, if the dance floor got even a little crowded, he was gone — sometimes leaving his wife stranded on the floor alone.

Dean's worst moments were in the summer of

1951, when he learned we were going to have to work in a submarine.

We were just beginning preproduction on *Sailor Beware* for Hal Wallis. Preproduction involves a lot of things, but for the two of us it mainly meant reading the script and finding out what we'd be doing in the film! We knew there had been rumblings around the studio for months about Wallis's plan to do a Martin and Lewis film in the Navy. When we heard the talk, we didn't much care. We had a contract, and we would do the work we were told to do. (Does it sound joyless? It wasn't always. But Hal Wallis did a lot to make it feel that way.)

Then we found out that *Sailor Beware* wasn't just about the Navy — it was about the Silent Service, submarines.

Holy Christ!

I spoke with Wallis about Dean's phobia, and he assured me that we would be working in mock-ups. No fourth wall, plenty of space when it was needed. I explained to Dean that he wouldn't have to be in a real live submarine, and he was relieved — until we got to the location, the Naval Training Station at San Diego, aka the West Coast Main Facility of Submarine Warfare and Strategic Information of the United States Navy. Very, very impressive. And, to my partner, very unnerving.

After we checked into the Grant Hotel in San Diego, we were summoned by our assistant director to meet at the dock at San Diego Naval Pier and to board the U.S.S. *Bashaw*, a war submarine that would take us for a trial run from the pier to the outer ocean beyond Point Loma. Dean was fine until the sub's commander, Captain Bob Froude, told us, in the kindest possible way, that no one could stand topside during a sub's movement, particularly in the bay area.

So we boarded the submarine, and were invited to the captain's wardroom, some thirty feet below deck. That's when I saw Dean waver. He didn't just waver. He bent, looking like a Slinky trying to find a place to hide. But down the conning-tower stairs we went — Dean, me, the captain, our assistant director, and some of the cast.

The padded walls of the wardroom were covered with plaques and photographs of the *Bashaw* in action — diving, trimming, sitting in port, under way. I stared, fascinated, until I noticed Dean getting really uncomfortable.

I asked the captain if we could talk. We walked to one side of the room, and as Dean stood with a bunch of fellow cast members, pretending to have a good time, I explained the problem to Captain Froude.

The captain nodded, understanding, then asked Dean and me to accompany him back to the conning tower and up the steps to the deck. Once we were up top, Captain Froude explained to us that since the sub would not be diving we could stay on deck the whole time. My partner looked at me with real gratitude.

★　★　★

The funny thing is, Frank was claustrophobic, too. Except that Frank never had to work with a partner.

★　★　★

Meaning what? That I crowded Dean? Smothered him with attention and affection? I suppose I did sometimes. Did I suck all the air out of the room? Sure, sometimes. I never claimed to be a shrinking violet.

Did Dean ever do anything for me?

The answer to that is a most definite yes. He might not have been a gift-giver, but for ten years he gave me the huge gift of his presence. And there were other important perks, as well.

For one thing, he protected me.

After all, that's what a big brother does, right? Maybe part of our problem, as I got older and stronger and surer of myself, was that I needed his protection less. But early on I needed it plenty.

The first time we played the Flamingo, in Vegas, was in 1947, just six months or so into our act. Bugsy Siegel, who'd taken on the ownership of the Flamingo from its original founder, Billy Wilkerson, and made the casino his personal obsession, was still alive (but not for long: He would be rubbed out that June). I had the chance to meet the handsome gangster himself when I got myself into a little bit of a jam — $158,000 worth — as a newcomer to the craps and blackjack tables. As I said, I talked my way out of that problem, but there was another

193

problem at the Flamingo that I talked my way into.

There was a convention of Tall Cedars of Lebanon members staying at the hotel, and they were all easily identifiable by their unique headgear: A green, pyramid-shaped fez with a long tassel, it looked like nothing so much as a dunce cap.

One night at our dinner show, I spotted that hat on one of the guests. Being as nuts as I was at that age (twenty years and change), I saw him as the defining moment of our act. 'If ever a man needed a hat job,' I said. 'Come on. Don't feel bad, I'll get you a number for Stetson.'

Everyone laughed but him.

We finished our show, changed our clothes, and went out front to hear that we'd done a good job. We strolled over to the bar and sat down. Dean ordered for both of us: very dry martinis. He loved olives, and I loved onions. As I ate them, he'd say, 'It's a good thing they're pickled, or you'd be alone on stage later.'

As we sipped our drinks, I felt the presence of someone standing very close to my back. Then a hand grabbed my jacket and slowly turned me around. (I was lucky that the stool swiveled.) There he was, old Dunce-head himself. 'If I don't get an apology, I might knock you into next week.'

Dean rose and, without saying a word, took the man's hand off my jacket, put one big hand between the man's legs and the other hand around his neck, picked him up as though he weighed nothing (he was at least 190 pounds), and hurled him into a shelf of glasses behind the bar.

The noise of shattering glass shook up the casino and management. One of the Flamingo's owners, Gus Greenbaum, strolled over to us and saw the Tall Cedars of Lebanon man plucking pieces of glass from the seat of his pants. (Gus was a Mob torpedo out of Chicago, but he was always a lovely man to me, and we would remain friends until his untimely demise in the late fifties, when he and his wife were both hit for an infraction I never understood.) Gus was calm, but serious. 'Look,' he told us. 'You guys need to go to your suite and let me deal with this.'

And deal with it he did. A little while later, the phone in our dressing room rang. It was Gus Greenbaum. 'Tell Dean that his punching bag got an urgent call and had to leave town tonight,' he said. I started to thank him, but he interrupted me: 'Case closed!'

A little while later, Dean gently reminded me: 'Look, Jer, before you shpritz someone ringside, just keep in mind who gets those ringside tables!'

'How am I supposed to know if it's a wiseguy?' I asked him.

'Oh, you'll develop a sixth sense about these things,' he assured me.

And I did. Dean's advice was sound, and I mostly remembered it.

★　★　★

There were times Dean protected me from others, but there were more times he had to protect me from myself. In 1952, Purdue University decided it wanted us to entertain at its homecoming festivities. Now, Purdue happened to be somewhere in northern Indiana, but since we happened to have just finished an engagement at the Copa and were on our way home to L.A., we agreed.

But — West Lafayette, Indiana? Deep in the cornfields of the Hoosier State? We asked for a very large sum of money (I mean *very* large) for the one evening, thinking we could get out of it that way. But Purdue promptly agreed. We were stuck, but good.

The whole crowd of us — Dean and I, Dick Stabile and our entire twenty-six-man band, our security guys, and our press agent Jack Keller — all flew to Chicago, then got on a bus and into a couple of limos for the three-hour drive south to West Lafayette.

One thing the planners hadn't counted on, though, was that the light snow that was falling as our convoy pulled out of O'Hare Airport would turn into a full-fledged blizzard. It looked like a grip on a sound stage had been cued to let the white stuff come full force!

The longer we drove, the darker it got and the more heavily it snowed. This was before the Interstate Highway System; we were slogging along on two-lane blacktop, making very slow headway into deepest Indiana. After five hours, it became apparent that we weren't going to reach the nice hotel in West Lafayette anytime soon.

Dean and I were in the head limo, along with Dick, Keller, our pianist, Louie, and our drummer, Ray Toland. The six of us started peering into the darkness for someplace to stay — six guys in a limo in the dark ain't the tunnel of love, folks! Tempers were beginning to rise when Dick, who was in the front seat alongside the driver and Louie, lit a cigarette. Which wasn't unusual in itself (we all smoked) — but after the match blew out, the four of us in the back (two in jump seats) began to smell an odd aroma.

Dean smiled. I wasn't sure what was going on until I heard Ray tell Dick, 'Gimme a hit!' Now I knew . . . Dick passed the reefer back, and Ray sucked in the smoke like it was his last day on earth. Then he passed it to Keller, who inhaled, and passed it to Dean — who puffed on it like a pro, then passed it back up to Dick.

'Hey!' I called. 'What is this shit? I'm twenty-five, going on twenty-six years old, for Christ's sake! Give me that thing!'

'Okay, kid, go slow,' Dick said, handing me the joint.

I inhaled deeply, as I would with one of my cigarettes — and Dean yelled, 'Let the coughing begin!' And did it begin. I must've coughed for five solid minutes.

Then I asked to do it again.

'Here's a new one, guys,' Dick said, and Dean handed it to me. We went around again, and pretty soon I was feeling exactly like Errol Flynn. How easy it would be, I thought, to step outside and leap over the limo . . .

After a while, none of us cared about the gig, the storm, or the hotel. We just kept riding into the night, as the windshield wipers slapped at the heavy flakes. Soon a chorus of snores echoed from the back seat. Dick was still awake up front, and I asked, 'What was that I smoked?'

'It's called Emerald Feet,' Dick told me. 'Comes from an island in the Indian Ocean. Very expensive — about a buck-fifty a joint.'

'Can we get more?' I asked.

Around two in the morning — eleven hours after landing at O'Hare — we rolled into West Lafayette. The night clerk at the hotel gaped at the sight of Martin and Lewis and a dozen other guys stomping in out of the snowstorm.

'I saw you guys on Ed Sullivan!' the clerk told Dean and me. 'You were great!'

As we thanked him, Keller made a remark too obscene to repeat — believe me — about Sullivan and a nice lady singer of the 1930s named Ruth Etting. We all screamed like chimps at a banana festival, and the night clerk stared some more.

But I was the one who couldn't stop laughing. Dean explained to me, in between my giggles, that a new pot smoker is very vulnerable and can stay high for days. I remember now that he had a worried look as he said it — he was thinking about our show — but at the time, I couldn't have cared less about any of it. As Dean and the security guys helped me up to our suite, I was singing my head off through the halls of the sleeping hotel. The guys tried desperately to quiet me, but to no avail. I was still singing as they bundled me into bed.

Finally, the house detective came up to ask

what was going on. I jumped out of bed and proceeded to tell him all about smoking pot, informing him that I would be all better in a couple of days. Eventually, Dean got me settled again.

The next morning, he came into my room to see if I was all right. Oddly enough, I felt perfectly fine, but I still had the sillies — I couldn't stop laughing.

Dick walked in. 'For God's sake,' Dean said. 'Is there anything we can give him to settle him down?'

'Hair of the dog,' Dick said.

'What?' Dean said.

Dick assured him that he had done it before — that it balanced the high. He took a joint out of his pocket, lit it, and handed it to me. 'Okay, Jer,' he said. 'Nice and easy. Just one or two small puffs, and you'll feel like a new man.'

Well, I took the puffs, and I was anything but a new man. In fact, I was right back to being Errol Flynn. I couldn't wait (I told Dean and Dick) to get to the rehearsal and let the band know I had tried pot!

Dean looked aghast. 'You can't say that to anyone,' he told me. 'It's against the law.' His expression turned to concern. 'Jer, are you going to be all right? I don't want to let you go on stage and humiliate yourself.'

I bit my lip. 'I'll be okay,' I assured him.

He watched me like a hawk during the rehearsal. Now I had totally lost my bubble — I was dopey and tired, not even sure I could do the show. And we were five hours from curtain.

'Take a walk with me, Jer,' Dean said.

Dean never walked if he could help it (before golf carts, he played gin), so I knew this was serious. We headed out across the campus. The bright sun reflecting off the snow was killing my bloodshot eyes, but the fresh, cold air began to revive me a little. As we walked, Dean explained what pot does to the body, and some of the differences between reefer and alcohol. Even high, I couldn't help but marvel at his big-brotherly wisdom, and at my good luck in being the recipient of it.

Then he looked me right in the eye. 'Look, Jer,' he said. 'If you don't feel like you can make it tonight, I'll cancel the whole gig.'

'Not on your life!' I said. The auditorium's 3,000 seats had sold out, and now that we were just across from the theater, I could see hundreds of people waiting for standing-room tickets. 'I'll be fine, Paul,' I told him.

Dean walked me around for quite a while, through the local park and then finally backstage to our dressing rooms. The orchestra played 'Blue Nocturne,' then Dick introduced me. As I came out, the crew, the staff, the electricians, the soundmen, prop men, curtain pullers, dressers, and makeup people watched anxiously. They all knew about my pot party of the evening before.

I did the normal welcoming remarks, then went into a pretty funny gag about Dean and me being in college again . . . Again? Not hardly! I segued into a bit about 'I will never go into politics because I do comedy already!' The audience laughed long and hard, while I went on to blast the U.S. government for taxing us so heavily, saying that if they weren't careful, everybody would wind up on food stamps and they'd wind up having to support us anyway.

This somehow transitioned into a rant about sex and youth versus sex and the elderly. I was aware the audience had quieted down, aside from some nervous coughing. I felt a little like I was working to an audience of Arabs and they knew what I was.

And then, thank God, my partner stuck his head out from stage right and yelled, 'If you don't hurry, I'll be too old to sing!' The relieved audience ate it up, and it certainly cued me. I introduced Dean, who came and did his three songs to huge applause.

We actually did one of our better shows that night, but we went slow, Dean establishing the tempo so I wouldn't run on — especially at the mouth!

When we got back to the hotel, Dean ordered me to take a nap, and I almost instantly fell into a sound sleep — and (of course) dreamed I was awake.

From then on, I swore to myself, I would stick to an occasional cocktail.

11

Dean's thirty-sixth birthday was a very different affair from his thirty-fifth. On June 7, 1953, we were in the middle of the Atlantic Ocean, aboard the beautiful new Cunard liner *Queen Elizabeth*, heading for our first-ever overseas engagement, at the London Palladium. Hal Wallis, a charter member of the Dress-British-Think-Yiddish sect of Judaism, adored all things English, and since there was no *Colgate Comedy Hour* in Great Britain to goose our movie-ticket sales, Wallis figured we'd better get over there and show them the merchandise in person. After extended three-way talks between Wallis, his pal Val Parnell, the manager of the Palladium, and our new agents at MCA, we were booked at the great theater for a week at seven thousand pounds sterling.

I'd had to do a little bit of explaining to Dean about the gig — first about that seven-thousand figure, which made him howl until I told him that a pound (at that time) was worth five bucks.

Then he asked me about the Palladium. 'Is it any good?'

'Good?' I said. 'My dad says there are only four theaters in the world that you'll play if you really make it in show business — the Paramount and the Palace in New York, the Olympia in Paris, and the London Palladium.'

He shrugged, always Mr. Cool. 'Okay.'

London Palladium, 1953.

So there we were aboard the great liner, a party of twenty-four — we took up three full tables in the first-class dining room! Patti and our two sons, Gary and Ronnie, joined us, along with the musicians, writers, dressers, and the rest of the group. The one person who did not make the trip was Jeannie: She and Dean had been having a little trouble lately, and though they'd kissed and made up, she decided to stay back in L.A. and take care of the kids.

Leaving her husband free to have the kind of fun he was so fond of having.

To begin with, the *Queen Elizabeth* had an elegant gambling salon, which Dean said he and I should enjoy. Major mistake! In less than three days playing gin rummy, I owed my partner $684,700. As always, he was most happy to assist me by letting me postdate the check, which I did. I made it out on June 5, 1953, but dated it August 5, 1956 (all in fun, little realizing what any date after July 24, 1956, would mean to us). For the next three years, Dean held on to that check, hoping to do something ridiculous with it one day. He never did. (He may have kept it longer, but I once asked Jeannie if she'd ever seen it, and she said no.)

The night of Dean's birthday, we had dinner with the ship's captain. That made me nervous. A captain away from the bridge for two hours, wining and dining and chatting with everyone that came over to say hello to him . . . Who was watching out for icebergs?

We were seated apart from the rest of our entourage, and in those days, when my wife

204

wasn't there, the Idiot was! Dean was squeezed between two old biddies, Mae and Clara. I remember their names to this day because — I later learned from the ship's social director — they owned a chain of department stores in Texas, making them two of the richest women in that very rich state. They were also (the social director said) on the lookout for husbands! We bird-watched those two for the whole trip. They had some pretty good moves, but no takers.

Also at our table were Anastas Mikoyan, trade minister of the Soviet Union (and later its premier), and Mrs. Mikoyan. Oh, they were a barrel of laughs . . . not!

The dinner started with a ceremonial hand-washing — hot towels passed all around. 'I just left my room — how dirty could I get?' Dean said. I kicked him under the table. Then the caviar was served — real Iranian caviar, about $11,000 a spoonful, and with it a nice small glass of vodka, which the Russian pushed away, motioning for the waiter to get him a tumbler, which he did. We watched in disbelief as Mikoyan held up the water glass, toasted everybody at the table, and gulped it down like Coca-Cola.

Dean took a sip and made a face. 'That boy's got a cast-iron stomach,' he said. 'This stuff is lighter fluid.'

I shushed him. 'Let's be polite,' I said. 'Just not *too* polite.'

Suddenly, my partner was wearing a very familiar grin and staring over my shoulder. I didn't have to be told what was going on; I just needed to know where she was. The answer was two tables away, sitting with a bunch of very theatrical types: an absolutely glorious, dark-haired young lady, twenty-one years old at the very most. She and Dean had locked eyes, and she was smiling in a way that told me I'd be seeing very little of him for the next few nights.

I won't say the girl's name here, but she was a celebrated young actress whose future seemed full of promise — yet would, in fact, be filled with heartbreak. At that moment, though, she was like the most beautiful blossom in a meadow, ripe for the plucking. She was also in the midst of a very public love affair with another one of Hal Wallis's actors, Kirk Douglas. Who was not aboard the *Queen Elizabeth*.

Dean's smile, and the young lady's, grew broader.

The next morning, the entire cruise staff were out rounding up pigeons for shuffleboard, horse-racing games, swimming contests, and, of course, the perennial amateur shows. At breakfast (Dean was still grinning), the two of us decided to enter the show in disguise. We had our bag of tricks with us — makeup, hats, wigs, beards, musical instruments . . . Christ, we could go on stage as anyone at all!

Dean decided to do his Bing Crosby impression (which he did quite well), in wig, golf hat, and mustache, and I would do my Barry Fitzgerald imitation (remember the little Irish actor who always played a priest? Well, believe it or not, I did a mean Barry Fitzgerald), in wig, mustache, and turnaround collar.

We auditioned in the *Queen Elizabeth's* mammoth showroom and were accepted for the show that night. Just what we were going to *do* in the show was another question — it wasn't as if we had a screenplay of *Going My Way* lying around!

Day turned into evening gradually and gorgeously, as it does at that latitude on the Atlantic: a soft twilight that seems to last forever. And then it was showtime.

At first, back in costume, we were laughing, but as the master of ceremonies got things going, it suddenly hit us again: What the hell were we going to do?

Then I had an idea. We watched the other acts. The juggler needed a day job. The trainer for the dog act forgot the doggie treats. The dog did nothing, except backstage he left us a gift.

Now it was the singer's turn. She was a beautiful blonde with flowing locks and extra lipstick on her teeth. She sounded like Tallulah Bankhead in heat. Thank God this was almost over. We were scheduled to follow the mind reader, who couldn't find his blindfold. A waiter was walking by backstage and I stopped him, gave him a twenty-dollar bill, and took his cummerbund. I slipped through the curtain and handed it to the mind reader, who was most grateful! Until the cummerbund's metal clips started pinching his temples. He went on, wincing in pain, until his assistant arrived with enough gas to go to Cleveland. I mean, she was whacked out of her mind, so everything the mind reader did, didn't work. They were on and

207

CBS was never happier!

off in short order, leaving the crowd hysterical. Now it was our turn.

We had the MC introduce us as O'Keefe and Merritt — the billing we'd finally settled on after going through McKesson and Robbins, Harris and Frank, and Liggett and Myers . . . anything but Martin and Lewis! (I'd wanted to use Dill and Doe, but Dean said no.)

We entered at the same time, Dean from stage right and I from stage left. I was carrying a small wooden box, which I put on the lectern in front of us. Then Dean sang 'Too-Ra-Loo-Ra-Loo-Ra' while I did a lot of face-making with the big meerschaum pipe I had clamped between my teeth. Then Dean kept on humming the song as I recited an ad-lib hunk of the speech Barry Fitzgerald gave in *Going My Way*.

When we finished, the audience went ballistic . . . for English people. Which is to say, more correctly, that they demonstrated a high degree of enthusiasm — most of them being, after all, rather prim and proper and stuffy types who looked like they should have had their pictures on Yardley Soap. The best part was, they didn't know we were who we were. As they applauded, I opened up the wooden box, removed a small bottle of whiskey and two shot glasses, and poured us each a drink. We toasted each other and drank, then took our bows and exited backstage. Both Dean and I thought we were a shoo-in to take first prize: We knew we had at least twenty-two people out there in our pocket! Then all the acts walked back out onto the stage so the MC could see who got the loudest applause.

He put his hand over the dog act first. Applause was sparse. Next, he indicated the mind reader and his drunken assistant, who got a polite hand. Then it was us. Thunder from our two tables in the back — and polite nods from the rest of the audience. Then the MC put his hand over the head of the singing blonde . . . who got a standing ovation! Dean and I slowly walked backstage, pondering our worst failure in quite a while. It might have been sad if it hadn't been so funny — of course, it took us a few minutes to see the humor.

We should have only known what lay just ahead of us.

★ ★ ★

For about ten days after landing, we went sightseeing in England and Scotland: Dean loved those great old Scottish golf courses. Then we headed for London. On Monday evening, June 22, we opened at the Palladium.

Everybody who was anybody in England was there that night, with the exception of the Queen, who would come a few days later. But Princess Margaret was in attendance, along with many other royals, most of Parliament, and a wagonload of British celebrities, including Laurence Olivier, Vivien Leigh, Morecambe and Wise, Benny Hill, Robert Morley, Alec Guinness (not Sir yet!), Jack Hawkins, Hermione Gingold, along with many friends from Paris . . . Maurice

Chevalier, Edith Piaf, and Pierre Etaix.

We did a terrific show, one of our best. Dean sang wonderfully and thought I had never been funnier. Dick and the band were great, and we played around with them, tooting along on our trumpet and trombone. We had that crowd in stitches. Then, as we were taking our curtain calls, I stepped to the microphone to thank the audience.

'When we return — ' I started.

'Never come again!' someone shouted from the balcony.

That stopped me in my tracks.

'Go home, Martin and Lewis!' someone else shouted.

And then the boos began. It's one thing to bomb in front of an audience — to hear an awful silence instead of laughs and applause. But boos are something else again. Something ugly and assaultive. All at once, it seemed as though that whole London audience was going nuts: a ton of applause and cheers, along with some very audible booing. Was it Dean and I who were being booed, or were our loyal fans showing their disapproval of the people who'd shouted at us? It was impossible to tell. Dean and I looked at each other, totally baffled, just as the curtain dropped. What was going on?

We went back to our dressing room, which looked like rush hour. There were Larry and Vivien and Alec and Jack and Hermione and Benny and Maurice and Edith, all smiling and drinking champagne. Had Dean and I heard wrong? Had none of the happy celebrities in our dressing room heard the boos? We didn't ask any questions. We were too busy shaking hands and talking to the press. It was bedlam!

We had to dress for the opening-night party Val Parnell was throwing for us at the posh Savoy Hotel. When we got there, we met with Jack Keller, who hadn't the faintest idea about the who or why of the booing. He spoke to a few of his English press pals but got no answers. And so the party proceeded, the good feelings gradually washing away the bad.

Then, next morning, came the London papers.

Jack Keller phoned us and said he'd meet us in Dean's suite. When I walked in, I found them in the living room, where Jack had spread the front pages of all eight London newspapers over the floor, every one blaring a variation of the same huge, black headline:

MARTIN & LEWIS BOOED
AT PALLADIUM OPENING

Jack was shaking his head, looking like he'd just taken a swift kick to the balls.

'What in Christ's name is this all about?' I asked him.

Dean chimed in: 'We did the best show of our lives, and they run headlines like that!' For once he had lost his cool. I'd never seen him so furious.

It turned out that a number of the papers ran great reviews, but not on the front page. Those headlines eclipsed everything.

Jack sat us down and tried to explain. 'Look, you guys,' he said. 'As great a job as you did last night, you've got to understand that ever since Lend-Lease, anti-Americanism has run pretty strong over here.' He was referring to the program that started the year before the United States entered World War II, when England was getting beaten up pretty badly by the Nazis, and we began sending them ships, planes, tanks, guns, food, and other supplies. Great Britain was going to make good on all of it, but file it under No Good Deed Goes Unpunished — lend someone money and, without fail, the recipient feels like a turd for needing it in the first place, then blames you for having it to give him.

Once again: Being the receiver of generosity isn't always the easiest thing in the world.

Now, though, something else was going on. The Red Scare was at its peak in America and Joe McCarthy was trying to prove everyone a Communist. Only days before we arrived, McCarthy's chief goons, Roy Cohn and G. David Schine, had stopped in London as part of their European tour to root out subversives. Both the English and European press had a field day making fun of these two turkeys. In addition, Julius and Ethel Rosenberg, convicted of giving American atom-bomb secrets to the Russians, had just been executed at Sing Sing. U.S. prestige, Jack reminded us, was at an all-time low overseas — especially in England.

A few weeks later, we found out that the shouting at our Palladium opening had been started by two left-wing students, and that most of the booing had been directed at their rudeness. But those headlines dogged us for the next two weeks, as we continued to play to standing-room-only crowds at the Palladium. Meanwhile, Dean seemed to keep getting angrier and angrier. I was mad too, but because Dean was taking it so hard, I tried to lighten things up in order not to make him feel worse.

'They'll never see me in London or Hong Kong, or even Burberry's in New York,' Dean swore. 'The English press are whores, parasites, and just low-down filthy scum.' And the sad thing was, I had to admit he was right. Remember, Fleet Street in London was the mother of tabloid journalism — and when you're in that spotlight, it isn't much fun.

After England, we toured the U.S. military bases in France, then stopped in Paris for some R&R. Time had passed, but Dean and I were both still stinging. When Art Buchwald, then writing for the *International Herald Tribune*, came to interview us over lunch at the Hotel George V, we didn't hold back. When I ordered my lunch, I asked for 'a nice roasted English reporter garnished with lots of French-fried potatoes.'

'I'm never going back to England,' Dean said, 'on account of the British press stinks. And you can tell them I said so. They tell you how much they like you to your face and what great admirers they are of yours, and then the next day you read in the paper that you stink.'

Dean sailed back to New York the next day, while Patti and I took a much-needed vacation in

France and Italy. I was mostly out of touch for the next few weeks, so I was unaware — at first — of how difficult my partner was finding it to let sleeping dogs lie. Dean just kept complaining about England to the American papers, and unfortunately, it didn't take too long for his bitterness to backfire.

He was stoking the headlines: 'DEAN MARTIN CALLS LONDON GARBAGE CAPITAL OF EUROPE,' one read. 'MARTIN AND LEWIS WILL NEVER GO BACK TO ENGLAND,' said another. Dean was quoted in one piece vowing, 'I will use all my power to see that no Martin and Lewis film will ever play in England again!' I began to worry that this kind of talk could affect our worldwide ticket sales, a major part of our income. Of course, Wallis was beside himself. I later found out he was phoning Dean, sending him telegrams, telling him, begging him, ordering him to cease and desist. And Jack Keller was frantically trying to get in touch with me. 'We've really got a problem here,' he said when we finally connected.

So I called Dean at home in L.A. 'Dean, please let it go,' I said. 'You're making this a very tough situation for us — '

He cut me off. 'Listen, pal, I've just begun.' I'd never heard him like this. Part of me wondered where all this anger was coming from. 'These motherfuckers can't get away with this bullshit!' he yelled. 'They're gonna be sorry they didn't go after Cohn and Schine instead of Martin and Lewis!'

I could see I wasn't going to cool his anger on

a staticky international phone. Patti and I continued our vacation, and I did my best to put the whole thing out of my mind. I did face some local press now and then, and they all had the same question: 'What really happened at the Palladium?' I said the same thing to all of them: 'We were great at the Palladium, and the English people loved what we did. The whole incident has been blown completely out of proportion.'

I was trying to put the best possible face on the situation, but I was still worried. When I got back to Los Angeles, Dean and I had a meeting at NBC about our radio show. It was the first time I'd seen him in three weeks. We hugged, but I immediately saw something different — the twinkle in his eye had dimmed. I tried desperately to jolly him out of his mood, to do whatever I could to ease the pain of what he'd had to read in the papers for the last few weeks.

But the American press was in full swing. The *San Francisco Chronicle* ran an editorial taking us to task for not being up to dealing with negative press. Walter Winchell and Hedda Hopper — the two biggest noisemakers in America at that point — both went after us. Winchell accused us of 'a Major Bubu: You never publicize the raps.' Hopper said we should have made fun of the bad reviews on the *Colgate Comedy Hour*. Dean was taking a lot of the heat. Ironically, he was getting all kinds of unwanted attention from the same people who usually ignored him.

It has taken me a very long time (a full half-century, to tell the truth) to finally learn the

216

sad lesson: If you knock even the most hateful human being, you will come out of the encounter looking less than heroic. People almost always side with the one being attacked.

The months passed, and as our memories of England faded, Dean and I got back up to all our old tricks. Still, my partner always seemed on edge. If he heard about someone wearing a coat made in England, he'd go off on a tirade. I'd have to work the room to get him settled. More and more I learned that there were certain resentments that seethed behind his cool facade. His tendency to bottle things up would soon come to hurt us both.

That's twenty-twenty hindsight, of course. At the time, I just kept wondering: Where was all this anger coming from?

12

The Caddy hit the theaters in August of 1953, and by that fall, the movie's big hit song, 'That's Amore,' was selling out of the record stores. Naturally, Dean was thrilled. The twinkle was back in his eye, and I could see a new lift in his step. I was pleased, too, even if I felt like something of a martyr, knowing that it had all been my doing. Some small part of me wanted to tell Dean about my generosity, to get the credit for it: That's human nature! But I also sensed that saying anything would take away from my partner's triumph, so I kept my mouth shut.

It was complicated. Christ, everything between two human beings is complicated! And in a relationship like Dean and I had (which was unlike any relationship I've ever known), it was much, much more so.

I felt guilty.

Guilty that for years, Dean had had to put up with the Bosley Crowthers of the world, to listen to Jerry this and Jerry that, to grin and bear all the horseshit about what a genius I was. The press utterly ignored the fact of Dean's genius. And many of the critics didn't just ignore his gifts, they demeaned and humiliated the man himself. One Thomas O'Malley, staff writer for an early-fifties magazine called *TV Forecast*, once wrote:

Although Martin is probably the best partner Jerry could ever have teamed up with, let's face it, Lewis could have paired off with Walter Brennan and been a sensation. He IS the team. If his stuff ever becomes ho-hum material, Dean certainly wouldn't be able to carry the slack.

You must understand, this was what Dean had to put up with. The drumbeat was incessant, and it would have destroyed a lesser man than my partner. I sure couldn't have lived with it for anywhere near as long as he did.

I *wanted* to flag-wave for Dean. I *told* any number of writers how brilliant he was, how much I owed him. Do you think that's what they wrote about? No. They didn't believe me.

So I tried to do things for Dean, to repay him, but I knew that part of his anger at the English press was really caused by the way the American critics treated him.

And I also worried that some of Dean's anger was at me, for getting the lion's share of the attention. If I had told him about buying him 'That's Amore' (a small voice in me reasoned), maybe he wouldn't be mad at me. But I was also a smart fella: I thought of Lend-Lease, and how furious at America it had made some Brits feel.

So I continued to keep my mouth closed.

Dean was in a funny place that fall. With his number-one hit song, he was feeling his oats as a performer for the first time. But at the same time, all the indignities he'd suffered had built up. And there were more to come. The last straw was floating down toward the camel's back.

★ ★ ★

In January 1954, Hal Wallis showed us the first-draft script for our next film, a circus story to be called *Big Top*. It was a story I had very high expectations for: I'd wanted to play a clown ever since I'd seen my idol Charlie Chaplin's 1928 picture *The Circus*. But when Dean and I read the script for *Big Top*, we were bitterly disappointed.

The screenplay had been done by a pal of mine, Don McGuire, who'd recently written *Meet Danny Wilson* for Frank Sinatra. That movie, a dark drama about an up-and-coming nightclub singer with a rough-and-tumble past, was a powerful and complicated version of Frank's own story.

Leave it to Hal Wallis to hire a writer for Martin and Lewis who didn't write comedies. Still, Wallis was aware of my friendship with Don, and thought it might make the project move along more smoothly to go with a writer I knew. And in fairness to Don, Wallis sat on him so heavily throughout the process that a Neil Simon would have been hard-pressed to come up with laughs.

There were a couple of other big problems. The biggest was that as the screenplay was written, Dean and I didn't have a lot of scenes together. The first twenty pages of the script — twenty full minutes on the screen — had ten minutes of my character, then ten minutes of Dean's, before the two of us even met.

When you have a Martin and Lewis picture without the 'and,' you don't have much.

For a few weeks, Dean and I let preproduction go on without us. In other words, we staged a sit-down strike, and for a while it looked as though the only Big Top Hal Wallis was going to get was the top he'd wind up blowing.

While Dean and I agreed we hated the first draft of *Big Top*, the fact is, we hated it for totally different reasons — selfish reasons on both our parts. At first we didn't really discuss what each of us found problematic. We should have, but we didn't. The truth is that Martin and Lewis lived very different lives when we were at home than when we were on the road. On the road, we worked together, ate together, lived in adjacent hotel suites. Back in Los Angeles, we had families, offices, agents, distractions. Dean had golf — lots of golf. Whole days went by when we didn't talk or see each other.

And where *Big Top* was concerned, all I could think about was how excited I was to be doing a circus movie, and about how really involved I would be in the moviemaking process. Selfish? Sure. Shortsighted? Absolutely.

Meanwhile, Dean stayed on the golf course, at a safe distance from unpleasantness. I think he knew, deep down, that coming clean about why he disliked this script was going to require a big-time confrontation. As a matter of fact, if he was to be completely truthful, he would have to face me with his dissatisfactions, which would be the hardest thing of all. That bottle stayed corked for a little while. The easier showdown (but still a very hard one for Dean) was with Hal Wallis.

We were both coming to hate the cookie-cutter scripts that Wallis wanted for all our movies. The formula had at least given me more room for experimentation than it had given Dean. In *Big Top*, he'd once more be playing my handsome sidekick, except that this time his character had fewer songs than usual and was even more of a heel.

After avoiding Wallis for a few weeks, having our secretaries field ever-angrier phone calls mentioning breach of contract, we finally agreed to a script meeting at Paramount. It was a big conclave in Wallis's office, full of agents, lawyers, and writers; the atmosphere was, to put it mildly, tense. I spoke my piece, but what shocked me was that Dean finally spoke his.

With Hal Wallis, 1948.
First screen test for crotchety producer.

222

More than that: He really let our producer have it. Tapping all too easily into the reservoir of anger that seemed to have built up over the last six months, he said that he didn't want to play a cheat, that he didn't even know what he was doing in the picture. 'Huntz Hall could play this part,' he told Wallis.

Wallis, no shrinking violet, gave as good as he got. He reprimanded us both for our 'belligerent attitude.' We shouted right back that he was selling us short with this script. After a lot of back-and-forth, we finally hit on what appeared to be a compromise that we could all live with. Dean and I would get into line and do our wardrobe and color tests for the picture, and I would work with our TV writers, Arthur Phillips and Harry Crane, on a revision of the script. Dean seemed completely satisfied with this solution.

More likely, he was just in a hurry to get back to the golf course.

★ ★ ★

We shot on location in Phoenix, Arizona, with the Clyde Beatty Circus, which should have been a delight. Unfortunately, the making of the movie that would eventually be released as *Three Ring Circus* was troubled in every way. (For starters, Hal Wallis only wanted to pay for one ring, not three! Fortunately, our director, Joe Pevney, was able to convince him that *One Ring Circus* didn't exactly cut it.)

But the shoot's main problems were between

my partner and me. Things got off on a bad footing a few days after production started, when *Look* magazine published a photograph taken on the set of our soon-to-be-released picture, *Living It Up*. The photograph was originally of Dean and me with our costar, Sheree North. But for some idiotic reason, *Look* cropped Dean out of the photo so that only Sheree and I appeared together.

Dean was furious, justly so. He crumpled up a copy of the magazine and threw it in Jack Keller's face. The slight seemed all too symbolic of the neglect he'd been enduring for years, a neglect that I can see came to a head with *Three Ring Circus*. The writers and I had worked hard on the script, but no matter how hard we tried, we just couldn't find much for Dean's character to do in the story. We tried to beef up his scenes and emphasize the musical numbers, but there was no getting around the fact that this was a circus picture and I was playing Jerrico the clown.

Perhaps after seven years as a team, Dean and I were displaying the classic symptoms of Seven-Year Itch. Our ideas about who and what Martin and Lewis were had begun to fray. For seven years, it had been enough for me to bounce around nightclub and theater stages like a crazy person while Dean smiled indulgently. Dean felt that still was enough. I didn't.

I was approaching thirty. I wanted to grow as a comedian, as an actor. I had, as Shakespeare said, immortal longings in me. Was Chaplin my idol? You bet your ass he was. If you're going to aim for the stars, why not pick the best? And the one thing that Charlie had — in spades — was something I'd barely tapped into: pathos.

Great comedy, in my mind, always goes hand in hand with great sadness: This is the grand Circle of Life, the mixture of laughter and tears. You can be funny without tapping into strong emotion, but the humor is more superficial. Funny without pathos is a pie in the face. And a pie in the face is funny, but I wanted more.

Dean didn't agree. In his mind, what we did wasn't broke, so why should we fix it? We were pulling in money by the bushel; why risk that by getting artistic?

Pathos was, to Dean Martin, the worst kind of flag-waving. Just keep 'em laughing, was his philosophy. Keep it cool and superficial. Audiences don't want to think when they see us. They don't want tears. If they want pathos, let them go to a Chaplin movie.

There was a skit we did on our TV show where I played a poor schnook who joins a friendship club. I tried desperately to make friends, but when everyone paired off to go get something to eat, I wound up alone, dancing with a mannequin. Dean hated that skit. He just kept saying, 'Why don't you cut out this sad stuff and just be funny?'

So in Dean's eyes, I was committing a double sin, flag-waving and acing him out at the same time. The problem had been simmering, and now — encouraged by some of his friends — it was all coming out. Dean kept losing his temper at me and everyone else on the shoot, saying he'd had it with playing a stooge. He often showed up late for work: One afternoon he came in at three o'clock, did a single scene, then walked off the set, saying, 'That's all you're gonna get from me.' Another morning, he came in an hour late, gave me a look that could kill, and said, 'Anytime you want to call it quits, let me know.'

I tried to tease my way out of it. 'But, Paul,' I said, 'what would I ever do without you?'

'Fuck yourself, for starters.'

This all felt like a nightmare. Literally. I couldn't sleep; I could barely eat. It was a schizophrenic existence: I loved hanging around with the circus people, I learned a ton from the Clyde Beatty clowns. I enjoyed shooting my scenes. But when the working day was over, that feeling of doom returned. My partner was drifting away from me. Or had he drifted away already? The uncertainty tapped into my childhood fear of being deserted. An icy look from Dean would turn me into a scared nine-year-old. My adult self knew how badly he was hurting, but the child in me could hijack my peace of mind in an instant.

And I was angry, too. It's satisfying, in a negative way, to lash back when you're being attacked. To think how right *you* are. But all the time I knew how dangerous this was, how unnecessary. One afternoon I summoned all my courage and knocked on Dean's door at the hotel. He was wearing his golf clothes. His face froze when he saw me, and I knew that he was struggling to control his anger. He didn't *want* to

226

hate me. 'Look, Jer, I'm headed out to the country club,' he said.

'We really have to talk, Paul.'

He sighed. 'Why don't you ride out with me.'

It was good luck, really, that he was on his way to play golf: It wouldn't have been half as easy to sit down and hash it out face-to-face as it was to talk sitting side by side in his car. I began by telling him how right I thought *he* was.

'I know there's less in this role than you deserve,' I said. 'I believe in you, Paul. I believe you could carry a movie all by yourself if you wanted.'

A glance at his face told me that this was something he'd given thought to but hadn't totally worked out. I felt certain that other people had told him this, and I could see that it confused him for me to say it. 'Well — ' He hesitated. 'I don't know 'bout that.'

'Well, I do,' I said. 'I'm absolutely sure of it. And I want to tell you something else. I know you're not a hundred percent with the direction we've been going in lately. I understand that, and I understand why. It's a tricky place we're in now — I'm growing, you're growing. Who knows where it'll all end up? But I think we can still have some fun, Paul. I want you to try and remember how good it can be when we're enjoying ourselves. Just give me this one movie, and I'll try like hell to get back to the good times.'

It was all I could do to hold back the tears when he held out that big hand of his to shake. I wished we could have hugged, like in the old days — but then, as I had to keep reminding myself, it wasn't the old days anymore.

* * *

Bad news travels fast, and word of the troubled shoot of *Three Ring Circus* was all over L.A. long before we returned from Phoenix. Our agent, Lew Wasserman, and our lawyer, Joe Ross, called us into the MCA offices to work things out. They were friendly but very firm: We had far too many commitments, they told us in no uncertain terms, to quarrel like schoolboys. Tens of millions of dollars were on the line. There were our contracts with Wallis, NBC TV, radio, club bookings, and product endorsements.

'You've got to try to get along, guys,' Lew said. 'For your own sakes, for everybody's.'

'We're doin' okay,' Dean told him. 'Right, Mr. Lupus?'

I could still see the coolness in his eyes. But that was all right, for now: Cool was better than cold.

Then a strange thing happened — or rather, a tragic thing with odd repercussions: Patti's mom died. I'd been very close to Mary, and I was almost as devastated as my wife was.

Dean and Jeannie were at the wake and the funeral. When our family returned from the cemetery to the house, my partner and his wife came along — solid, soothing, sympathetic. While everyone was sitting around, speaking in quiet tones, Dean came up and asked if we could talk. 'Of course we can,' I said. We went into my den and shut the door. We both admitted that we'd said some stupid things, and that we owed it to ourselves and our families to be the total pros that we knew we were. And when we were finished talking, we hugged.

Maybe, I thought, we could be OK just as long as we weren't on a movie set . . .

★ ★ ★

That August, we were booked into Ciro's for two weeks. We might have had our troubles with *Three Ring Circus*, yet as far as our fans were concerned, we were still very much at the top of our game. And the illustrious citizens of Hollywood had always been among our biggest fans.

Why was that? Film people knew what it was to make magic with a script, perfect photography, and brilliant editing. The fact that on stage Dean and I could work wonders with none of the above simply awed them.

The insanity started five weeks before we were to open: Everyone tried to book a table for opening night, and soon there were no seats left. I had made reservations for some of my closest friends.

Then one morning, with only two days left before our opening, I got out of bed and started to brush my teeth. When I looked in the mirror, I saw that my face was yellow to the gills. I phoned Dr. Levy, who made a house call (they still did that then). He told me I had hepatitis and the only way I'd be able to recover from it was complete bed rest. For eight weeks.

With the opening on top of us, there were two options: We could cancel, or Dean could go on alone. With the buildup we'd had, cancellation seemed out of the question. But I wasn't sure how Dean felt about doing his first single in eight years.

He came to visit me at my house that afternoon. When he walked into my bedroom, I was ready — in a coolie hat and a Japanese waistcoat, with a record of 'Japanese Sandman' playing on the phonograph. Dean almost fell on the floor laughing. After a minute or two, he settled down and sat on the edge of the bed, looking serious. 'Listen, pally,' he said. 'I talked with Dr. Levy. You gotta be careful with this thing, okay?'

'Listen, Paul — I may play one, but I'm not a fool,' I told him. 'I'll do whatever it takes to get better. You know how much I want to get back to work.'

'Good,' he said. He slapped me on the knee. 'Now I'm gonna go play some golf.' And he started to walk out of the room.

'What? You're about to do a single for the first time in eight years and you're not planning a strategy so you don't step on your balls?'

He stopped and looked at me, genuinely puzzled. 'Strategy?' he said. Then he smiled. 'Hey, as long as the seats are facing the stage, I'll be fine!'

'You're not going to rehearse?' I asked him.

'Rehearse what?' Dean said. 'All's I need is our music books. I pick a couple of tunes, throw in a couple of ideas that feel right, and have some fun. What are they gonna do? Kill me?'

'Would you like to share those ideas with me?' I said. 'Maybe I can help.'

He was still smiling, but I thought I detected a long-suffering look in his eyes. 'Help what?' he said. 'It's gonna be okay, I promise.' And with that, he blew me a kiss and left.

★ ★ ★

On opening night, I sent the following to Dean's dressing room at Ciro's: a case of Scotch, a case of Jack Daniel's, two cases of Schweppes club soda, ten cartons of Camels, a case of his favorite red wine . . . *and* bottle openers, tall glasses (the ones he liked that no one carried), and Old-Fashioned glasses. I had Paramount print a thousand cocktail napkins reading 'DEAN MARTIN AND JERRY LEWIS,' with a big black X through my name.

★ ★ ★

I lay in bed as nervous as a cat, wondering, hoping, and praying a little. I expected not to hear anything until morning, since the show at Ciro's didn't break before midnight. But I was wrong. At 12:15, Jack Keller called me and said, 'Can I come out to see you?'

'When?' I asked.

'Now!'

I figured if Jack Keller, who hated to drive, was ready to make the forty-minute trip out to my

231

house in Pacific Palisades, it had to be important. I told him to come on out.

He walked into my bedroom at 1 a.m. — where, of course, I was ready for him in my Japanese outfit. Barely cracking a smile, Jack sat down on the opposite side of the room. If God Himself had told Jack that I wasn't contagious (which I wasn't), he'd still have sat across that room: Jack was a world-class hypochondriac.

'Was everything okay?' I asked him.

'Okay?' he said. 'It was unbelievable! It was fantastic!'

I sat up straight in the bed. 'Tell me!'

Keller says: 'They introduce him, and the audience, who were in his corner from the get-go, all stand up as he walks on stage . . . But instead of opening with a song, he signaled for quiet. You could've heard a pin drop. And Dean said, soft and serious, 'Ladies and gentlemen, thank you for coming tonight, because it's a very special night. A night I've been praying for, for the last eight years . . . to be alone on stage without that goddamn noisy Jew.'

'The house came down,' Keller said. 'Then, as the uproar died, Dean called to a stagehand. 'Please,' he said, 'bring me that other item.' The stagehand comes out with a mike stand and a mike, exactly like the one Dean has in front of him. 'I can't really feel comfortable,' Dean says, 'if he isn't here next to me. So, all kidding aside, I'd like everyone here to say a silent prayer that my partner gets better very soon.'

'That audience applauded and whistled and stamped their feet,' Keller said. 'It was electric!

Then Dean did a song and broke it up with some silliness. Jack Benny stood up and asked him if he needed any help. And Dean says, 'Sure, Jack, but no money!' Jack looks around as only Jack can, then walks back to his seat with his head down, and the crowd screamed. Dean then went into a Martin and Lewis routine, breaking up his own song in your voice, and playing to the mike stand as if it was you.

'So help me God, Jerry, it was just like you were there, and Dean was never better . . . '

Talk about mixed emotions! I was bursting with pride and seething with jealousy at the same time. *He did so well!* part of me thought — while the other part of me thought, *How dare he do so well without* me!

13

The Martin and Lewis movies would never have drawn such big audiences without our wonderful leading ladies. There were so many, so talented in so many different ways — and, like Dean and me, so much better than the material they had to work with. Some of their names might surprise you: Did you know we appeared with Donna Reed? Agnes Moorehead? Anita Ekberg? But the dozens of lesser-known actresses who acted in our films all added immeasurably to our work. (And, despite rumors and innuendoes, Dean and I did *not* sleep with *all* of them — names will be made public upon request!)

However, to my vast regret, the one actress we never performed with was Marilyn Monroe — and how great she would have been in a Martin and Lewis picture.

Dean and I first met her when we were receiving the *Photoplay* magazine award as Best Newcomers of the Year (whatever the hell year it was) and Marilyn was the Best Female Newcomer. God, she was magnificent — perfect physically and in every other way. She was someone any man would just love to be with, not only for the obvious reasons but for her energy and perseverance and, yes, focus. She had the capacity to make you feel that she was totally engaged with whatever you were talking about. She was kind, she was good, she was beautiful, and the press took shots at her she didn't deserve. They got on her case from day one — a textbook example of celebrity-bashing.

In the late fall of 1954, Marilyn's marriage to Joe DiMaggio had just ended, and she badly needed friends — and laughs. Dean and I had seen her here and there over the years since the *Photoplay* awards, and when we invited her out for an after-work snack at Nate'n Al's (then and now the best deli in Beverly Hills), she accepted instantly.

She had a delicious sense of humor — an ability not only to appreciate what was funny but to see the absurdity of things in general. The three of us huddled in a booth in a far corner of the restaurant, making fun of some of the late-night Hollywood regulars who drifted in and out. We laughed for a couple of hours, and then we drove her home in Dean's blue Cadillac convertible. It was a warm November night; she was living, temporarily, in the Voltaire Apartments in West Hollywood. Marilyn asked us to have a drink with her, and we did. She hated to be alone, especially late at night, when she couldn't sleep. She mentioned Joe a couple of times, but I think Dean and I both saw that there was a lot she couldn't or didn't want to talk about, so we tried to keep it light.

Soon it was close to two in the morning, and we had to get up early for work. (We were all on films at the time, with a 6 a.m. wake-up.) On the way out, I asked Marilyn if she would consider going to dinner with Dean and me one night that week.

'How about tonight?' she said.

'Tonight is perfect!' we said in unison.

Dean and I spent most of that day trying to figure out where the hell to take Marilyn Monroe for dinner. 'I know!' I finally yelled. 'Let's go to Perino's!'

It was the most elegant restaurant in L.A., on Wilshire Boulevard not too far from Slapsy Maxie's. Great food, great service; strictly a wear-a-tie type of place. I had my secretary make reservations — for four, on the chivalrous assumption that Marilyn might bring someone. We were to meet at the restaurant, because she was shooting later than we were. We set the time for 8:30.

Dean and I left the set after work, and Christ, did we dress that night. I won't even go into how much cologne was applied.

We stepped into Perino's precisely at 8:30 — and there at the waiting bar was Marilyn. Alone, sitting on a stool, and looking drop-dead, as always. Dean asked, 'How come you're alone? Where's Milton?' It was well known that she had started seeing Milton Greene, the photographer. But Marilyn told us he had a family and had to be with them every now and then.

She said it with a slight note of sadness, but it was all Dean and I could do to keep the grins off our faces. We were seated in the center of this very open restaurant, with all eyes on . . . guess who? She might as well have been having dinner with Price and Waterhouse! We ordered drinks and made lots of small talk. At one point, Marilyn teased: 'Dean, don't you think you'd make a perfect leading man for one of my films?'

Dean laughed and said, 'Well, you know, every good screen team has a dog!'

I spoke right up in the Idiot's voice: 'I will not be a dog for anybody!'

Marilyn laughed, the captains laughed, the waiters laughed. And that's what we did the whole night — laughed and laughed.

How amazing it is to think that it was only seven years after that night — both a short time and a lifetime — that Dean was cast as Marilyn's love interest in *Something's Got to Give*, for 20th Century Fox. By that time, poor Marilyn was falling apart. She was fired from the picture and, not long afterward, took her life. Christ, what a loss!

★　★　★

In that same eventful fall of '54, Frank Sinatra invited Dean and me to visit the set of his latest movie, *The Man with the Golden Arm*. Based on the novel of the same name by Nelson Algren, the film is a harrowing story of a former card dealer and heroin addict named Frankie Machine struggling to get his act together after he's released from prison. Frank played Frankie, and his performance was, I think, his greatest, even more spectacular than the work he'd done in *From Here to Eternity* two years earlier.

The Man with the Golden Arm was being shot at the Goldwyn Studios, and the man in charge was Otto Preminger, the director from hell! He was good, but nasty to actors. The fact that I never worked with him probably added twenty years to my life.

Frank introduced us to Preminger when we walked onto the set, and the little director was quite cordial — he even told us that he'd caught our show at Slapsy Maxie's and thought it was the best he had ever seen in a nightclub. We thanked him and stayed out of the way.

They were shooting a scene they'd rehearsed all morning — the climax of the movie, in which Frankie, who has slid back into addiction, goes through heroin withdrawal. Everyone was a little anxious, as people get when a big scene is about to explode. The set got extremely quiet. Prop men moved materials into place. The cinematographer checked last-minute light. Preminger called the roll, then cried, 'Action!'

In the scene, Frank was in the corner of his bedroom, screaming at the top of his lungs as he underwent his horrific ordeal. Dean and I were standing directly beside the camera, and as close as we were, and as well as we knew that it was just a movie, we both had gooseflesh watching Frank's incredible performance. It ran for the better part of four minutes, and was simply explosive. He hit every beat and every nuance. Then Preminger yelled 'Cut!' and Frank got up off the floor and lit a cigarette. He walked toward the director to see how he liked it. 'That was great, Frank,' Preminger said, 'but we need one more take!'

Frank whirled around. 'Another take?' he said. 'For what, if that one was so good?'

I'm sure Preminger wasn't surprised. Frank's

approach to a film never varied: He learned his dialogue, knew every scene by heart, rehearsed as much as the director wanted (though Preminger was the first filmmaker Frank ever rehearsed happily for), and was ready for the camera. He knew that any extra takes would lose spontaneity, and he was dead right. That's why he was so good in everything he ever filmed. 'One take and print it!' was his motto. It made directors a little testy, because it meant the actor was in charge, and the one thing that directors can't stand is losing control. Frank walked back to his dressing room, calling Dean and me to follow, and we did.

Frank poured himself a tumbler of Jack Daniel's, which he needed after that scene. We couldn't stop telling him what a great job he'd done and how strongly it had affected us. 'I knew it was perfect and that I'd never get it that way again!' he said. I knew exactly what Frank meant — I never wanted to do a comic scene twice. I would prepare it all day and shoot it once, strictly for the spontaneity, and in comedy that really is vital.

Preminger stopped by the dressing room and said (in the kind of voice that let me know he wanted something), 'Frank, are you sure you want me to print that last take?'

Frank just looked at him while taking a sip of his Jack Daniel's. 'Uhhuh,' he said.

And that was that. When Dean and I saw the film in a theater, we knew Frank had been right. The scene knocked our socks off, and the audience's, too. Frank definitely should have gotten an Oscar for that performance, but ultimately, I think, the film's subject matter (which caused the Production Code to refuse it a seal of approval) was just too controversial for its time. Frank always did push the edges.

★ ★ ★

Not long after New Year's, Hal Wallis and I traveled to New York to find an ingenue for the new Martin and Lewis movie, *Artists and Models*. It's funny: As contentious as Wallis and I could be about business — and there were times I could have murdered that humorless skinflint — we could have a ball just hanging out. One thing we had in common was that we both loved to shop for shoes and clothes, and the New York trip featured plenty of that, as well as theatergoing. One cloudy Wednesday afternoon we were discussing what to do, and I said, 'Let's go to a musical — I love musicals!' I looked in the paper and my eyes immediately went to the listing for *The Pajama Game*, choreographed by my friend Bob Fosse.

But Wallis told me he had to meet with some lawyers and that I should go to the show myself. We would meet back at the Plaza for dinner. After dinner, Paramount had set up a cattle call in the hotel's main ballroom so that Wallis and I could scout the talent and, we hoped, find the right girl for our movie.

I called the St. James Theater and easily arranged for a single ticket. I settled into my seat, not too happy about being alone (in fact, now that I think of it, this may have been the one and only time I ever went to the theater by myself). It made me feel all the more wistful to remember that the St. James was the very same theater to which Dean and I had brought June Allyson and Gloria De Haven to see *Where's Charley?* six years earlier. I missed Dean — it was hard for me to admit how much I missed him.

Then it's two o'clock, and there's no downbeat and no curtain. And suddenly, a man walks to center stage and makes an announcement.

'Ladies and gentlemen — due to an ankle injury, the role played by Miss Carol Haney will be played this afternoon by her understudy, Miss Shirley MacLaine.'

There was a loud sigh of disappointment from the audience. Now, please understand: At this point, Shirley MacLaine was still Shirley Who? Carol Haney was the fabulous protégée of Gene Kelly, around whom Bob Fosse had built *The Pajama Game's* showstopping 'Steam Heat' number. *Oh well*, I thought. *I'm here. Let's see.*

Then the show went on, and the rest is Broadway legend, the kind of story line that, if it happened in a movie, most people would simply find too far-fetched to believe. Shirley came on and absolutely electrified me and everybody else in that audience. By the final curtain, we were all on our feet, yelling for her to come out again and again.

Then I ran out of the theater, hailed a cab, and went back to the Plaza. I wasn't in my suite three minutes before Wallis called, saying he was back and had plans for us that evening. I said, 'I'll be right over!' I ran down the hall to his suite, banged on the door, and almost screamed in his face: 'You have plans for tonight! I don't think so! You must let me take you to the theater to see the girl we're looking for!'

'Really,' he said with a smirk — as if to say, '*You* found the girl?'

I picked up the phone and asked for the hotel's concierge. I told him I needed two orchestra seats for that night's performance of *The Pajama Game*, for Mr. Wallis and myself.

Wallis shook his head. 'I'm not going to the theater tonight!' he said. 'I've got other plans!'

I looked him in the eye. 'If you trust my instinct,' I said, 'you'll change your plans.'

He pursed his lips, thought a second, and said, 'All right, I'll humor you.'

Humor? I thought. *Where will he get it?*

As we were riding to the theater in the limo, I was suddenly struck by a thought: *What if Carol Haney got better, and the girl I saw will never be heard from again?* I was ready for the Intensive Care Unit until we got to the theater and picked up our tickets at the box office, where the sign said:

In Tonight's Performance,
Miss Carol Haney's Role
Will Be Played by Miss Shirley MacLaine

I breathed a sigh of relief, and in we went.
At 11 p.m., Hal Wallis and I were on our feet

along with the other 1,700 people in the St. James Theater. I thought Shirley had been terrific at the matinee — but that night she simply exploded on that stage. Not long afterward, Wallis gave her a screen test, then signed her to a contract, and my partner and I had a leading lady for *Artists and Models*, a lady who would go on to make a great career for herself, and whose path would cross again with Dean's.

★ ★ ★

Often, others see us with the sharpest eyes. Then again, even the sharpest eyes can miss the whole truth. There's a series of wonderfully vivid verbal snapshots in Shirley MacLaine's Hollywood memoir, *My Lucky Stars*, of my partner and me during the shooting of *Artists and Models*. Shirley remembers what look like good times: The two of us going wild in the Paramount commissary, throwing food as Marlene Dietrich and Anna Magnani watch in horror, smearing butter all over the suit of production chief Y. Frank Freeman as Y. Frank, the courtliest of Southern gentlemen, sits in discreet shock (his real shock was yet to come). She recalls us racing golf carts around the studio lot, honking horns; jumping into strangers' cars and screaming that we're being kidnapped. She remembers the way Dean used to light a Camel with one of his gold cigarette lighters, blow out the flame, and throw the lighter out the window. These were all hijinks we'd been pulling for years, but Shirley was young and admiring, and witnessing them for the first time. It wouldn't take her long to see the strain beneath the jolly surface.

★ ★ ★

So we had a leading lady; we also had a new director. The last half-dozen of our films, with the exception of *Three Ring Circus*, had all been under the watch of Norman Taurog or George Marshall. I had the utmost respect for Norman and George, but Wallis's new discovery, Frank Tashlin, was a man I would come to revere.

Frank — or Tish, as I renamed him — started out as a newspaper cartoonist, then did some animation directing at Warner Brothers and other studios. A side job writing gags for Hal Roach's low-budget comedies led to more gag-writing for live-action pictures (including a couple of the Marx Brothers' and Bob Hope's), then screenwriting, then directing. By the mid-1950s, Tish was a full-fledged movie director — the only important director ever to make the transition from animation to live action. But his background in cartoons always gave him a priceless instinct for outrageous comedy. (They said about him that he directed his cartoons like live-action comedies and his live-action comedies like cartoons.) He had an incomparable mind for the kind of humor that was right up our alley.

Unfortunately, Hal Wallis was standing halfway down the alley with a blackjack in his hand.

Wallis initially hired Tashlin not because Tish

244

With Ben Hogan.
They won't let me mark my ball.

was a great comedic director but because *Artists
and Models* was a story about comic books and
cartoons. Hal Wallis was always a cut-and-dried
fellow, and it was as cut-and-dried as that.
Remember, Wallis knew as much about comedy
as he did about atomic energy. But then,
Hollywood deals always start with a smile and a
handshake and a good deal of blindness about
what's going to happen next. I think that Tish
never knew precisely what he was getting into.

Frank and I liked each other right away. He
was a big bruiser — six-three and 250-plus

pounds; brush crew cut, mustache, and horn-rimmed glasses — and, for a guy who made his living out of nonsense, was surprisingly direct. His personality was what you might call extra-dry. He watched you, made his judgments, and spoke his mind only when he was good and goddamn sure what he wanted to say. He had a patient, long-suffering air about him. I amused Tish — I tried very hard to amuse him — but I think that what he saw in me was a perfect instrument for his ideas. I will always think of him as my great teacher.

Which didn't mean he favored me over my partner. Not by a long shot. In fact, *Artists and Models* was a kind of liberation for Dean, especially after *Three Ring Circus*: In the new film (which Frank cowrote), Dean played my roommate and fellow wannabe comic-book writer, and he not only got as many lines as I did (a first) but (another first) had substantial comic material, as well as several terrific musical numbers.

Not surprisingly, for the first time in a while, there was zero tension on the set between the two of us. But at the time, I'm afraid, my ego was still ballooning. Frank Tashlin's strategic decision to let me in on the technical aspects of the movie was creating not just a future filmmaker but a kind of monster. I spent much of the shoot engaged in range wars — or pissing matches, call them what you will — with Wallis over everything from his attitude toward the crew to how much of my off-camera time I could spend attending to Martin and Lewis business. I was

246

locking horns with the Big Guy, ego versus ego. It was quite a tussle.

Meanwhile, Dean stood by smiling and practicing his golf swing. He was delighted with *Artists and Models* — and delighted to watch Wallis vs. Lewis from the sidelines.

The funny thing, though, is that on nearly every single issue, Wallis ultimately backed down. It wasn't the power of my personality (though at the time I thought it was) so much as it was the power of the Martin and Lewis franchise. We were just too big a moneymaker for the producer to risk rocking the boat.

Instead, Wallis took out his ire on others.

One day toward the end of the shoot, Tashlin came onto the set looking like someone had rammed a twelve-inch pin in one of his ears and out the other. I went into his dressing room on Stage 5 and asked, 'Anything I can do, Frank?'

'You've worked for Wallis long enough,' he said. 'You know him, and if you want to help, find out how I can get out of my contract with him. I just will not allow him to diminish me the way he does. How can a man with so little knowledge about comedy ... ' And he proceeded to go into a tirade about what I understood all too well: the great Wallis's utter tone-deafness when it came to humor on film.

I heard Tish out, then said, 'Frank, if you're really serious about getting out of your contract with Hal Wallis, there's a very simple thing you can do.'

He blinked. 'Simple? What's simple about it?' he said.

'Listen, Frank,' I said. 'Wallis loves cutting film better than seeing his own kid grow up. He believes himself to be the ultimate filmmaker — and in certain cases he is, but not with what *we do*. Now, if you write him a note saying you think he *cuts like a butcher*, I bet you're out of your contract before he finishes reading it.'

Frank wrote what I suggested and sent it to Wallis's office at about 3 p.m. Later, he phoned me at home to tell me that Wallis had called him at 5:15 to say he was out of his contract. Wallis didn't want to work with him anymore!

Wallis cut *Casablanca, Fugitive from a Chain Gang, The Life of Emile Zola*, and *Jezebel*. He cut those films very dramatically and very well — and that's the last nice thing I'll say about Hal Wallis. He was a strange man. He had to win. He acted as if his very life depended on making his point. He justified all his actions with this pontification: 'Great film can be put together by many men, but it is made by one man.' Without that one man, he felt, nothing could go forward. Maybe he was right, but he handled everything with such life-or-death conviction that he beat many around him into the ground. Yet away from his office he was a joy to be with. When he wasn't behind that desk, he not only had a human side but a wonderful sense of humor. He could be generous almost to a fault. But behind that desk, he would cut your heart out if it saved him 50 cents.

Poor Frank. Free from his contract, he sat out our next (and also next-to-last) picture, *Pardners*. But then Wallis somehow sweet-talked him into returning to direct our last film, a total debacle all too aptly titled *Hollywood or Bust*. (The 'or' in the title should have been replaced by an 'and.') After Dean and I broke up, Tish and I made a half-dozen pictures together (*The Geisha Boy, Rock-a-Bye-Baby, Cinderfella, It's Only Money, Who's Minding the Store,* and *The Disorderly Orderly*). I continued to learn priceless lessons about film, and comedy, from him. But I think that the give-and-take of the movie business, and especially the stress of having to go up against people like Wallis, probably led to Frank's much-too-early death, at age fifty-nine, in 1972.

★　★　★

Despite Wallis, and at the expense of Frank Tashlin's nervous system, *Artists and Models* became what many regard as one of the best Martin and Lewis pictures. After the film wrapped, Dean and I took Dick Stabile, our twenty-six-man orchestra, and the rest of our staff and went on a two-week theatrical tour throughout the Midwest, then jumped east to the Boston Garden. We put all the pressure and contention and bitterness of the movie business behind us, and for seventeen charmed days in May of 1955, it felt just like old times . . .

14

That lovely trip reminds me of another one: At the precise midpoint of our ten years together, in July of 1951, we played Grossinger's in the Catskill Mountains.

Now, that might not sound so strange to you, but in 1951, the likelihood of such an engagement was not even a long-shot bet — no bookie would have taken your action.

Martin and Lewis in the Borscht Belt, even in the heyday of the Borscht Belt? Lewis, yes. Martin, no way!

By that summer, we had turned down Grossinger's for three years straight, and we planned to keep turning them down. We always had something else going on, and the fit didn't feel right.

But Paul Grossinger was a young man who didn't know how to take 'No' for an answer. He felt — no, he *knew* — that everything has a price. That was Paul's way of thinking, and he was a nice, warm, and friendly man, and personally, I hoped we could do it just on account of his being a terrific guy.

So Paul's agent called ours: 'We want Martin and Lewis for an exclusive one-night show at Grossinger's.' (*Exclusive* meaning that we could not play any other hotel up that way — as if we'd finish that show and dash off to Kutsher's!) The agent went on to say, 'We know how many times they've turned us down since 1948. They said no to $25,000 and no to $50,000, and they said no to $75,000! We now feel we have to go the last mile and make them an offer of $100,000 for the night.'

Our representative said, 'Let me call you back.'

At this point, I, in my house in Las Vegas, whip out my handy inflation calculator and note that $100,000 in 1951 translates to approximately $733,462.38 in today's dollars. Approximately.

These were not the kind of numbers offered by agents over the phone. Our representative hung up and got me at my office at Paramount. I said, 'But we turned them down each time because we were either doing a film or were otherwise unavailable.'

'You know that, I know that, Dean knows that. But *they* don't know that.'

I said, 'Let me talk to Dean.'

I ran out of my office to Dean's dressing room, just across the way. He was smoking a Camel, watching a rerun of some old movie, and waiting for Artie, the barber, to come and give him a haircut. I walked over and turned the set off.

'Hey, they were just about to show the murderer!' Dean yelled, getting out of his chair to turn the TV back on.

'Don't bother!' I said. 'I saw it! It was Henry Fonda.'

(Note: Henry Fonda never played a murderer in his entire career.)

'What's so goddamn important, and why are you puffing like a tired racehorse?' he asked.

'Because,' I whispered, 'Grossinger's wants to give us *one hundred thousand dollars* for *one show*. One night. The most money ever paid to anyone in the history of show business . . . Including Frank, Bing, Caruso, and Mario Lanza.'

For one of the few times I can remember, Dean was hooked. 'Tell me you're joking,' he said. 'Tell me I can't really pick up fifty grand for doing one performance!'

'I'm telling you you can pick up a hundred grand for that one show, but I get half. So work it any way you want — just tell me to okay it!'

He jumped onto his couch and bounced up a couple of feet in the air. 'What the hell are you still doing here?' he yelled. 'Go and say yes!'

A Saturday night in the Catskill Mountains in the early 1950s was a lot like Times Square on New Year's Eve. There was no other hotel like Grossinger's. The dining room fed 1,600 people at a time (with two sittings, like a cruise ship), at big round tables seating twelve. Before that there were cocktails. There was milling, there was *shmoozing*, there was *kvelling* and yelling. There was *tummling*, by busboys who would grow up to be comedy headliners. In short, Jewish pandemonium! And tonight the pandemonium was compounded by our presence at Paul Grossinger's table.

Watching Dean on this turf was priceless. All the little old ladies would come to the table and just flat-out kiss him on the face, rub his hair, pinch his cheeks.

And Dean was loving it. He was loving it, but

I also recall that he *was* hungry, and anxious to get into the half-grapefruit already sitting in front of him, with a little American flag stuck in the center. There were also pickles and horseradish and rye bread — but no butter. Kosher is kosher. Dean picked up a slice of bread and scanned the entire table for butter. No one would say anything, so I told him: 'Butter you get here for breakfast and maybe lunch, but not for a meat meal!'

Dean shouted, 'Then I'll eat what I need to eat to get some butter!' I glanced over at Paul Grossinger, who gave me a look as if to say, 'No way!'

I crept around the table, knelt by Dean, and whispered the ground rules to him. 'We just traveled three thousand miles,' he said. 'You couldn't tell me to buy butter?'

'And no milk,' I tell him. 'And no cream.'

'So why do the Jews hate cows?'

★   ★   ★

Now we move forward four years to the spring of 1955. You may remember a friend of mine named Charlie Brown — the man, not the cartoon. Charlie and his wife Lillian were hotelkeepers who let me busboy and bunk at the Arthur, their Lakewood, New Jersey, resort, when I was just starting out. I had sweated through the earliest performances of my record act on their stage. In the interim, Charlie and Lily had moved their establishment to the Catskills, and now Brown's, in Loch Sheldrake,

New York, was one of the important hotels of the Jewish Alps.

So when Uncle Charlie called me and asked if Brown's could host a gala premiere, in early June, for the thirteenth and latest Martin and Lewis movie, *You're Never Too Young*, I was absolutely thrilled. Charlie was offering to pay for everything — transportation, accommodations, food, cocktail parties, and press receptions. He was even offering to permanently dedicate Brown's newly constructed theater, the site of the proposed premiere, to Martin and Lewis, with a ribbon-cutting ceremony at the Dean Martin — Jerry Lewis Playhouse! It was irresistible . . . I thought back to my early days at the Arthur Hotel in Lakewood, perspiring as I lip-synched to Frank Sinatra and Danny Kaye, then imagined myself returning to the Browns, a celebrity.

When I brought up the idea at a meeting of our production company, everyone there — Hal Wallis; director Norman Taurog; Paul Jones, line producer for York Productions, the company Dean and I had started; the Paramount head of publicity; and Jack Keller — found it equally irresistible. Wallis, in particular, was ecstatic at the idea of Charlie's footing the entire bill. 'Terrific deal!' he said. 'Can't go wrong! This oughta save us fifteen, twenty thousand bucks!'

Then I told Dean.

It was the following morning, and my partner did not look pleased. In fact, he gave me such a glare that the little hairs rose on the back of my neck. Suddenly, all the ill will that we'd sidestepped for months came flooding back. 'You should have consulted me first,' Dean said.

I fought back feelings of panic — *alone, he's going to leave me all alone.* But I could always act as tough as anyone, even Dean. 'I'm consulting you now,' I told him. 'Give me the word and we'll do it. If not, we won't.'

He took a long, slow breath. 'Actually, Jerry, I really don't care where we hold it.'

I took this to be tacit approval. (We hear what we want to hear.) And so I got right on the phone with Uncle Charlie, who went straight to work on the extensive preparations for the big event.

The night before our fifty-plus-person party was to get on the east-bound Super Chief, there was a knock on my office door at Paramount. It was Mack Gray.

Mack, aka Maxie Greenberg, was a onetime prizefighter who had worked as George Raft's man Friday for twenty years. He'd been very much present at Raft's pool party on our first night in Hollywood. When Raft couldn't afford to keep him on anymore, Gray went to work in the exact same capacity for Dean. I always had a full staff buzzing around me; Dean mostly just had Mack. Mack was a gofer. If Dean needed a pack of cigarettes, or a girl driven home at 7 a.m., Mack was his guy. He wasn't the sharpest tool in the shed, but I liked him. Thought I did, anyway.

Now he was staring at me with that sad tough-guy's face. 'Your partner isn't making the trip,' he said.

'Are you putting me on?' I said.

'Look, Jerry, I'm relaying this straight from Dean's mouth. He said he's tired. He's going to take Jeanne on a trip to Hawaii. What else can I tell you?'

I felt like somebody had kicked me in the stomach. At the same time, some part of me couldn't help but marvel at how Dean had once again avoided confrontation by sending Mack. He had also stuck it to me by bailing at the very last minute. It was all too symbolic — my partner and I were headed thousands of miles in opposite directions. I got on the train the next morning with my family and the rest of our large party and traveled east in a miserable rage, unable to explain my despair even to my nearest and dearest.

★　★　★

Meanwhile, before heading to Hawaii, Dean sat down with syndicated columnist Earl Wilson and fired another couple of shots across my bow: 'I want a little TV show of my own, where I can sing more than two songs in an hour,' he told Wilson. 'I'm about ten years older than the boy. He wants to direct. He loves work. So maybe he can direct and I can sing.'

Then Wilson asked him why he hadn't gone east with me. 'Outside of back east,' Dean said, 'who knows about the Catskills?'

★　★　★

A trickle of blood had first leaked into the water when we had our troubles on *Three Ring Circus*, but the press was slightly more discreet in those days, and then the story of Martin and Lewis's troubles died down.

Now, however, it was back again in full force, and there was a crowd of hungry reporters waiting for me when I got off the train at Penn Station on June 9. I was completely unprepared for their questions.

'Where's Dean?' 'Why didn't your partner make the trip?' 'Are you feuding?'

I must have looked like a man on his way to the gallows. 'No comment' was all I came up with.

'Then where is he? Can you comment on that?'

'No. You'll have to ask him.'

They were all yelling at once. 'Have a heart! C'mon, Jerry, you're not helping us!'

'If I commented, it wouldn't help me.'

The drive north to the Catskills was more miserable with each passing mile. Route 17 was plastered with billboards announcing the appearance of Martin and Lewis at Brown's Hotel. And when we pulled into the driveway of the resort, there were Uncle Charlie and Aunt Lil standing on the big front porch, beaming out into the light rain.

I was moved; I was terrified; I was mortified. I gripped Patti's hand for dear life. 'Momma, what am I going to tell them?'

'Whatever you think is best,' my brave wife said.

The clichés about show people are true: We *do*

smile when we're low. And the lower you feel, the bigger and broader a grin you need. We arrived on Friday afternoon, and from the moment I stepped out of the car until the premiere on Saturday night, I was completely in character as the kid half of Martin and Lewis, impersonating a bellhop, a busboy, a waiter; kibitzing with the guests. After the screening of *You're Never Too Young*, there was a two-hour show: Alan King performed, and my wife the former band singer directed a number, 'He's Funny That Way,' right to me. And then another King showed up — Sonny King, the guy who first introduced me to Dean! Sonny and I did a little shtick together. It all felt like a weird episode of *This Is Your Life*.

By the time the big show was over, I simply couldn't take any more. The facade cracked. Another gang of reporters was waiting for me at the foot of the stage, and I could no longer hold back the tears. The theater went dead quiet. 'Maybe I'm using the wrong words,' I said, and then my voice broke for a moment. 'But I don't know the right ones. Maybe the lawyers wouldn't want me to say anything at all. But you've been wonderful. I want to thank you all for saving me embarrassment by not asking questions I couldn't answer.'

Everyone in the place stood and clapped, and my tears weren't the only ones flowing. But when the applause stopped, the questions started. *Lawyers? Did he say lawyers?* And the word started to rocket across America: *Martin and Lewis are having a feud.*

★　★　★

It's hard to explain to a 999-channel, Internet-connected, all-entertainment-all-the-time world what it felt like to be a big act in a much simpler time, having very public trouble. Then imagine the commercial implications of a rift between Dean and me. We had commitments out there worth literally tens of millions of dollars. We owed Hal Wallis five more movies, for starters. We had TV and radio contracts, theater bookings, and commercial endorsements. And we had some very big shots — most notably, Wallis and our mega-agent at MCA, Lew Wasserman — very, very concerned.

Still, I'd come to the point where I couldn't take it anymore. The day after I got back to L.A., I marched into Lew's office and said, 'Please do something, anything, because I can't continue working this way.'

'What about Dean?' Lew asked. He was, after all, agent to both of us.

'How do I know?' I said. 'We don't talk to each other. Just get me out of my commitments and I'll be happy.'

'But, Jer — '

I cut him off. And I didn't let up until Lew promised to hold a meeting with Paramount, and to tell Dean what I'd decided.

In the meantime, my partner (who was getting more press-savvy by the minute) answered me in the newspapers. On August 3, he told a UPI reporter, 'To me, this isn't a love affair. This is big business. I think it's ridiculous for the boy to

He just wouldn't shut up.

brush aside such beautiful contracts.'

Again with 'the boy.' I was going to be thirty in a few months, for Christ's sake! Anyway, I got my meeting, all right, and I didn't have to wait for Lew Wasserman to tell Dean what I'd decided — Dean was right there. The parley took place on Monday morning, August 8, in Y. Frank Freeman's office at Paramount, and besides Y. Frank and Martin and Lewis, Lew, Wallis, and our lawyer, Joe Ross, were all present. Another heavy sit-down at Paramount, and, once again, very serious business.

It was the first time Dean and I had seen each other in over two months, since before our separate trips to Hawaii and the Catskills. There was no hugging. I eyed him warily, but he was all smiles and cool assurance. I knew there was something cooking under there, but I also knew my partner well enough to realize that he'd be damned if he was going to show any weakness to *me*.

We sat around a big conference table, and while Y. Frank's secretary, Sydney, filled our water glasses — for some reason, my mouth was very dry — Y. Frank and Lew and Wallis and Joe proceeded, one after another, to explain to us just how inextricably tied up the two of us were, with our contracts and with each other. After a while their voices turned into a hum in my head that repeated the same message over and over: *You're stuck, boy — stuck good and proper. For now, anyway.* As the businessmen talked, I kept stealing glances over at Dean, who was squinting coolly in his cigarette smoke. He hadn't touched his water.

Jack Keller announced to the press, and the press announced to the world, that Dean and I had reconciled. The truth, of course, was more complicated. My partner and I were beginning to speak to each other again, and my emotions were wildly mixed: On the one hand, I couldn't shake the childish hope that, just like a fairy tale, everything would be all better. On the other hand, I knew that Martin and Lewis's days were numbered. I thought of something that my dad had told me: 'You and Dean have been the greatest shooting star in the history of show business. Recognize that it tails off. But don't wait until it's gone before deciding, 'Well, let's do something.' Uh-uh. You gotta do it while the star is still cresting.'

★ ★ ★

You want to see brilliant faking with a not-so-subtle psychological subtext? Watch the *Colgate Comedy Hour* we did that September, where I play a goofy quiz-show contestant who has to be isolated in a tank of water so he won't hear the answers. Dean, of course, is the master of ceremonies, and *he keeps pushing my head under water.* He won't stop! Could he possibly be getting some sadistic pleasure from this? 'Wait,' I finally say, bobbing up and gasping for air. 'Haven't you heard? The feud is over!'

The studio audience screamed with laughter.

There was another reason the two of us were stuck together. Soon after I had returned from the Brown's fiasco, I'd been met with more bad news: a letter from the Internal Revenue Service using the very attention-getting phrase 'tax evasion.' The IRS claimed that Dean and I owed them $650,000 in back taxes. And unfortunately, when I had my accountants check and double-check the matter, it turned out that the IRS was right.

The timing couldn't have been worse. Despite the money that was rolling in, almost all of it was rolling right back out again: Both Dean and I were running very high overheads — mansions, servants, cars, offices, staffs — and I knew that neither of us had that kind of cash lying around.

Moreover, we were not really speaking to each other.

So I did the only thing I could think of: I went to Y. Frank Freeman for help.

The 'Y' stood for Young, and Y. Frank was from a fine old Atlanta family that had managed to hold on to its money. How a well-off and cultivated Georgia boy had managed to find his way west and make good in the motion-picture business is a saga in itself. In fact, along with four other men, including his East Coast counterpart, Barney Balaban, and founder and chairman Adolph Zukor, he ran Paramount Studios.

Y. Frank Freeman was like no studio executive I had ever met or have encountered since: He was a white-haired gentleman of the old school, who lived by the principle that a man's word is his bond. In a town full of sharks, he actually believed in the handshake. Since our first days with Hal Wallis, I'd shaken hands with Y. Frank on a number of York Productions matters that, at any other studio, would have kept squadrons of lawyers busy for weeks. The suits at Paramount would have loved to get thousands of pages in ironclad legalese holding Martin and Lewis to account if we did anything that even smelled as if it conflicted with the studio's interests. But Y. Frank trusted us because I shook his hand, and Dean and I did nothing to abuse that trust.

Y. Frank and I had a special relationship, one I was very careful to nourish and protect. He allowed me to enter his office whenever I wanted, no appointment necessary, through a private entrance that opened onto the back lot. When he was entangled in business that had nothing to do with me, I could always see it in his face. 'Not now, Y. Frank?' I'd say.

'Give me fifteen and come back,' he'd answer.

A lot of the time, Y. Frank and I would just sit in his office and rap about the industry and the people in it. And more than once he expressed his displeasure with Bing Crosby, who was a very closed man, even with his sons. I always thought Bing was so insecure that he had no fun, and a man that can't have fun can't have love.

But back to our tax problem. After exhausting

all other possibilities (including the fantasy of approaching Hal Wallis for a loan, which I instantly realized was insane), I went to see Y. Frank. Knowing that I had a short break from shooting and was due back on the set, he was waiting for me in his office. The moment I sat down, he could tell from my body language that I was in some kind of trouble.

'Nothing can be that bad, Jerry!' he said.

'I'm afraid this one is, Mr. Freeman,' I said.

He smiled. 'Mr. Freeman?' he said, in those wonderfully warm Southern tones. 'What happened to 'Y. Frank'?'

'Excuse me, Y. Frank, but this is gonna be tough.'

'Just spit it out and get it over with,' he said kindly. 'I'm not about to bite you, son.'

And so I told him the story, and mentioned the amount that the IRS was demanding from Dean and me.

He whistled. 'That is a big number.'

'Yes, sir,' I said. 'It sure is.'

He frowned. 'Even though I'm positive that Martin and Lewis will be good for that amount and much more in the coming months, you know that Paramount Pictures Corporation has a policy — '

My heart was sinking. 'I see,' I said.

' — that has never been broken, making it impossible for any officer of the company to make a loan in dollars to anyone.' He frowned. 'That's strictly a corporate matter,' Y. Frank said. 'Nothing personal.'

'I understand.'

'Personally, though, I've always been impressed by the way you've honored your commitments.'

'Well, you know how much they mean to me, Y. Frank.'

He looked me in the eye. 'I tell you what I'm going to do, Jerry. I'm going to write you a check for the $650,000, as a personal loan from me to you — as long as you can tell me when you'll pay me back!'

Once I got my breath back, I said, 'Y. Frank, if you give me sixty days, which comes out to . . . let me see, September 13, 1955, at 3:55 p.m., I can pay you in full. And you have my personal guarantee that I *will* pay you in full, and it won't be one minute late.'

I knew we had percentages on our last four pictures coming in, equal to slightly more than the $650,000 — and Y. Frank knew it, too. 'I'll skip tea that day and be here waiting for you,' he said. Smiling, of course.

★   ★   ★

On September 13 at 3:30 p.m. I was in Y. Frank Freeman's outer office, waiting to be announced. I hadn't wanted to go in the back way. Sydney pushed the button on her intercom and said, 'Mr. Freeman,' but before she could utter another word, Y. Frank's voice came through the intercom speaker, saying, 'That must be Jerry Lewis. Have him come in!'

I entered the office, holding a certified check for $650,000.

'You're early,' he said.

'I'm sorry, Mr. Freeman, I know how busy you are.'

'It's twenty-five minutes till 3:55. Do you realize what kind of interest you can pick up in twenty-five minutes, Mr. Lewis?'

I was trying hard to keep a straight face. 'Would you please take this check so I can go back to work?'

He put his arm around my shoulders and looked me in the eye. 'Jerry, you did right. You kept your bond.'

'How did you know it was me out there, Y. Frank?' I asked.

He picked up his desk calendar and showed me the notation for September 13. 'Jerry Lewis here today at 3:55 p.m.' it read. 'I never doubted for a minute that you'd show up,' he told me.

★ ★ ★

A couple of weeks later, Mr. Freeman phoned me, sounding slightly embarrassed. 'Jerry, I don't mean to seem like I'm calling in a favor, but I could really use your help,' he said. He told me he was the chairman for a benefit to be given in early November at the Shrine Auditorium in Los Angeles for his pet charity, the City of Hope, an organization for under-privileged children. Would Dean and I be willing to perform?

Absolutely, I told him, knowing in my heart of hearts that Dean would agree to this — must agree to this — after the colossal hole Mr. Freeman had just dug us out of.

'How do I know, Mr. Lewis, that I can depend

on you and your partner to be there?' asked Y. Frank.

'Mr. Freeman, you can rest assured that Martin and Lewis will be at your benefit. Don't worry about it, we'll do your crappy little show.'

He laughed happily, but after we hung up, I started to get that feeling in the pit of my stomach again. It had only been four months since I'd agreed to something big without my partner's say-so, and look how that had turned out. When was I going to learn?

I ran over to Dean's dressing room on the Paramount lot. His smile when he opened the door was complicated: I could see affection, suspicion, and caution, all rolled into one expression. 'Hey, pal,' I said, 'I hate to okay this without your approval, but something important has come up.'

'Is it a contract?'

'Sort of.'

'Okay, then sign it. You'll do it anyhow.' The TV in the dressing room was on, of course — with a Western on, of course — and Dean sat back down, watching the screen.

'No, this is a little different,' I said. 'Y. Frank needs our help at the poor-children's benefit on November tenth.'

'Sure, he's got it.'

The answer had come too fast, too easily. His attention was divided. I sat in a chair next to his and spoke deliberately. 'Dean, hold on, now,' I said. 'This doesn't involve money or contracts. This is Y. Frank, the guy who kept our cars from getting repossessed. Do you understand what I'm saying?'

One eye was still on the TV screen. 'Hey, man — I told you. It's okay.'

'Well, I'm gonna ask you to do something for me so I can rest easy,' I said. 'I want you to stick your big grubby Italian paw in mine and agree that you'll do the benefit for Y. Frank.'

And Dean gave me that big hand, saying, 'Jerry, for Chrissakes, I know how important this is. You got it.'

I let out a big breath. It felt like the first time I'd relaxed in months.

★ ★ ★

It was Thursday afternoon, November 10, and I was starting to get my usual preperformance butterflies, part excitement, part nerves, only today there were more butterflies than usual, because my partner was off the radar screen. He wasn't in his dressing room, he wasn't at home, he didn't seem to be at the Lakeside Country Club. When we were on the road, I always knew exactly where Dean was, but when we were back in L.A., it was a very different story. He might have been anywhere at all — having a business meeting, driving in his car, engaging in a bit of hanky-panky. It was a big city.

And so I did the best I could, writing him a note reminding him about the benefit, and having three copies made. The original went by messenger to his dressing room at Paramount; the copies went to Jeannie, to Mack Gray, and to

Lakeside Country Club. I kept myself as busy as I could for the rest of the day, then drove down to the Shrine Auditorium.

There was no sign of Dean at the Auditorium, and it was looking like there wasn't going to be any. I *hoped* he would show up at the last minute, with a big smile on his face, telling me he'd just been taking a nap — but I *knew* that was the old days. The backstage loudspeaker blared: 'Martin and Lewis, you're on next!'

I rushed to the wings, where I stood next to Bing Crosby and watched along with him as Red Skelton tore down the house.

'Where's the sleepy one?' Bing asked.

I blinked and told a bald-faced lie. 'He's not well — he's at home,' I said.

'I wish Hope would do that!' Bing said.

Then Red was off, to huge applause, and the announcer was saying, 'Ladies and gentlemen, Dean Martin and Jerry Lewis!'

I walked out from the wings. I'd always gone on first, but never alone. And tonight I was alone and scared. *Just go on and do*, my brain told me. *Just go on and do.*

As I entered the spotlight, excitement began to replace some of my fear. I opened my mouth, and this is what came out: 'Good evening, ladies and gentlemen — I'm so glad to be here, and I wish I could share that with my partner, but I can't, because he isn't here. It happened about six-thirty this evening, while he was dressing — he was taken suddenly drunk!'

They shrieked with laughter. The more I did bits about his not being there, the more the people laughed . . . I wound up being a hit with fifteen minutes of ad lib that I had never even thought about.

Y. Frank phoned me the next morning and told me not to take it too hard. 'These things happen, Jerry,' he said. 'Don't worry about it.'

He was a gentleman to the end, but I knew I had let him down.

★   ★   ★

Dean was in his dressing room. I walked right in, fuming. 'You crossed me, Paul.'

'What are you talking about?'

'I'm talking about your *handshake*. You gave me your word that we'd do Y. Frank's benefit.'

'You're out of your mind. I don't know a thing about it.'

'Where were you last night?' I asked.

'When did my life become your business?'

'I didn't mean it that way. I mean, I sent notes to your dressing room, your wife, your valet, and your country club. So you mean to tell me you didn't know you were supposed to be at the Shrine at eight o'clock last night?'

Cool as could be: 'Nobody told me there was going to be a benefit.'

I was struck dumb. Meanwhile, he was going through the motions of looking for something to write on. Finally, he found a typed sheet of paper, turned it over, and started to scribble a note on the back. 'Listen, Jer,' he said. 'I need two prints of *Living It Up*. Could you handle that for me?'

He handed me the note. On the other side was the memo I had sent him.

15

I dream about Dean pretty often, maybe once a month since he died. In my dreams, he's almost always young, tan, still unbelievably handsome — indestructible. Sometimes, though, in these ultravivid late-night movies, bad things are happening — to him, to me, to both of us — and I'm powerless to stop them. Sometimes, my wife tells me, I cry out in my sleep. Other times, I dream I'm Super Jew, making everything right, doing all the things I might have done, when the pressures on us were so enormous.

Fortunately, my dreams mostly take me back to the beginning — like our time in Atlantic City, summer of '46. Dean and I, all of twenty-nine and twenty, are staying at the Princess, a block off the Boardwalk and a bit away from the fashionable district. Down the Boardwalk is the Million-Dollar Pier and the great hotels: The Ritz-Carlton. The Shelburne. The Marlborough-Blenheim. Names that drip diamonds! In our neck of the woods, the hotels have names like The Overlook Villa. The Pink Swan. The Aladdin. The Harem Arms.

During the day, before our shows at the 500 Club, Dean and I sit on the beach, hoping to sneak a tan so we won't need makeup — and anyway, to stay in our non-air-conditioned room would be like committing hara-kiri! There we are on the hot sand, hoping to catch a stray ocean breeze, praying that someone will go home and leave their umbrella. When they do, we're all set, perched like kings under the canvas, out of the July heat.

This was the time our wives, hot and lonely at home, decided to come down with the kids, meaning Dean and I would have eight mouths to feed between us, one little room to house all these people, and not much money to swing any of it. We agreed we had to tap our greatest — and as yet untested — resource: Dean's gambling ability.

In our travels up and down the beach, we had become exquisitely sensitive to the gradations of class in Atlantic City. The Ritz-Carlton, with its gorgeous beachfront restaurant and swimming pool, was the crème de la crème, and it hadn't escaped my partner's notice that many of the Ritz's high-rolling guests amused themselves by playing gin rummy on the beach in front of the hotel.

'I can take these guys, Jer!' Dean says, his eyes lighting up. 'All I need is a bankroll . . . '

So we make one. We pool our funds, a big $95 apiece, figuring that with $190 you're good for at least three hands. The games are Penny A Point, Hollywood, and Boxes, and if you know what you're doing, you can walk away with big bucks. And Dean knows what he's doing.

We get about seventy dollars in singles and a few twenties, and put it all together to make a wad big enough to choke a horse — one that, with the twenties on the outside, actually looks impressive. Dean knows exactly how to carry himself, just how to flash his cash without being too showy. And before I realize what's happening, he's sitting down to play some gin.

Three hours later, with a big grin on his face — and shaking hands all around, to make sure there are no hard feelings — he gets up from the table with sixteen hundred dollars.

Sixteen hundred! Christ, it would take us almost six weeks to make that kind of bread! Now we'll be able to take another room at the Princess to handle the wives and kiddies.

But Dean's ambitions go a lot higher than an extra room at the Princess. 'Now that we've got a little money in our pockets, why don't we go check out the Turf Club,' he tells me.

The Turf Club was a spiffy private establishment just off the main drag: You had to have a member invite you inside, and you had to have a jacket and a tie, not to mention at least $200 for tips. I tell Dean the tab alone will kill us, but he says that that kind of worrying is for chumps. So one night after our families arrive, having wangled an invitation from one of Dean's new friends, into the Turf Club we march with wives, children, bottles, and strollers, and ask the headwaiter for the best table in the house.

He stares at us for a moment, but after Dean slips him a twenty, he leads us to the perfect table. This is the night I learn how far you can get by greasing a palm.

Then I discover what Dean has known all along: The Turf Club is a gambling club. Dean and Betty and Patti and I are having drinks, and the children are behaving nicely, when Dean whispers, 'Come on, Jer. I'll show you the real world.'

As we glide up the stairs, leaving the families to order, I suddenly realize we are heading for trouble. And I swear as the Almighty looks down upon me, we aren't in that gambling hall for eight minutes before Dean has lost eleven hundred dollars at the craps table — and he hasn't even thrown the dice! When they finally come around to him, he whispers, 'Watch this, kid!'

Oh, I watch, all right, and I become ill before Dean even tosses the dice. We both know who runs this joint, and as funny as my partner and I might be, these guys have no sense of humor. Whatsoever. This is where they make their living. It isn't personal, *just business*!

Dean proceeds to throw three crap rolls, and we are officially out of funds.

He hands me the dice, only because he didn't seven out yet. So we're still alive — without a sou. My partner asks for a $500 marker — a loan from the house — and, because the pit boss knows who has invited us, Dean gets his chips. He lays $250 on the front line, and I throw the dice.

They come up seven. We win!

I throw another seven. We win again!

Now Dean puts a hundred on the hard eight — a sucker bet; you get eight to one if you throw two fours.

I throw two fours.

We win eight hundred bucks, plus the front line, which was three hundred. We now have eleven hundred again, and I can't lose. I throw a six. Dean bets it back, and I make the six. We win the six bet and the front line once more, and we collect more money than I ever knew existed anywhere in the world, or even Europe. Christ, we'll never have to work again!

We now have $3,700 of the house's money, and the pit bosses from all the other tables are crowding around. They're curious as much as anything else: They rarely see anyone throw nine passes and still stay at it! But they're nervous, too: They have absolutely no idea how to stop this crazy, screaming monkey and his handsome friend.

'Go for it!' Dean shouts.

'Yeah!' I answer. 'Let it roll!'

We're now getting close to the house limit, which is a thousand dollars a bet. Holy Christmas — I just threw a ten, made all the bets you can make on that tough number, and now I throw the ten right back . . . And all we can do is laugh, while the men around the table glare at me like IRS agents.

One hour and fifteen minutes later, we go to the cashier and collect $23,000 . . . all hundreds . . . hundreds . . . *hundreds*!

We pick up the wives and kids and check into the Ritz-Carlton for the night, in the biggest suite they have. We order up room service in spite of the fact that they all just ate. We order brandy, champagne, Cokes, chocolate milk . . . What a night! The eight of us are out of our minds with joy, though Gary is already asleep, and Craig and Claudia and Gail are well on the way.

And in the morning we head straight over to see Mike Schwartz, the crazy car dealer, who would make anyone any deal on the face of the earth. Dean and I have decided we are now going to be partners in travel. So we buy ourselves a brand-new 1946 Chrysler Town and Country sedan, with wood doors and roof rails, and a spiffier vehicle you have never seen! That night we park it in front of the 500 Club for all the world to see — but we're not telling Atlantic City anything it doesn't already know. In that town, at that time, word of mouth wasn't just about your nightclub performances. It spread even faster when you beat the Turf Club for over twenty G's!

A couple of nights later (the families have gone back home) it's showtime, and as Dean and I do our thing, we notice a few familiar faces at ringside. They just happen to belong to some of those pit bosses from the Turf Club. Just looking at the silly bastards that made them look like silly bastards. They don't want anything from us, just to get even. After our show, they invite us to sit down and have a drink. We oblige, happily, and laugh and drink till our midnight show. They stay for that one, too. We start changing the material so they don't get bored.

Before the night is over — having seen all *three shows* — they invite us for breakfast at the Turf Club. We understand it's in our best interests to accept. We go. We eat. It's 4:15 a.m. when Dean sits down at the blackjack table

— and proceeds to beat them again . . . for another $8,000. We tell the pit bosses we're tired and have to get to bed. They say they understand and invite us to come back — anytime!

At the hotel, we jump up and down on the beds, throwing hundred-dollar bills in the air, until the security man bangs on our door, shouting, 'Roseland Dance Hall is down the block, knock it off!' We hush, but can't stop laughing till we drop off to sleep.

Dawn comes at a terrible time in the night. Just when you're getting your best sleep, the sun shines on your face — meaning, time to get up! No, there were no blinds at the Princess: Sunup meant get up.

We've tried eyeshades. They don't work, only because when we see each other in them, we start calling each other 'Zorro.' Every once in a while, Dean drops his sophisticated pose and — just for a few moments — is downright silly. Clowning with those masks was one of those times.

Anyway, we now have a bank account that requires both our signatures! We've got about twenty-six grand left after paying five thousand for the Chrysler. Ten days pass, and Dean and I are discussing what to do with the money we have in the bank, when the answer comes to him like a shot.

'Why don't we do what the big guys do?' he says.

'Yeah, like what the big guys do, and what are we really talking about?' I say.

Dean explains to me that the only reason these

guys at the Turf Club have so much money is that they had so much to gamble in the first place. And now that we have so much money, why shouldn't we do the same?

I'm nervous that this won't fly, but I figure Dean's nine years older, he's been around the block a few times. He must be right. Right?

So we decide to go to the bank the next morning and draw out our money. (Bad idea? You bet, but who knew?) We get to the bank, close out the account, and ask for hundred-dollar bills! They give us 260 hundreds, and we race to the Turf Club — even though it's only 11:30 in the morning . . .

Up we drive in our Chrysler, ready to take on the world. Since it's before noon, none of the 'big boys' are around. We walk up to the blackjack table. We can't have been there more than fifteen minutes when all of a sudden the boys appear . . . wearing open shirts, sweaters; all caught off guard, apparently. But when they heard we were there, they knew their twenty-six grand had come home to roost.

We're served drinks and sandwiches, and Dean is on a roll. We win the first eight hands, and he starts pressing (increasing) the bets. And all of a sudden — miracle of miracles — the house limit has vanished. By the end of an hour, we've lost all the morning's winnings — as well as the $26,000. Plus Dean took a marker for $10,000.

Not all at once, of course. The house wouldn't give ten grand all at once. It's called Dribs and Drabs . . . or, in gambling parlance, Grind Him

280

Down ... Burn Him Out ... Chill the Sucker ...

As we're attempting to leave and check into the nearest ICU, the head pit boss cordially invites us to sit down in his office. Call him Mr. Cashman.

'Coffee, fellas?' Cashman says. 'Any refreshment?'

He looks at each of us. When speech isn't immediately forthcoming, he smiles. 'So,' he says. 'How do you fellas plan on paying off your marker for the total sum of ten thousand big ones?'

Dean's voice is practically a whisper. 'Well, we haven't exactly come to terms with that issue just yet,' he says. Meanwhile, I'm sitting there like Edgar Bergen left Charlie McCarthy alone on a stool.

Mr. Cashman shrugs. 'No big deal,' he says. 'When do you guys close at the 500 Club?'

Since I'm the heavy-duty businessman, I pipe up: 'Whenever we close, that's it!'

Cashman frowns. 'This isn't the time for funny, kid. I mean, you can't play off your marker working in two places at the same time.'

'You mean you want *us* to play here?' Dean asks. This is, I think, his first clue that we are actually heading into the big time. The Turf Club is upscale, heavyweight.

'Unless you have a better idea,' Cashman says. 'Like giving us the cash!'

'No, no,' Dean says quickly. 'We appreciate the chance to pay it off.'

Cashman smiles. He has a scary smile. '*Play* it

281

off,' he says. 'We'll give you guys five thousand a night for a Saturday and a Sunday night at two shows a night, and we'll be clean.'

Dean and I look at each other, realizing that's twenty-five hundred fuckin' bucks a show. Christ, we're only making $750 a week apiece at the 500 Club — a total of $1,500 between us, and we're doing twenty-one shows a week, which comes to about $74 a show. This man has just offered us $2,500 a show!

Cut to: Skinny D'Amato's office at the 500 Club. Same day.

Skinny listens while turning in his leather chair behind the desk he only sits at when there's trouble. 'According to the contract you guys signed, I got you exclusive for any work in and around Atlantic City for the next three years!'

The silence is deafening. Skinny sees our pain. Skinny is our friend, and now he proves it. 'I'll tell you what,' he says. 'You can play their gig, but just this once. I know these people, and I wouldn't want them angry at either one of you — or me.'

So we're broke again, but we have a car, and we're thrilled to think that we're going to headline at the Turf Club. Skinny was such a good friend that he allowed us to close on the Friday night of the weekend we promised Mr. Cashman.

And so comes the fateful Saturday. We rehearse all day, thrilled to learn that the Turf Club's orchestra is eleven men. A band of eleven musicians — as opposed to the 500's four. Fortunately, the leader of the Turf Club's orchestra is a great guy, and he writes us some charts that same day, so we're in good shape . . .

Until that night.

The joint is loaded with the cream of Atlantic City, all those people who have heard about Martin and Lewis but wouldn't go to Missouri Avenue to see them. This is an audience that waits until you come to them, and nothing has changed over all the years. The venue doesn't matter; these people lurk around show business because it's the thing to do. Not to enjoy themselves, but to see and be seen. It's like owning a twenty-carat diamond ring and hating the weight of it, but loving people to look.

Well, we had them all that night. They're so stiff, they have to be propped up in their seats. The average age is deceased . . . (That's where the joke comes from — either the Turf Club or West Palm Beach, take your pick.)

Dean and I have no idea what has hit us. All you hear is a cricket when there should be applause. Dean sings his little heart out, and they talk through his songs. They watch me a little because I remind them of their grandkids, but they hardly laugh. For about an hour and a quarter we struggle. This isn't worth twenty-five thousand, let alone twenty-five hundred.

As we're sitting in our dressing room after the first show, a lightbulb goes on over my head. 'There's nothing in our agreement that stipulates how much time we do,' the Jew tells the Italian. 'Let's get even, and they'll never know the difference.'

We go out there, Dean does two songs, I start

our bits rolling back and forth, and before you know it — we've been on about thirty-five minutes — we close the show with a song and get off.

And the audience is ecstatic, because they're so old, they can't wait to go home and go to sleep. And the big boys are even happier, because while the show is on, nobody gambles!

★ ★ ★

The saddest thing in life is that the good times, no matter how good and no matter how long they last, always come to an end. And so my thoughts return to the winter of 1955–56, when Dean and I shot *Pardners*, in Phoenix, where the weather was almost as miserable as our relationship.

Silence. Coldness. And the worst thing for me: dishonesty. When things were good with my partner, what we had was Truth. When we were clicking on all cylinders, the joy and the wildness — the very things that really got to people — came straight from our hearts. People knew it and could feel it, which sent them to our movies — where, even in the best of conditions, the joy and wildness got freeze-dried. Between the script, makeup, setups, lighting, and multiple takes, the spontaneity (which was the essence of our work) tended to wither.

In the worst of conditions — like Phoenix in the winter of '55–'56 — not only was the spontaneity missing, so was any semblance of fun or joy. Both Dean and I had become cynical and tough. Unpleasant to be around. Unpleasant even to ourselves. My memories of shooting *Pardners* are of a seemingly endless parade of cold and rainy days, only occasionally relieved by the sun that allowed us to shoot. And then of doing my best to make funny faces under my ten-gallon hat. When I'd catch my partner's eye — or try to — he would be staring over my shoulder.

The best thing about *Pardners*, for Dean, was — after having been in love with Westerns all his life — he was actually starring in one. If he could have known then that in only four years he'd be making *Rio Bravo* with John Wayne, he would have been in heaven.

Dean and me and two Star Search losers.

285

The best thing for me was learning, from a man named Arvo Ojala, to quick-draw and twirl a pistol, two skills I would eventually develop to world-class levels. (In fact, I don't mind telling you that I was the fastest draw in Hollywood — no small distinction when you're talking about the likes of Clint Eastwood, Jim Arness, and Duke Wayne. And the second fastest was . . . are you ready? Sammy Davis Jr.)

The hardest thing about the picture was the crushing irony of Dean and me singing the film's title number, written by Jimmy Van Heusen and Sammy Cahn:

You and me, we'll always be pardners,
You and me, we'll always be friends . . .

But there was worse to come. Despite Jack Keller's best efforts, and those of the Paramount publicity department, rumors still abounded that Martin and Lewis were about to break up. And so the studio prevailed upon us to slap on a little coda, after 'THE END' came up on the screen. I yelled, 'We're not ready for 'The End' yet!' Then Dean and I drew our pistols and fired, shattering each letter as if it were glass. When we were done, we stepped out of character and spoke directly to the audience.

'We have something to say to you, right, Dean?' I said.

'We sure do, Jer. We want you folks to know we sure enjoyed workin' for ya, and we hope you enjoyed the picture.'

'Yeah, and we hope you'll keep coming to see

us, because we like seeing you.'

I've often wondered how movie audiences reacted to seeing that little epilogue on the day *Pardners* was released: July 25, 1956, the day after Martin and Lewis broke up.

16

In the mid-fifties, Don McGuire, who'd written the screenplay for *Three Ring Circus*, told me the legend of Damon and Pythias, friends so close that when Pythias was sentenced to death, Damon was willing to pledge his life as bail. That story fascinated me, reminding me of my friendship with Dean at the height of our partnership.

I asked Don to write a screenplay based on the legend, and he came up with what I thought was a terrific story: I would play a not-too-bright street kid named Sidney Pythias who gets mistaken for a criminal, and Dean would play Mike Damon, a cop who befriends and protects Sidney.

But when Dean saw the script, he was furious. 'Are you saying that I play a cop in this thing?'

'That's right,' I told him.

'In a uniform?'

'Of course.'

'No,' he said. 'All my life, I ran from cops who wore those goddamn uniforms. I won't play one. That's low class to me.'

I think Dean somehow feared that everyone in Steubenville would feel betrayed if he played a cop. But by now, I couldn't see beyond my exasperation. 'Then we'll have to get somebody else,' I said.

'Start looking.'

That was the last straw. Both Dean and I had built up such backlogs of fury that, short of going to see a couples counselor — something not too many comedy teams would have thought about in 1956 — we had no recourse but to vent at each other.

Which meant we had no recourse.

Dean, as we know, didn't vent. As for me, my partner loomed so large in my psyche that the idea of giving him both barrels was simply unthinkable.

Others around us got the brunt of our anger.

The two of us had remained civil during the shooting of *Pardners*, but mainly because that picture was for York Productions, our own company. Now we were about to start work on our sixteenth film, *Hollywood or Bust*, with Hal Wallis producing (and Frank Tashlin directing), and neither one of us was about to treat Wallis or his movie with kid gloves.

I was (by far) the worse offender. Dean's modus operandi was distance. Me, I'd stick around and get right in people's faces. Especially if they were people I could push around. It's not a pretty thing to admit, but I was a bully in those days. And on the shoot of *Hollywood or Bust*, I'll be the first one to tell you, I was officially off the rails.

My emotions were all over the place: One minute I'd be mad as hell at my partner, the next I'd be hoping against hope for a reconciliation. The result was that I paid almost no attention to what I was doing. I barely bothered to learn my lines. I came up with unfunny ad libs that threw off the rhythm and the schedule of the shoot. After every take, I'd pace around the set grumbling, 'That scene is shit' — when I was the one who had messed it up. I constantly picked fights: with Wallis, with most of the cast and crew.

Except Dean.

I see now that he was the one I was really trying to get to, but Dean was not about to let anyone, even me — especially me — get to him.

And (of course) the cooler he acted, the madder it made me.

I had one brief scene with Slapsy Maxie Rosenbloom, the former prizefighter and Holly-wood character who had given his name to the L.A. nightclub. The scene should have taken half a morning; I made it last three days, hitting Wallis where it hurt him most: the checkbook. I sprinkled obscenities into every take; I made fun of Maxie for being punch-drunk. He had the good grace not to put my lights out.

But the person who took most of the heat from me was poor Frank Tashlin. I was doing my level best to make Wallis's life miserable, but he didn't have to be on the set every day. Tish did. For six weeks I gave him crap, challenging his directions like a surly adolescent. Astonishingly, Frank took it all in stride. It was everyone else on the production who got upset. And after a while, it didn't matter that Tish could stay cool. His cast and crew were suffering, and that meant Frank had a big problem on his hands. Control is always the issue with a director. Once he loses it, his production is in trouble.

One afternoon, Frank reached his limit. I was starting to disagree, loudly, about a scene we were about to shoot, when he stopped the production. He called the crew around, then pointed his finger at me.

'I want you off the set,' he said.

'You what?'

'I mean it, Jerry. Off! You're a discourteous, obnoxious prick — an embarrassment to me and a disgrace to the profession.'

Everybody on that sound stage was staring at me. I blushed to the roots of my hair. 'Hey, Tish, whoa — calm down. When did you get the right — '

'Jerry, as director of this picture, I order you to leave. Go. Get your ass out of here and don't come back.'

That walk off the set and out to my car was the longest of my life. I drove home in a daze, lay on a couch in my den for hours, staring at the ceiling, wet-cheeked with self-pity, trying to figure out how I'd gotten myself into this mess.

That night I called Tish at home. He wouldn't come to the phone. I kept calling back. At last he picked up. 'Yes, what is it?'

'Tish, I'm sorry. I can't tell you how sorry I am. I was wrong. All I ask is, please, let me come back.'

He thought about it for a moment. 'Will you behave?'

I gave him my solemn promise that I would.

'Okay,' he said. 'Report to work in the

morning. The shoot is at seven o'clock.'

'I'll be there at six. And Tish . . . thanks.'

'For what?'

'I don't know, maybe for saving my life.'

★ ★ ★

I behaved. I did whatever Tish told me. The set calmed down, and the cast and crew stopped looking miserable. What didn't change was the relationship between Dean and me. It had ended. Outside of the lines we spoke to each other in the script, we weren't talking at all. Just try doing comedy with someone when you're not on speaking terms. As the two of us passed each other on the sound stage, or on the way to our cars after work, our eyes never met. Oh, we were cool. Tough and manly.

For Dean, this was business as usual. Whatever mixed feelings he had for me, his habit of not letting his emotions show — even to himself — kept him from feeling his own pain, which I have to believe was on a level with my own.

And while I don't want to glorify my own anguish, I really was suffering. My partner's aloofness (and the effort of pretending to be cool, myself) hurt so much it affected me physically.

On Friday night, May 18, I was toastmaster at a Screen Actors Guild dinner for Jean Hersholt, the actor turned humanitarian, who was dying of cancer. Between the gravity of the occasion and the stress in my own life, I was able to strike the right note. The dinner badly needed laughs

— and not from the Idiot, but the thirty-year-old Jerry Lewis. I respected Mr. Hersholt, and the audience approved.

Afterward, as I walked out to my car, I was struck by a wave of intense nausea. I took a deep breath and it passed. Probably just the rubber roast beef I'd eaten.

But when I walked in the door, Patti looked alarmed. 'What's wrong? You're as pale as a ghost.'

I shrugged it off, but all at once my legs turned to rubber. I sat down, breathing hard. My chest hurt like a son of a bitch.

'I'm calling Dr. Levy,' Patti said.

An ambulance took me to Mount Sinai Hospital, where my physician, Dr. Marvin Levy, ran a battery of tests and found that the heart attack he'd feared was in fact just an arrhythmia. Dr. Levy, who knew me — and what was going on in my life — very well, said that what I'd suffered was probably a reaction to all the fury I was holding inside.

He looked me in the eye. 'I'm gonna write you a prescription,' he told me. 'Do a single.'

⋆ ⋆ ⋆

The only sound under the oxygen tent was the hypnotic hiss of the life-giving pump. The tent itself was made of thin plastic, translucent but not transparent, and when I saw a shadow flicker across the surface, I knew someone had come into the room, but I had no idea who it was.

Could it be — the wild fantasy actually

crossed my mind for a second — my partner?

The tent had a flap in it so the doctors could check my vital signs or the nurse could hand me a drink. Suddenly, the flap opened. It was my dad.

'Jerry, what happened to you?'

I was in a haze of painkillers. 'Nothing,' I told him. 'Getting a tan.'

He pushed his face in closer to mine. 'Do you know what you're doing to your mother?'

★ ★ ★

Ten days later, I was back at work, feeling like a different man. My frightening episode had made me realize that something simply had to change between Dean and me: We couldn't go on this way. So one afternoon on the lot, I took a deep breath and walked right up to him.

'I've got to talk to you.'

'Talk.'

'You know, it's a hell of a thing,' I said. 'All I can think of is that what we do is not very important. Any two guys could have done it. But even the best of them wouldn't have had what made us as big as we are.'

'Yeah? What's that?'

'Well, I think it's the love that we had — that we still have — for each other.'

He half-closed his eyes, gazing downward for what felt like a long time. Then he looked me square in the face. 'You can talk about love all you want,' Dean said. 'To me, you're nothing but a fucking dollar sign.'

*   *   *

Put it in context. He was as hurt as I was that the partnership was coming to an end. The writing was on the wall, the ink was dry. Martin and Lewis were going to be no more.

So Dean needed to lash out. He was furious because I couldn't fix it, and at the same time, he didn't *want* it fixed. People around him were saying, 'Get on with it; you don't *need* him; you'll be better without him.'

And as hurt as I was — and believe me, Dean couldn't have hurt me any worse if he'd kicked me in the nuts — I too needed to take my work somewhere new, and I had to go there by myself. Terrifying.

But at the time, all I knew was that my heart was broken.

*   *   *

On June 7, Dean had a party for his thirty-ninth birthday at L'Escoffier, a fancy restaurant on the eighth floor of the new Beverly Hilton hotel. Patti and I were not invited. On the fifteenth, Paramount held a preview of *Pardners* at a ranch north of Los Angeles: studio executives, publicity people, two hundred reporters, and me. No Dean. We waited and waited; finally, two hours late, he phoned in sick.

I'd like to tell you I suffered these injuries nobly, except it isn't true. Yes, I was heartsick, but I was also enraged. I went to Lew Wasserman and told him I wanted to cancel all our contracts, to formally dissolve Martin and Lewis.

I knew Warner Brothers had asked Dean to star opposite Doris Day in the movie version of *The Pajama Game*. I wanted to go ahead solo, at Paramount, with the Damon and Pythias project.

Lew responded like the master agent he was: cautiously. Still speaking of Dean and me as a team, he said, 'Here's your potential for the next year and a half: eleven million — apiece.' I tuned out while he detailed movie, television, night-club, and concert deals. Then there was a silence, and I tuned back in to see Lew staring at me through his big horn-rimmed glasses. 'Good heavens, Jerry, compromise. What in the world is perfect?'

But I knew I couldn't live with it, even though nothing is simple when a lot of people and money are involved. Y. Frank Freeman called Dean and me to a meeting at Paramount with Wallis and him. You could have cut the atmosphere with a knife. Thank God for Mr. Freeman's warmth and good manners. If he hadn't been there, the three of us might have killed one another. Y. Frank told us that Paramount president Barney Balaban was ready to release us from our contract. Hal Wallis, on the other hand, was ready for no such thing.

Our agreement with Wallis stipulated that we work as a team no matter who was producing the picture, and he was adamant we abide by the contract. Y. Frank reasoned with him. 'For heaven's sake, Hal,' he said. 'These boys both want to stretch their wings. Can you blame them?'

Amazingly, Wallis gave in — a little. He said he'd let us do one picture apart if we did three more for him as a team. If we wanted to get out of that, he told us, it would cost us. Big: a million and a half dollars, plus ten percent of the money we'd earned on our last two movies.

Meanwhile, our agents went to the suits at NBC, who also set our ransom high. They would sign with us as individuals rather than a team, but at $5 million a year rather than $7.5 million. We would then owe the network thirty-four TV specials over the next five years, seventeen from each of us as a solo act.

A solo act. What on earth would that be?

With so many agents, lawyers, producers, and studio and network executives involved, it didn't take long for the news to leak to the press. On June 18, it was formally announced: Martin and Lewis were over.

The following day, we wrapped *Hollywood or Bust.* It's the single one of my movies that I've never seen, and never will.

★   ★   ★

Incredibly, we still had uncancellable obligations. We both had committed to attending the premiere of *Pardners* in Atlantic City at the end of June, and then, for old times' sake (and for Skinny D'Amato, who was in financial trouble), we were going to put our feelings on hold and do ten nights at the 500 Club.

297

Imagine — ten nights in Atlantic City with a partner I wasn't speaking to. Ten years after our shining beginning: same place, same time of year. Somehow we made it through those twenty shows, persuading the audiences to laugh without ever once exchanging a warm remark, a reminiscence — anything — when we were offstage. At one point, the *Today Show* interviewed us, live, at the Club. There's a kinescope of that segment, and it's painful to see: Dean and I can hardly bear to look at each other.

We stayed at the Ritz-Carlton. Naturally. Different suites, different floors. Naturally. I don't recall ever giving a thought to the Princess Hotel, if it was even still in business at that point.

In early July, we did a twenty-one-hour muscular dystrophy telethon, broadcast from Carnegie Hall by a local New York TV station. It was our final television appearance together. More songs, dancing, comedy. More silence between us.

And then the Copa.

* ★ ★ ★

In time-honored Copa tradition, we opened on a Thursday night — July 12, 1956. We would do three shows a night, seven nights a week, for a total of thirteen days, winding up on July 24, our tenth anniversary as a team.

We played to the same New York audiences that had always come to see us at the Copa, except now there was an extra electricity in the air, a morbid curiosity: 'Are they *really* going to split up?' When Dean accidentally stepped on my foot during some onstage horsing around, fracturing two of my toes, I let out a yell louder than an air-raid siren, and the Freudian-minded New York press had a field day.

'Was that *really* an accident?' somebody asked. 'Or has the feud turned physical?'

'Purely an accident,' I said (after counting to ten). 'Next question.'

And since everyone in New York takes a special pride in being in the know, the interest around those Copa shows built as the days passed toward our last performance together, ever. The club stopped taking reservations for the last three Martin and Lewis shows a week before we opened.

During that time, friends had told me the gossip going around Manhattan, in spite of the city's worldly facade, was touchingly hopeful. Otherwise sophisticated people just didn't want to believe that the two of us were really going to break up. 'Are they crazy? Look at the money they're making.' And 'How would they get along without one another?'

One night during that week, the National Children's Cancer Society held a benefit at the Versailles, a nightclub in the East Fifties, and Dean and I were invited to appear, between shows at the Copa, to do a brief performance. It was the last thing either of us felt like doing, but where children and cancer are concerned, how can you say no? So we went, and we acquitted ourselves like pros.

The comedian Joey Adams was the master of ceremonies. After we did a couple of numbers, he came out to take us off the stage. But then, instead of going on with the rest of the show, Joey called, over the applause, 'Hey! You guys come on back out here for just a minute!'

And so we did — Dean on Joey's right side and I on his left. Joey threw his arms around our shoulders. 'Ladies and gentlemen!' he shouted. 'Do we want these two men to split up?'

The audience rose to its feet, yelling: 'No! No! No!'

'Shouldn't they think about us — who love them?'

'Yes!' the people roared.

Dean was as embarrassed as I was. I quieted the crowd and took the mike from Joey. 'Thank you all very much,' I said. 'Thank you for your support, your love, and your loyalty. We both appreciate all you've done for us for these past ten years. *But* — ' And I stared out at the audience for a long moment.

'But,' I continued, 'just as Dean and I would not go to your home and try to talk you back into a marriage that wasn't working, we cannot allow anyone to alter what we have decided is best for us. Thank you and good night!'

The audience heard us. They knew Joey Adams's heart might have been in the right place, but even Mother Teresa can screw up if she lets her feelings get the better of her judgment.

When we reached the car that was waiting to take us back to the Copa, Dean actually spoke to me for the first time in weeks. 'You did that good, pal,' he said.

'Thanks,' I said, and then we were quiet. Very quiet.

★ ★ ★

Tuesday, July 24, 1956, was a mostly ordinary summer day in New York City. The Yanks were out of town, but the Brooklyn Dodgers beat Cincinnati 10–5 at Ebbets Field, and the New York Giants lost a squeaker to Milwaukee at the Polo Grounds. The morning dawned warm, gray, and muggy; a late-afternoon thundershower briefly broke the heat. If you were anywhere in the vicinity of the Plaza Hotel in the early evening — maybe taking a cooling-off stroll near the southern end of Central Park — you would have noticed a crowd starting to form at Fifth Avenue and Sixtieth Street. Several mounted policemen were on hand. The focus of the activity was the red awning of the Copacabana Club, at 10 East Sixtieth. By 7:30, the crowd was thick and pushy and excited, and the flashbulbs started to pop . . .

Nine hours later, I was lying in my hotel bed, my heart racing. I had just hung up the phone after speaking to my partner for the last time.

'*We had some good times, didn't we, Paul?*'

'*We sure did, kid.*'

'*I don't know where either of us is going from here, but I'll be carrying you in my heart wherever I go, because I love you.*'

'*I know. I love you too, Jer.*'

It was the first time he had ever said those words to me.

When I awoke on Wednesday afternoon, I understood how an amputee must feel.

★ ★ ★

About ten days later, Elvis Presley started shooting his first movie, *Love Me Tender*, at Paramount Studios. In April, he'd signed a seven-year deal with Hal Wallis, who knew as much about rock and roll as he did about comedy. Much like Martin and Lewis, Elvis — whom I later got to know when we were making movies on the same lot, and who was one of the nicest young men I ever met — would have a career that boomed because of — and in spite of — the lousy but very popular movies he made with Wallis.

America had someone new to scream over.

17

When Dean and I split up, there really were some very angry people in this country. It was as though we'd broken into their homes and disrupted a pleasurable routine. Well, the public didn't own us, so we had little or no feeling about what *our* pain was about to do to *them*. In truth, neither of us gave a shit.

As I said before, most of the people who had contracts with us worked things out — except Julie Podell, Mr. Tough Guy of the Copacabana.

Julie maintained he had a deal with Martin and Lewis, and *they would play his place*, either together or individually. He only cared about the Copa, probably because that's the way the Mob wanted it. He was just a gofer, but I never realized that until much later.

About a week after I got home from our last show, Podell sent a — let's call him a messenger — to my home in Bel Air.

It was early on a Sunday morning when I heard my front doorbell ring. Through the window, I could see my family, who had just piled into the car to go to church, driving out our gate. I opened the door to find a very well-dressed gentleman standing in front of me. He stuck out his hand and introduced himself. 'Hi, Jerry. I'm Bobby Brown-Eyes from New York.'

I shook his hand, as any gentleman would. 'All

the way from New York and so early!' I said. 'How can I help you?'

He looked a little embarrassed. 'Well, first I need you to know I don't like having to do this,' he told me. 'I mean, you've given me and my family years of laughs and great times, so this isn't exactly how I imagined I would meet up with you.'

It was evident he was struggling, and I tried to make him comfortable: 'Won't you come in?' I asked.

'No, no. I'd rather stay right here and say what I gotta say and go.'

I found this strange, but I chose to see how it played out. 'Okay, shoot,' I said.

Bad choice of words!

Bobby cleared his throat. 'Jerry, Julie Podell of the Copacabana Club said he wants you to know that he expects you to free up your schedule and play the Copa for him no later than September 21 — the first day of autumn, next month.'

I hadn't expected this. 'Wait a minute,' I began.

The man drew himself up and looked me in the eye. 'No, you wait a minute,' he said. 'Podell says you will play the Copa or he will disrupt this nice family you have, and you wouldn't want that, would you?' He cleared his throat again. 'Those were his words. I'm just the messenger.'

I was stunned. 'He said *what*?'

'Jerry, don't make me repeat it. You heard what I said. Now, have your people call Julie and get it resolved.' And he slapped his palms together like someone rubbing off dirt.

My mouth was hanging open. I was staggered — and furious. 'I hear you' was all I could say.

Without another word, Bobby nodded, stepped off the front porch, and got into a waiting limo. The big black car pulled through my gate and vanished into the quiet streets of Bel Air.

As I closed the door, I thought, *Okay — now's the time. I've heard for a decade: Anytime we can do something for you, will you please let us know?* So I did.

I called Chicago. More specifically, I called Tony Accardo, who had been the boss of bosses in the Windy City ever since Al Capone had gone away for good. As a young man, Tony had earned the nickname 'Joe Batters' for his skill with a baseball bat, and let's just say there were no baseballs involved. Reputation aside, I knew him as a kindly, quiet (but still imposing) man who lived in the most enormous mansion I had ever seen, complete with indoor pool, not one but two bowling alleys, elevators, pipe organ, and gold-plated bathroom fixtures. Dean and I once visited him there in the early fifties, because Mr. Accardo wanted his son and daughter to meet us (it was an invitation we couldn't refuse), and he'd had a warm spot for both of us ever since.

'It's good to hear from you, Jerry,' Tony said after I mentioned my recent visitor. 'I'm sorry it had to be this way.' He then asked me to tell him exactly what the messenger had said. That was easy: I remembered it word for word. Mr. Accardo was silent for a couple of seconds. Then he said, 'Forget about it!'

'But according to Podell — '

Joe Batters repeated what he'd just said, only more firmly: 'Forget about it! Now, get on with your life!'

I thanked him sincerely and hung up — but couldn't help still feeling uneasy about the whole thing . . . until a couple of days later, when I got a call from a very connected friend in Chicago.

'Hey, long time, buddy,' I said.

'Yeah, long time. Listen — I was told to touch base with you and let you know that the little problem in New York is solved, and you should have a good rest at home with your lovely family.'

'Thank you,' I said. 'And please extend my thanks to The Man.'

He said he would, and that was that.

P.S.: I *never* played the Copa without my partner!

★ ★ ★

Back in July, as things were winding to a close with us, Dean turned down the lead in Warner Brothers' movie version of *The Pajama Game*. We didn't speak about it — we weren't speaking about anything at the time — but here's what I believe was on his (and MCA's) mind: Warner's was offering him a big role opposite a big star, Doris Day, and I think Dean was tired of sharing the spotlight. What he really wanted was to establish himself as a leading man in his own right. So instead, shortly afterward, he signed with MGM to do a picture called *Ten Thousand Bedrooms*.

My first thought, when I heard about his new

I love being in the middle.

project, was to hope that the film would be great for him. If that sounds saintly, let me correct you. It was actually quite selfish. My reasoning was as follows: *If Dean falls on his ass, I will have guilt for the rest of my life, because I could have prevented it.*

How? Because the day that we had our big conclave at Paramount with Y. Frank Freeman and Hal Wallis, *Dean had been willing to go on with the act.* I was the one who pushed the breakup.

And now the word on the street in Hollywood — and Hollywood is a town where the word on the street always matters — was that I would do fine as a comic, director, and producer, but Dean was probably washed up. If you believed what the critics wrote, Dean was just a pretty good actor with a pleasant singing voice, period. If you believed the gossip, my ex-partner would fade gently into the sunset.

Regardless of the press, I was panicked: I felt incredibly alone and desperate. The fact that everyone around me seemed sure that I'd land on my feet made things worse. I didn't know what the fuck I was going to do.

It's hard to explain. Intellectually, I knew all the things I *could* do — knew where my talents and ambitions could take me. But in those midsummer weeks in 1956, I was unable to put one foot in front of the other with any confidence. I was completely unnerved to be alone, and the Podell episode hadn't done wonders for my peace of mind.

'You need a rest,' Patti told me. 'Let's go to the desert.'

It sounded good to me. So we headed off to Vegas, along with Jack Keller and his wife Emma, for a little fun and sun at the Sands. For a blessed few days I pretended to be someone else — someone without a care in the world. We played blackjack, we went to shows, we lay in the sun. For four days I totally stopped thinking about my career.

And it worked — I began to smile again. Sure, I knew that this was just a pause in the action, that the pressures would return. But I didn't care. I wasn't thinking about tomorrow.

On Monday, August 6, I was packing to go back home, when the phone rang. It was Sid Luft, Judy Garland's husband and manager.

'What's up, Sid?' I asked.

'Jerry, Judy's got a strep throat. She can't sing. Is there any way you could go on for her tonight at the Frontier?'

'Hey, I'd love to, Sid, but I'm practically on a plane — '

Sid Luft was a real charmer: He could have sold Popsicles to Eskimos. 'We're in trouble, Jerry. You can postpone the flight. Come on, kid, for old times' sake.'

And that's how I found myself on stage at the Frontier Hotel, in front of a thousand people who were very much expecting someone else, wearing the one dark-blue suit I'd brought with me and a pair of black socks I'd borrowed from Jack Keller. Judy was sitting in a chair at stage left, and once the audience laughed at my first remark — 'I don't look much like Judy, do I?' — my nerves settled and I found my groove. I did thirty-five or forty minutes of silly mischief, playing to her, because that's what I sensed the crowd wanted. There were a lot of complicated feelings in the house that night: The breakup was still a fresh wound, and the audience felt for me; they had also come out to see Judy Garland — but they *were* getting to see her, if not hear her, and they were also getting a surprise, a guy who hadn't done a single in ten years.

Yes, I'd played Y. Frank Freeman's benefit at the Shrine Auditorium alone, but that had been just fifteen minutes of ad lib. This was a full act, and unless you're a performer, you'll never understand what it feels like to go out in front of a big audience on a moment's notice to charm them for the better part of an hour. But somehow, it worked. The crowd at the Frontier loved the interplay between Judy and me (with those expressive features of hers, she could do more without saying a word than most performers could singing their hearts out). Inevitably, though, after around forty-five minutes, I felt myself running out of gas. So I turned to the conductor and said, 'How does Judy get off? What's her closer?'

' 'Rock-a-Bye,'' he said.

Thank you, God. You've given me what I needed. 'Rock-a-Bye Your Baby with a Dixie Melody' was one of Al Jolson's signature numbers, his showstopper, and my dad, who built his act around his Jolson impersonation, sang it all the time. I not only knew it by heart, but my key was close enough to Judy's that when the conductor hit the downbeat, I was ready to go.

I had so much adrenaline pumping through me that I barely thought about the fact that I hadn't sung on stage in twenty-five years. My previous solo had been 'Brother, Can You Spare a Dime?' at the President Hotel in Swan Lake, New York, in 1931 — at which time, as you'll recall, I was five years old.

Now I was thirty. I got down on one knee, just the way Jolson had, just the way my dad had, and sang with no mugging, no funny business. When I was done, the place exploded. I walked off the stage knowing I could make it on my own.

What happened next is a perfect illustration of the rule that when it comes to good luck, the best kind is the kind you make yourself. The reaction to my singing had been so strong that two weeks later, thinking *Why not?*, I went to Capitol and asked them if they'd be interested in cutting an album of me singing standards, straight.

Was that bold of me? Egotistical? Sure it was. Capitol certainly thought so. They were friendly and polite, but brief and to the point: No, thank you.

So I took out my checkbook. I hired the conductor-arranger Buddy Bregman, paid for a forty-five-piece orchestra, and rented the same Capitol studio where Dean and I had recorded 'The Money Song' in 1948. What a difference eight years can make. This time around, I recorded four demo disks — including 'Rock-a-Bye' and another Jolson standard, 'Sitting on Top of the World.' The result sounded pretty damn good to me, and I took it to Capitol.

Again: Thanks, but no thanks.

Now, another man might have folded his tent, but I've always been a stubborn bastard. I shlepped my demos to the other record labels in town, and the people at Decca liked what they heard. If I recorded a half-dozen or so more songs, they told me, they would put out an album of me singing straight.

In September I recorded eight more songs, and in November, *Jerry Lewis Just Sings*, along with a single of 'Rock-a-Bye,' was in the stores.

I never expected what happened next: Both the album and the single hit the *Billboard* charts. The single rose as high as No. 10 and remained near the top for almost four months, eventually selling a million and a half copies. The album hit No. 3 on the LP charts.

Along with all the other hats I wore, I was now officially a singer.

I have no idea what was going through Dean's mind then, but I know this couldn't have been easy for him. Not one of his albums had ever made the charts, and only two of his singles, 'That's Amore' and 'Memories Are Made of This,' had done as well as 'Rock-a-Bye.' His most recent hit single, 'Watching the World Go By,' had only reached No. 83. Certain would-be humorists in the entertainment business had nicknamed my album 'Music to Get Even with Dean Martin By.'

I wasn't trying to get even. At the time, I thought I was just getting on with my life. *The Delicate Delinquent*, with Darren McGavin playing the cop role that Dean had refused, had wrapped in October, and I thought it was terrific. NBC and I were firming up an agreement for my first solo TV special in January. And on the strength of my surprise appearance at the Frontier, I suddenly had a lot of club dates lined up.

I won't kid you — the breakup was still much on my mind. I missed Dean like hell. But action is a great pain reliever: When you've got a lot going on, there's only so much time you can devote to introspection. The public, however, still didn't want to let go. And so when *Look* magazine came and interviewed me in January, I tried to be as thoughtful and honest as possible: about myself, about Dean, and about the two of us.

'As early as 1949, things began to be different,' I said in the piece. 'Dean divorced Betty and married his second wife, Jeanne, and suddenly our families weren't friendly anymore. As time went on, I grew to believe that Dean wasn't the strong, self-reliant character I thought he was, but, if anything, felt even more insecure than I. We both discovered that we were completely different in temperament and in our outlook. I don't blame Dean . . . it probably developed out of his tough childhood — but he was never as warm and outgoing as I hoped he'd be.'

That was definitely the hurt talking. I didn't feel I was being unfair, but Dean hit the roof.

Apparently, my mentioning Jeannie had set him off. 'Jerry was jealous of Jeannie,' he told a reporter. And: 'I respect other wives. I could talk about Patti and Jerry knows it, but I wouldn't.'

If my hurt could talk, so could Dean's. At the end of January, a new NBC TV show featured live coverage of a party at the Beverly Hilton. Dean was there, he'd had a couple of drinks, and the enterprising interviewer, seeing an opportunity to further stir things up between us, ambushed him. Dean finally vented some of his own feelings, saying some not very complimentary things about me and my artistic aspirations, and the press — having set him up for the fall — hit him hard for it afterward.

And then *Ten Thousand Bedrooms* came out.

The critics really killed Dean this time, and none more enthusiastically than his old nemesis at the *New York Times*, Bosley Crowther. 'More than a couple of vacancies are clearly apparent in this musical film,' he wrote. 'One is the emptiness alongside of Dean Martin, who plays the lead without his old partner, Jerry Lewis, and that's some emptiness indeed. Mr. Martin is a personable actor with a nice enough singing voice, but he's just another nice-looking crooner without his comical pal. Together the two made a mutually complementary team. Apart, Mr. Martin is a fellow with little humor and a modicum of charm.'

On one hand, this was just one more nasty critic giving Dean the same crap the critics always had given him, but this time Crowther was trying to finish Dean off. And unfortunately, he was right about the movie itself, which simply wasn't very good.

★ ★ ★

So 1957, the year Dean turned forty, was a tough one for him. They loved him at the Copa Room at the Sands, where he'd just signed a five-year contract. He would always have a home in Vegas. But that was only a few weeks out of the year. He had to let the rest of the country know who Dean Martin really was.

Still, I want to tell you something about who Dean really was. One night while he was on stage at a club in Pittsburgh, a rowdy fan yelled out something derogatory about me and Dean stopped the show. 'Sir,' he said, 'I want you to know that even though we've broken up, I have the greatest respect for Jerry.'

It put that audience in the palm of his hand. Almost fifty years later, it puts me in the palm of his hand, too. There he was, getting slammed by the critics — and still taking the high road.

That July I played ten nights, as a single, at the 500 Club. Skinny D'Amato's financial woes had worsened, and I wanted to do what I could for him. (Frank and Sammy, too, would both step in and help him out that summer.) But there I was again: July in Atlantic City — except that this time I was alone. It was a strange feeling. And strangest of all was how small and seedy Skinny's club looked to me now that I'd had a taste of the best. It seemed frozen in the past. But I kept my head in the right place, played my ten nights, and moved on.

I was on a kind of furious tear, a single-minded quest to become the King of Show Business, and over the next decade, to the degree that I succeeded, it was at great cost to myself and those close to me.

Then, at the end of 1957, Dean's solo career began to turn around. He would succeed beyond his wildest dreams.

Ed Simmons, who with Norman Lear had cowritten *The Colgate Comedy Hour* for us, had always been a big believer in Dean's comic skills. Now that Simmons and Lear had broken up themselves, Ed was looking for a new gig. So he went to Dean and offered to write some material for his nightclub act.

Dean's first reaction was 'I'm just gonna sing.' But Ed told him, bluntly, that everyone already knew him as a singer, and it wasn't enough — that image, by itself, fixed him in the past. *Just another nice-looking crooner* . . . .To really make his career take off, Ed insisted, Dean needed to continue being funny on stage.

Then Dean had a stroke of genius. Everyone knew he was going through a tough time — why not have a little fun with it? In our act, he'd often used a glass of apple juice as a prop, pretending it was Scotch. He'd also taught me the trick of keeping anyone who annoyed you at bay by making believe you've had a few. Suddenly, he put two and two together and came up with the shtick that would work for him till the end of his life: He would play a drunk on stage. 'Write me some stuff like that,' he told Simmons.

Simmons wrote it, Dean lent it his brilliance, and it was a smash hit. Dean went from being someone people liked to see at the Sands to being someone they *had* to see, everywhere. His nightclub bookings took off.

But then something even more important happened. In the aftermath of the breakup, Lew Wasserman and Herman Citron at MCA had decided to put all their efforts into making sure that, despite the word on the street, Dean wouldn't fail. *Ten Thousand Bedrooms* had largely been their doing, and they felt terrible about it. Now Citron had an idea about how to make Dean a serious movie star.

A couple of years earlier, Frank Sinatra's career had been in the dumper, too — and then he played Private Maggio in *From Here to Eternity* and won an Oscar. Now, in the summer of '57, a new World War II movie, *The Young Lions*, starring Marlon Brando and Montgomery Clift, was about to start shooting in Europe. There was a third major role in it — a devil-may-care former draft-dodger — that Citron felt was tailor-made for Dean.

There was only one problem: Tony Randall had already been signed to play the part.

Citron pled his case to the producer, and the producer brought the idea to Clift — who, as the box-office megastar of the moment, had creative control over the project. All Montgomery Clift knew about Dean was that he had been the straight man of Martin and Lewis. 'Good God, no!' he reportedly said.

317

Legend has it that Clift then went to see the latest Tony Randall movie, a light comedy, and decided that Tony had a brilliant future — in light comedy. *The Young Lions* was a very serious picture. Clift decided to give Dean a shot.

The role would pay less than Dean was earning for a week at the Sands. What's more, he was petrified at the thought of acting next to the great Brando and Clift. In the meantime, there had already been tension between the two hypersensitive Method actors. But then magic happened: When Dean flew to the film's location in France, his sense of humor and easygoing personality charmed his temperamental costars. Marlon and Monty recognized what a natural Dean was as an actor and fell all over themselves trying to charm him right back. The end result was that the three of them wound up getting along — well, like a charm. The tension between Clift and Brando evaporated, both did some of their best work, and Dean — helped by Clift's coaching — found depths in his acting that he'd never imagined.

The Young Lions was a critical smash when it premiered in the spring of 1958, but most notable was Dean's emergence as a brand-new acting talent. 'It's inevitable,' *Variety* said of Dean, 'that his performance . . . will be likened with what *From Here to Eternity* did for Sinatra.'

Take that, Bosley Crowther!

The Young Lions went on to become one of the biggest hits of the 1950s, and Dean's success in it gave him a whole new public image — as an actor to be reckoned with and a multitalented superstar.

He had also never stopped recording, though without a major hit. Maybe he just needed to get out of 1957. In January 1958, Dean recorded a new song called 'Return to Me.' In early April, the same week that *The Young Lions* opened, the song hit the *Billboard* charts, where it would remain for five months, rising as high as No. 4. In July, he would record another hit, 'Volare.'

When Dean opened at the Beachcomber in Miami that spring, *Billboard* wrote, 'If there's any doubt that Dean Martin can make it as a single, cast the doubt aside.'

The word on the street had shifted a hundred and eighty degrees: Dean Martin had a big, big future. And a big present. His first NBC special aired in late 1957, and the next year he was all over the small screen. Along with all his other successes, he was at the beginning of a brilliant TV career, one that would last for over a quarter of a century.

We had both made it — but only after causing each other a world of hurt.

* * *

Dean's association with Frank Sinatra, the partnership that would lead to the formation of the Rat Pack, began toward the end of 1958, when Frank called Dean and asked him to costar with him and Shirley MacLaine in a new movie called *Some Came Running*.

319

Frank and I had been friendly for years. We had great esteem for each other, but at the same time we never let it get too formal. I called him 'Wop'; he called me 'Jew.' (When Frank won the Oscar for *From Here to Eternity* in 1954, I wrestled him to the ground, in full view of the photographers outside the theater, and kissed him smack on the lips.)

With Dean and Frank, of course, it was very different. They admired each other enormously, but Dean had always kept him at the same slight distance he kept everybody. When Dean and I broke up, though, I think Frank decided that Dean needed some extra attention, and he actively sought Dean out.

I wasn't in on the phone conversation, but I can imagine roughly how it went. 'Hey, drunkard,' Frank would have said. (That was, and would remain, his nickname for Dean.) 'How's your bird?'

'Hey, pally. What's up?'

'How'd you like to do a picture with Shirley and me?'

'Sure — why not?'

And that's probably how Dean got to costar with Frank Sinatra and Shirley MacLaine in *Some Came Running*, the critical and box-office success about postwar, small-town America, based on the James Jones novel. Dean played Bama Dillert, a dying professional gambler — and a drunk. The role was tailor-made for him, but I noticed an interesting thing: Dean's Southern accent. He first had exaggerated his drawl for our act — it was partly an affectation, but it worked well with his stage role. In *Some Came Running*, though, he sounded as if he really did come from Alabama. It was perfect for him and for the movie.

Early the next year, along with John Wayne, Dean started shooting *Rio Bravo*, a Western directed by the great Howard Hawks. A Western, starring Wayne and Martin, and directed by Hawks. As I said before, Dean was now in movie heaven. As a drunken coward named Dude, he did his strongest acting ever — and got pretty damn good reviews, too.

But something else happened in early '59 that kicked Dean's personal and professional life into a whole new gear. Back in the mid-fifties, Frank had spent a lot of time hanging around with Humphrey Bogart, his wife Lauren Bacall, and a group of the couple's drinking buddies informally known as the Holmby Hills Rat Pack. (Dean and I had both been friends with Bogie and Betty Bacall, too, but I was never a drinker and Dean was never a joiner.) Besides Bogie, Betty, and Frank, the group included Judy Garland and Sid Luft, David Niven, Jimmy Van Heusen, and several others.

Frank idolized Bogie, and he was crushed when Bogart died of lung cancer in 1957. But Frank still loved the idea of the Rat Pack: He liked to drink, and he liked to hold court. Not long after Bogie's death, Frank started his own group: It included Van Heusen (who wrote some of Frank's greatest hits, like 'Come Fly With Me' and 'Love and Marriage'), Sammy Davis Jr., Peter Lawford, Joey Bishop, and Shirley

321

MacLaine. At first they called themselves the Clan, but that sounded a little too much like that other clan, the one that begins with a K, so they finally settled, as a tribute to Bogie, on the Rat Pack.

At first they all just drank and played cards. Sometimes they went out and raised a little hell. But Frank was having so much fun — these were his bachelor years — that he wanted to try and bring some of it to the stage. And meanwhile, he was courting Dean.

Dean hadn't changed. He still wasn't about to join any groups, and he still liked to turn in early at night. But he admired Frank, and after doing *Some Came Running*, Dean knew they worked well together. In early January, Frank conducted the orchestra for Dean's new album, *Sleep Warm*, and at the end of the month, the two of them performed together for the first time at the Sands.

A remarkable thing happened when Dean and Frank got on stage together. Among friends, Frank was a funny guy, a great talker and story-teller, but in the past, he'd never been able to convey his humor to his audiences. For most of his professional life, he had done no more than announce the title and the writer of his next song. Eventually, he might add, 'Rodgers and Hart — two nice men that I met, and they would love the way you people reacted to their song.'

Frank admired many things about Dean, but one of the biggest was Dean's ability to ad lib on stage. That drawl, that perfect timing — it struck Frank with the same kind of awe that Dean felt for Frank's phrasing with a song. Performing together felt like a perfect career move. And what happened the instant Dean and Frank stepped onto the stage at the Sands was that they did a version of Martin and Lewis, with Dean assuming my old role — the cutup, the wise guy (less physical, of course) — and Frank playing the straight man.

It worked beautifully. It let Frank be funny on stage, and it finally demonstrated to the world what a brilliant comic Dean was. He could do absolutely anything.

Dean still wasn't about to go out drinking and hell-raising with Frank and the others. But the act paved the way for him to get on stage with Frank, Sammy, Peter, and Joey. It wouldn't take long before the Rat Pack was complete.

★   ★   ★

If I was making a serious stab at being the King of Show Business, Dean was giving me a serious run for my money. I sure didn't have to feel guilty anymore. But I also sure missed him: We hadn't spoken in over two years, and if I'd known then that it would be eighteen years more, I don't think I would have survived.

18

Life moves along by its own mysterious sets of rules. By the mid-1960s. Dean and I were in totally separate orbits, in our work and our private lives. For seven years, Patti, our six sons, and I had been living in Louis B. Mayer's old house on St. Cloud Road in Bel Air. Dean, Jeannie, and their large brood lived in a big place on Mountain Drive in Beverly Hills, just a mile or two away. It might as well have been a hundred miles — our paths never crossed.

I'm sure many young fans were only vaguely aware that we'd once been a team. Dean had continued recording, building strength on strength: In 1964, the year the Beatles invaded America, he knocked them off the top of the charts with his hit 'Everybody Loves Somebody.' He'd also continued making movies — fun ones like *Ocean's Eleven* and *Robin and the 7 Hoods*, and, of course, Westerns, like *The Sons of Katie Elder*. Whether the pictures sank or swam, there was no denying he was a major international star. And after years of doing successful TV specials for NBC, in 1965 he signed a multimillion-dollar deal with the network to star in his own weekly series. In various incarnations, as *The Dean Martin Show*, *The Dean Martin Comedy Hour*, and *Dean Martin Celebrity Roasts*, it would become one of the most successful shows of all time, running until 1984.

Meanwhile, I was trying to concentrate on filmmaking. I made sixteen movies in the 1960s, and either produced, directed, or wrote (or did some combination of the three) on ten of them. Features like *The Bellboy, The Ladies' Man*, and *The Nutty Professor* were hits.

Television was more up and down. After a successful stint guesthosting on the *Tonight Show*, I tried a couple of series, a variety show, and a talk/variety show that didn't quite jell. And in 1965, the same year Dean's TV career soared to a new level, I suffered an on-air disaster.

I was doing a guest spot on *The Andy Williams Show*, with a dance number like a thousand dance numbers I'd done before. Andy Williams, his chorus girls, and me, all singing and high-stepping around the stage — except that all of a sudden I hit a little wet spot and went down like a ton of bricks.

Everyone around me figured I was just doing another one of my pratfalls — after all, I'd been throwing myself around on stage for a good twenty-five years. The director kept the tape rolling and I finished the number.

Then I went straight to the hospital.

I had not only fractured my skull, I'd also taken a chip out of my spinal column, and the results were disastrous: nausea, dizziness, double vision, and horrendous pain. The doctors put my neck in a metal brace and prescribed codeine and Empirin.

The pain got worse.

Over the next year, the doctors eventually told me, a fibrous knot built up around my spinal injury. The pain became constant and agonizing. The medicine they gave me didn't touch it. Heat and massage didn't help.

Then one of my doctors prescribed Percodan.

To my absolute astonishment, one pill made me feel like a human being again. The pain that had affected every waking moment, every interaction, suddenly receded, restoring my smile and leaving me free to think about all the things people normally think about. The pain was still there, of course, but in the background, always reminding me that it might come back full-force whenever it chose.

I didn't want any pain at all. And so, after a little while, I tried taking a second pill during the day. Bingo — no more pain! Suddenly, I was head over heels in love with Percodan. It felt like the best thing that had ever happened to me. But I couldn't help wondering: If two pills made me feel this good, what would happen if I took a third?

I felt even better.

The third pill had nothing to do with pain; it was all about elation. On three Percodans a day, in the mid- to late-sixties, I felt just the way I wanted to feel — a bit larger than life. Buoyant. Optimistic. Funny.

Then, little by little, the third pill wasn't doing it for me anymore. And so I took a fourth.

★　★　★

By the early seventies, I have to admit, Dean was not the first person on my mind. I knew he and

Jeannie had divorced in 1969, and I felt terrible about it. Jeannie and I had had our conflicts — we both loved the same man, after all! — but I still thought she was a great woman. I still think so. To this day, I believe she was the true love of Dean's life. The relationships he had afterward were all just flings.

But it was hard for me to concentrate on anyone else's problems but my own. I had a lot going on, and not much of it (with the exception of the Muscular Dystrophy Association Telethons and the film course I taught at USC) was good. For one thing, my son Gary, who'd had a successful recording career himself in the mid-sixties before enlisting in the Army and going to Vietnam, came back from the war a wreck, unable to sleep, unable to erase the horrible images of combat from his mind.

Then, in 1972, Frank Tashlin died. Later that year, my dad had a stroke.

Professionally, things weren't going much better. The kind of family films I'd been making for a quarter of a century was rapidly going out of style. I was losing my fan base: Kids were staying at home watching television, and a new sort of audience was coming to movie theaters, one that was more in the mood for sex and violence than comedy. Suddenly, I was having trouble financing my pictures. I made a serious Holocaust film called *The Day the Clown Cried* and lost two million dollars out of my own pocket when my producer skipped town, leaving me unable to finish postproduction. The movie has never been seen. It was like losing a child.

A couple of years earlier, I'd gone into business with a big company called Network Cinema Corporation to start a chain of Jerry Lewis Cinemas around the country. The theaters would only show G-rated pictures. But with the increasing scarcity of that kind of product, the cinemas were running into financial trouble. In 1973, a group of frustrated theater franchisees hit me with a $3 million lawsuit and won.

And then there was Percodan.

By the early seventies, I was up to six of the yellow beauties a day. I'd developed a whole ritual: I would take the first pill in the morning with hot water, believing that the heat and the liquid broke up the medicine and got it into my system faster. On a similar theory, I took the other pills, throughout the day, with Coca-Cola.

The pills kept me going, but there were physical repercussions you wouldn't even want to hear about, deeply embarrassing things. My marriage was sputtering. I was on a mood roller-coaster, most often headed straight down: When I wasn't furious, I could be mean as a snake.

On my twenty-ninth wedding anniversary, October 2, 1973, I felt I couldn't watch the red second hand go around the clock face one more time. I locked myself into my bathroom, took a .38 pistol out of a padlocked drawer, and stuck the barrel in my mouth. I cocked the hammer. I was ready to go. All the pain, all my troubles, would vanish. I sat there like that for what felt like forever. Then, through the door, I heard my boys, running and playing somewhere off in the house. I took the gun out of my mouth and locked it back in the drawer. I would struggle along somehow.

But there was still plenty of pain to come.

My career was down to two things: the Telethon and personal appearances. While I was on the road, I would often tip a hotel bellboy to come into my room in the morning with a passkey, crush three Percodans in a spoon, and dissolve them in hot water so I could take them and get my day started. I'd lie in bed for twenty minutes until the medicine kicked in, then I'd get up and pop a Dexadrine.

The funny thing was that performing was its own drug. It remains true to this day. No matter how shitty I feel when I get out of bed in the morning, the moment I step onto a stage, the adrenaline takes over. Back then, I would often avoid taking the Percodans before I performed, so my head would stay relatively clear and my timing would be sharper.

After I got off the stage, it was another story.

While I did a number of shows drug-free in those days, there was such a thick haze of Percodan before and after that it's hard for me to remember them. In fact, I'm ashamed to say that there's an entire block of MDA Telethons — some four or five years in the mid- and late-seventies — that I have no recollection of whatsoever.

Except one.

★ ★ ★

329

I was on stage at the Sahara in Vegas, doing 'Telethon '76,' for the greatest cause on the planet (of course, I'm prejudiced). As I was singing 'Rock-a-Bye Your Baby with a Dixie Melody,' I found myself thinking, *Why do I feel something's about to happen?*

I finished the number and introduced Frank Sinatra, who came on to a standing ovation . . . just for being there. He sang a couple of songs and stopped the show cold — as he always did. Then Frank and I talked about his healthy grandchildren, and he made a five-thousand-dollar contribution to the Telethon. While I was thanking him, he interrupted, saying, 'I have a friend who watches what you do here every year and thinks it's terrific. I'd like to have him come out.' Frank then yelled, 'Hey, send my friend out here, will ya?'

And out walked Dean Martin, my partner, and I was in a time warp. My hands got sweaty, my mouth turned dry. I tried to stand tall as he approached me, and we hugged hard, very hard. He kissed me on the cheek, and I did the same to him. The audience in the theater was going wild! For the first time in twenty years, we stood side by side — as always, Dean stage right, me stage left. 'I think it's about time, don't you?' Frank said. The two of us nodded *yes* in tandem. We talked . . . a little. I prayed to God for something to say that wouldn't make me sound like an emotional idiot.

'You workin'?' I finally asked, looking directly into Dean's eyes.

★   ★   ★

I wish I could say Dean and I reconnected then and there, but it took a little while. I had to get my own house in order first. My spine pain was like an insatiable monster. I was living in a private world of agony and addiction, and my family saw me — when they saw me — at my worst. I kept those who had been nearest to me at the greatest distance, and some permanent emotional scars formed. My long-suffering wife suffered the most. My boys came a close second.

Meanwhile, I traveled around the world, not just performing but also seeking out doctors of every description, trying to find one who could bring me some relief. A famous surgeon said he'd be glad to operate on me, but that there was a good chance I'd get worse instead of better after the procedure, and a 50 percent chance that I'd be paralyzed for life. I've always liked to gamble, but I didn't like those odds.

It seemed as though there was no way out. I don't even like to think about the desperation I was feeling by 1978, when I was up to thirteen Percodans a day. Even hardened survivors of drug addiction get wide-eyed when they hear that number. My self-medication was a full-out assault on my internal organs.

Then fate stepped in, with a little sleight of hand. I've always liked magic tricks — the key is getting the audience to look one place while the trick happens somewhere else. It was a bit like that in my case: God played a card trick.

One night at the end of September, I was at

PAUL KAMMET

Friendship is priceless.

the Sahara in Vegas, talking with the hotel's music director, my pal Jack Eglash. Jack had always suffered from migraines, but that night he had a particularly incapacitating one. I got an idea. 'Well, Jack,' I told him, 'you should have a specialist check you out. As a matter of fact, there's a top medical team at Methodist Hospital in Houston. I can call and make the arrangements.'

'Forget it,' Jack said. 'I'm scared to death of doctors. And hospitals.'

But I'm a stubborn SOB, and for whatever reason, Jack's case got me going. The next day, I phoned the world-famous heart surgeon Dr. Michael DeBakey at Methodist Hospital. Michael had been a member of the MDA Scientific Advisory Committee since 1970, and over that time he'd also become my best friend. I talked with him at length about Jack's condition, and Michael felt he ought to be seen. I had a room set aside for him at the hospital.

Jack dug his heels in. 'I'm sorry, Jerry. I can't do it. I'm not going.'

'Jack, Dr. DeBakey has a team of specialists waiting. Don't be a baby. I'll take you there myself.'

We were in Houston the next day. Jack was in his hospital room, getting a workup, and Michael DeBakey, his assistant, and I were headed down the hall to see him when I keeled over.

I came to in a hospital bed just a few doors down from Jack. Dr. DeBakey thought I'd had a heart attack — the pain in my stomach and chest was excruciating — but tests soon ruled out a coronary. When they X-rayed me, they found an ulcer the size of a lemon in my abdomen. The Percodan had masked the pain as the ulcer grew. Michael said that if it had remained undetected, I probably would have bled to death in two weeks.

Jack went home, but I stayed. When Michael sat down and talked to me about my condition, I fessed up about my addiction. He knew I'd been taking Percodan, but he'd thought it was two or three pills a day. When he heard what I'd actually been swallowing, he knew we had two goals: to eliminate the ulcer, and to kill the monkey on my back. Dr. DeBakey put me under heavy sedation, with a drip feeding me liquid nourishment, and gave me periodic steroid injections for the spinal pain. I lived in a twilight state for the next ten days as my blood circulated through an instrument and came back clean. When I woke up, my ulcer was gone and so was my addiction.

There was one important thing, Michael DeBakey told me: Coke and Percodan, he explained, were the same to me as coffee and cigarettes were to many smokers — inextricably bound, one triggering the need for the other. I must never let Coca-Cola pass my lips again. My dentist was delighted.

★ ★ ★

The following year, I was able to go back to moviemaking for the first time in almost a decade. The picture was called *Hardly Working*.

We shot it in Florida, and the whole experience was a very mixed bag. I directed, cowrote, and starred, and I have to admit that the awful strain of the past ten years showed in every part of my work. The movie didn't really hang together, and not so surprisingly, I looked terrible in it.

Still, *Hardly Working* had some good moments onscreen and off. When the film was released in Europe, it turned out that audiences had missed me: They bought $25 million worth of tickets. And once we were finally able to get a distributor in the States (it wasn't easy, because of how long it had been since my last picture), the critics, who had a field day putting the movie down, were amazed to see it sell.

But the best thing that came out of *Hardly Working* was a little scene I did with a fresh-faced young dancer from North Carolina named Sandra Pitnick, nicknamed SanDee, or Sam. Out of that scene came a friendship, from that friendship came a relationship, and from that relationship came a new life. After Patti and I made the agonizing decision to bring our long and difficult marriage to an end, Sam and I became husband and wife in February 1983.

It was just a couple of weeks later that Sam and I went out to dinner in Beverly Hills with my manager Joey Stabile and his wife Claudia, who ran my office. The restaurant was La Famiglia, on Rodeo a couple of blocks north of Wilshire. We'd picked it out because we all felt like some Italian food. Who knew that it was Dean's favorite restaurant?

I spotted him the moment we'd been seated:

He was alone in a red-leather booth by the front door. After a moment, I caught his eye and waved. He waved back. I got up and walked over to his table.

My first reaction as I approached was a double take at how much Dean had aged. I know I was no Prince Charming, but my partner had always looked so magnificently handsome and youthful. He was about to turn sixty-six. There are young sixty-sixes and old sixty-sixes, and Dean was definitely the latter. Whether it was the effects of the sun for all those years, or the accumulated sadnesses of his life, or just the genetic luck of the draw, I don't know. But it saddened me deeply.

'You workin'?' I said, putting on a brave smile.

He laughed at that, and it made him look younger. 'You wanna have a drink?' he asked.

'No, I don't drink,' I told him. 'I used to work with a guy that drank all the time and breathed on me — I've had all the booze I can take for one lifetime.'

He laughed again. It was all very playful. But at the same time, I felt that I was imposing on him. With age, his reserve had grown. (Mack Gray, the one man who was at all close to Dean in later years, had died in 1981.) Dean could have had almost anybody in the world in that booth with him — a gorgeous girl, Frank, anyone — but he truly wanted to be alone. I touched his arm, gave him a wink, and went back to my table.

Ten minutes later, a waiter brought over a champagne bucket, covered with a cloth napkin.

I finally went to hell.

'Compliments of Mr. Martin,' the waiter said.

I removed the napkin and saw six bottles of Diet Coke sitting on ice.

I laughed out loud, not just at the joke — it was classic Dean! — but with a kind of relief. He hadn't closed me out. I patted Sam on the hand. 'Come on,' I told her. 'I want you to meet him.'

She hesitated. Sam is deeply sympathetic to others' feelings, and that's just one of the reasons I'm so nuts about her. She didn't want to impose — on Dean's privacy, on my relationship with him.

But I felt strongly about this. 'Come,' I said. 'This is important to me.'

We walked over to his table. Just for a second, I went into the Idiot voice: 'Thank you for the lovely champagne.'

He laughed, and I had my opening. 'Paul, I want you to meet my wife, Sam.'

He looked up at her with a grin. 'I always knew you'd marry a guy.'

We all laughed. We stood there chatting for a couple of minutes, and it was nice, but once more I picked up on his wish to be by himself. We went back to our table.

I couldn't take my eyes off Dean after that. Staring across the restaurant, trying to get my mind around how much he had changed. A million images of the old days, when we were both kids, flashed through my brain . . . Christ! *Don't get old*, I thought.

What's the alternative?

As we ate, I watched him eat. It's a very strange thing to watch someone you know well eating alone. I tried my hardest not to be sad, but the feelings washed over me. One thing I did notice: Dean had an Old-Fashioned glass in front of him, and it sat there, full, for his whole meal. He never touched it.

Then, one day not long after that, I found — it both surprised me and didn't surprise me at all — that I missed him. So I called him up. As simple as that.

'Hey, Paul — how ya doin'?' I said, bright and chipper.

'Hey, pally. How are you?'

'What, you forgot my fuckin' name already?'

We had a few laughs, chatted for a few minutes. Nothing important — it was more about the music than the words. It was easy, and lovely, and it didn't last one second more than it had to.

So every couple of weeks afterward, I called him again. It went on that way for four years.

★   ★   ★

Dean had seven children, and he loved them all dearly, but Dean Paul Martin Jr., his second son and his first child with Jeannie, was the apple of his eye. Dino, as they called him, truly was a golden boy. Blond like his mother, and sharing both his parents' good looks, he was a talented musician (like my son Gary, he'd had a successful rock recording career in the mid-sixties) and a brilliant athlete — for a time he played tennis on the professional circuit. He also did some acting in the movies and on television;

still, it wasn't any picnic trying to succeed in that profession as Dean Martin's son. In his mid-thirties, Dino was working hard to make his own way in the world.

And Dean admired the hell out of that. He could tolerate very few people, and he admired almost nobody, but God, he looked up to that boy. To top it off, Dino was a captain in the Air National Guard: He flew jet fighters every weekend. To Dean, who wasn't crazy about air travel, that seemed amazingly brave.

On March 20, 1987, Dean Jr. was on maneuvers over the San Bernardino Mountains when his F4-C Phantom went off the radar screen. The wreckage of the plane was found five days later. Dino and his weapons officer had been flying into a blizzard in white-out conditions. When they lost radio contact with air-traffic control, they crashed into Mount Gorgonio.

I was playing at the Bally with Sammy when I heard about Dino's death. I immediately flew to L.A. for the funeral. I walked into the back of the church at the beginning of the service, and I stayed there. Dean didn't know I was present, and I didn't want him to.

Afterward, I said to Sam, 'Honey, it's just a matter of time. Dean's gone. That boy was the most important thing he had in his life.'

Early that evening, Greg Garrison, Dean's television producer and a friend of both of ours, phoned to say that he'd seen me at the funeral and told Dean. Greg said that Dean was so touched that I'd been there. What he didn't say, but what I understood, was how moved Dean had been that I'd come and gone in anonymity. Going unnoticed has never been my strong suit. But I felt it was a gesture I owed to both my partner and Dino.

Late that night, after my second show at Bally's — it was about 3 a.m. — the phone in my dressing room rang. The voice on the line was instantly recognizable.

'Hey, Jer.'

In our phone relationship of the last few years, I'd always been the one to place the call. That was just the way it went with Dean, and I never minded, but this night was very different.

We talked for an hour. He cried, I cried. I said, 'Life's too short, my friend. This is one of those things that God hands us, and we have to somehow go on with our lives. That's what Dino would have wanted.' I was trying to get him to see that he had to find a way to go forward. But all he kept saying was, 'Jer, I can't tell you.'

I wanted to get together with him, but I sensed Dean preferred talking on the phone, so I respected that. I called him whenever I could, as often as I could without feeling I was intruding. The conversations always began the same way.

'Hey, Paul, how you doin'?'

'How you doin', pally?'

'You *still* don't remember my fucking name?'

Now and then, he even laughed.

★   ★   ★

341

In the spring of 1989, I saw an announcement that Dean was going to play Bally's in Vegas. I was impressed: *He's found a way to go on*, I thought.

I stayed away, though, not even sneaking in to see him perform. I wanted him to have his own space.

Then one day I looked at my calendar and saw that it was June 6. The next day, unbelievably enough, would be my partner's seventy-second birthday.

I phoned Claudia Stabile and told her to buy the biggest and best cake she could possibly find, have it delivered to Bally's, and get somebody to guard it until I got there. We planned the whole thing with military precision. I found out what time Dean went on stage and arrived at the club a few minutes later. The management knew me well, of course; everyone was in on the plan, including Dean's conductor and pianist, Ken Lane.

I went backstage while Dean was on and watched him from the wings for around twenty minutes. He was wonderful. Ken had told me there was a certain point in the show when Dean bowed off and exited — stage right, as always. After that, Ken would play the introduction to the next number and Dean would come back out. This all went exactly as planned, except when Dean returned to the stage, Ken stopped the music and I yelled from the wings, 'How the hell long are you gonna stay on?'

Dean looked startled, turning toward the familiar voice, Ken cued the band into 'Happy

Birthday cake at Bally, 1989.

Birthday,' and I wheeled that giant cake out onto the stage. The place went apeshit.

'You surprised me,' Dean said. He held his arms out. His eyes were full of tears. I blinked hard, not wanting to start bawling in front of 1,500 people.

As we hugged, he said, loud enough for the audience to hear, 'I love you and I mean it.'

And this is what I said, also loud enough for everyone to hear: 'Here's to seventy-two years of joy you've given the world. Why we broke up, I'll never know.'

'Nuff said.

AFTERWORD: GOOD-BYE, HELLO

I heard the news flash while I was in Denver, on tour with *Damn Yankees*. The devastating bulletin came at 8:30 in the morning on Christmas Day. I was stunned, terrified, not believing any of it, and still knowing it was real. It had happened. I had lost my partner.

When I finally pulled myself together, I hired a private jet to fly to Los Angeles as soon as possible, to be with his family — and with *him*.

My four-year-old miracle daughter came home from school around 3:30 — and when I saw her face, the pain of the reality of that day shook me again. I hugged my Princess . . . thinking of the life we'd lost, but holding on to this new life. Danielle helped me pull it all together.

Sam and Dani went with me to the airport. I didn't want them to have to go to a funeral. In fact, if it hadn't been Dean's, I wouldn't have gone at all. I believe funerals are fundamentally uncivilized. If you have something good to say about a person, for Christ's sake, say it to their face while they're still alive. It doesn't mean squat to them after they're gone!

I arrived in Los Angeles in time for the memorial service — thank God, I missed the burial itself. I was asked to speak, and I prayed I would have the strength to say what I had to say without breaking down: I knew Dean would have called me a wuss if I had.

I told the people, 'You are so lucky that you knew my partner and my friend. I will not fall into that drone of pain about death, but I will ask you all to just yell 'Yeah!' that he lived . . . that he was with us for all that time. 'Yeah!' 'Yeah!' And that, my friends, is my celebration of his life. Long may he drink!'

I stepped down from the podium and walked to my seat. I stopped along the way to kiss Jeanne . . . He loved her so much. I sat down next to Lew and Edie Wasserman. The names who were there would have made the *Hollywood Reporter* envious.

Outside, I met Frank. He grabbed my hand and said, 'Well, we lost the big gun, my friend!'

I said, 'We didn't lose him, God just placed him elsewhere.'

Frank said, 'Yeah, I know. How you holding up, Jew?' That's all Frank ever called me, for fifty-one years, and I loved it. We held hands like two kids, not knowing what to say next. Thank God, I had to get back to the plane. I boarded the jet — and the tears came.

I lost my partner and my best friend. The man who made me the man I am today. I think of him with undying respect. I miss him every day I'm still here. I've considered the idea of our getting together again someday, but I believe when we die we are just put away and life goes on. My prayer to be with him again isn't realistic, but I'll live the rest of my life with the memory of a great

and wonderful man, my partner, Dean Martin
. . . G.R.H.S.

★   ★   ★

So many memories flash and flicker around my
brain — and the strangest ones come up at the
strangest times. Why am I thinking, now, about
those first crazy shows we did, way back before
we were even a team, at the Havana-Madrid in
the spring of '46?

I've told you already about all the insane
things I did to get Dean's attention while he was
performing, just to try and make him laugh. And
how scared I was, at first, that he wouldn't like
what I did — and then, when I came out of the
kitchen with that goddamn hunk of raw meat on
a fork, he smiled, and it was like the sun coming
out on the rest of my life.

Something else just popped into my mind.

The third or fourth night into my relentless
menu of stunts, I realized that no matter what I
did, short of lighting a stick of dynamite on
stage, Dean would do takes, throw lines, and just
go right on singing. (Most songs run two and a
half to three minutes; with my help, his could
run eleven or twelve.) That was the wonder of it
all, the fun and joy of it all — but being nineteen
years old, I couldn't help but want to try to top
myself. Then I had an inspiration.

As I said before, the staff at the Havana-
Madrid was even more enthusiastic about our
go-for-broke craziness than the few patrons who
were still around in those early-morning hours.

347

And so when I approached the guy who ran the lighting board with my idea, I knew right away that I had a willing accomplice.

Dean had gotten a little ways into 'Pennies from Heaven' — up to the line that goes, 'Save them for a package of sunshine and flowers' — when I hit the main switch and the whole place went black.

The musicians fumbled along for a moment, then stopped dead.

And Dean — of course! — never hesitated for a second. You think he had any doubts about what had just occurred, and who was behind it? No, going on with his number (even a capella) was a matter of pride for him at that point — and in one of those lightninglike inspirations I would soon learn he was capable of, he instantly figured out a way he could be seen as well as heard. He took out his gold-plated Zippo cigarette lighter, flicked the flint, held the flame under that unbelievably handsome face, and finished his song in the mellow flicker of its flame just as though nothing at all had happened.

No, scratch that. He finished up that goddamn number even more stylishly than if the spotlight had been right on his face.

ACKNOWLEDGMENTS

I would like to start by acknowledging Jerry Lewis himself, who was not only the first person I ever saw on a movie screen (in a trailer for the re-release of *At War with the Army*, in Hazleton, Pennsylvania, circa 1956), but who, in all his super-complicated essence, and in all his complex associations for me — Jersey landsman, coreligionist (both in Judaism and comedy), friend, writing partner, and indubitable father-surrogate — has compelled me ever since our first meeting, for a *New Yorker* profile I wrote in 2000.

The following people were also essential to this project: Peter Bogdanovich (who introduced me to Jerry in the first place), the tireless Chris Lewis, Peter W. Kaplan, Claudia Stabile, the delightful Penny Rice and Violet Ostrowski, Jeff Low, Hillery Borton, and Neil T. Daniels, of the Dean Martin Fan Center.

I must also acknowledge the superlative Joy Harris and the magnificent Phyllis Grann.

And, as ever, Karen, Jacob, Aaron, and Avery.

— James Kaplan

We do hope that you have enjoyed reading this large print book.

Did you know that all of our titles are available for purchase?

We publish a wide range of high quality large print books including:
Romances, Mysteries, Classics
General Fiction
Non Fiction and Westerns

Special interest titles available in large print are:
The Little Oxford Dictionary
Music Book
Song Book
Hymn Book
Service Book

Also available from us courtesy of Oxford University Press:
Young Readers' Dictionary
(large print edition)
Young Readers' Thesaurus
(large print edition)

For further information or a free brochure, please contact us at:
Ulverscroft Large Print Books Ltd.,
The Green, Bradgate Road, Anstey,
Leicester, LE7 7FU, England.
Tel: (00 44) **0116 236 4325**
Fax: (00 44) **0116 234 0205**

Other titles published by
The House of Ulverscroft:

THINGS I OVERHEARD
WHILE TALKING TO MYSELF

Alan Alda

Acclaimed actor and internationally bestselling author Alan Alda has written an account of some impossible questions he's asked himself over the years: What do I value? What, exactly, is the good life? (And what does that even mean?) Alda listens in on things he's heard himself saying at critical points in his life — from the turbulence of the 1960s, to his first Broadway show, to the birth of his children, and to the ache of September 11. He notes that 'doorways are where the truth is told', and wonders which particular things help lead to a 'life of meaning'. In a book that is as questioning as it is incisive, Alda amuses and moves us with his uniquely witty meditations on questions great and small.

BORN STANDING UP

Steve Martin

Acclaimed author and Emmy Award-winner Steve Martin tells the history of his career in stand-up comedy. It is a portrait of a man dedicated to the art of making people laugh. He reveals how in his search for comic originality, fame fell on him as a by-product, and admits that he was not naturally talented, but working around that minor detail made him inventive. Steve Martin was not self-destructive, although he almost destroyed himself. However, it was during his research of this crucial part of his professional life that he was reminded why he did stand-up and why he walked away. Twenty-five years later, he now views that time with surprising warmth, and even feels 'an affection for the war years'.